THE PLANTFINDER'S GUIDE TO

GARDEN FERNS

THE PLANTFINDER'S
GUIDE TO
GARDEN FERNS

Martin Rickard

David & Charles

Timber Press
Portland, Oregon

For Catherine and Edward

PICTURE ACKNOWLEDGEMENTS

All photographs are by **Marie O'Hara**, except pages 50–1, 56–7, 60–1, 66–7, 72–3, 80–1, 102–3, 106–7, 116–17, 134–35, 138–39, 146–147 and 156–7 by **Karl Adamson**, and pages 11, 17, 19, 24 (bottom left), 24 (top right), 31, 32, 34, 36, 39, 47, 49, 53, 54, 55, 63, 64, 95, 115, 125, 145, 158, 161, 165, 166 and 169 by **Martin Rickard**

Illustrations on pages 10, 11 and 173 by **Coral Mula**

Note: Throughout the book the time of year is given as a season to make the reference applicable to readers all over the world. In the Northern Hemisphere the seasons may be translated into months as follows:

Early winter – December	Early summer – June
Midwinter – January	Midsummer – July
Late winter – February	Late summer – August
Early spring – March	Early autumn – September
Mid-spring – April	Mid-autumn – October
Late spring – May	Late autumn – November

Copyright © Martin Rickard 2000, 2002
Hardback edition first published in 2000
Reprinted 2001
Paperback edition first published 2002

First published in the UK in 2000 by David & Charles Publishers
Brunel House, Newton Abbot, Devon
ISBN 0 7153 0806 8 (hardback)
ISBN 0 7153 1536 6 (paperback)
A catalogue record for this book is available from the British Library.

First published in North America in 2000 by Timber Press Inc.,
133 SW Second Avenue, Suite 450, Portland, Oregon 97204, USA
ISBN 0–88192–476–8 (hardback)
ISBN 0–88192–567–5 (paperback)
Cataloging-in-Publication data is on file with the Library of Congress.

Project editor: Jo Weeks
Book design by Ian Muggeridge
Printed in Spain by Edelvives

Photographs:
Page 1 *Asplenium scolopendrium* on the Hermitage, Kyre; page 2 *Polystichum yunnanense*, a tough, robust, evergreen fern; page 3 *Dicksonia sellowiana*, a South American tree fern surprisingly hardy in Britain; page 5 *Dryopteris lepidopoda*, a wonderful red-fronded species from the Himalayas.

Contents

Preface

There have been an awful lot of fern books published in the past, with over 400 different books appearing in English prior to 1900 alone. I can only make a wild guess at how many have been published during the twentieth century, but I would not be surprised if it were as many as 1000. This volume could easily be something like number 1400. So, why do we need another?

In fact, it is not a difficult question to answer because the vast majority of published works are taxonomic and scientific – books for gardeners are relatively rare. In addition, gardening is progressing in leaps and bounds in England, and no doubt elsewhere, too. Because success at a nursery level depends on always having something new and exciting to offer, new species and cultivars of ferns, as well as other plant types, are being introduced in greater numbers than ever before, and information on these new introductions, and the new techniques sometimes needed to grow them, is inevitably sparse. I hope, therefore, that this book will be of some assistance to the reader in recognising and growing some of these wonderful new plants as well as many of the old favourites.

Of special interest in Britain is the sudden availability of tree ferns, mainly *Dicksonia antarctica* from Australia. These are being widely grown with great success, so far with little or no protection from the cold. Whether this is down to global warming or plain good luck and mild winters only time will tell (I prefer to protect my plants in any case). Up to now information on tree ferns has

been sparse and fragmented so I hope the account in this book will provide a concise and useful introduction to how to grow these magnificent plants, and also give information on some of the other tree fern species that might be worth trying.

Alpine plants are very popular. Many ferns fit into this category, none more appropriately than the dwarf desert ferns in the genera *Cheilanthes* and *Pellaea*. Information on recognition of the more common species and notes on how to grow them has generally been scattered in obscure publications. The introduction given in this book aims to encourage their wider cultivation.

Another aim of this book is to highlight the old favourites, especially the 'living antiques' surviving from the Victorian heyday of fern growing, which are great favourites of mine. Fortunately there is still a hard core of growers who covet these rare forms. I hope the inclusion of these plants will make them more widely known with the knock-on effect of making them more widely grown. The National Council for the Conservation of Plants and Gardens (NCCPG) is doing a great job in this area, along with the British Pteridological Society.

The A–Z section is as comprehensive as I can make it. Most of the ferns included are, or have been, grown by me. My comments are, therefore, usually based on personal observation.

I look forward to seeing a continuing influx of new ferns for our gardens. My current dream is to find a tree fern that is truly hardy in the climate of central England.

Graceful ferns enhance the beauty and mood of a Georgian waterfall at Kyre Park.

Part One Introduction to Ferns

I The Botany and History of Ferns

True ferns are the principal components of the plant group known as the Pteridophyta. In an evolutionary sense the Pteridophyta fit between the Bryophyta (mosses and liverworts) and the Gymnospermae (conifers or gymnosperms). Of all the plants known today, the Pteridophyta are the most primitive with vascular tissue (tubular cells that carry food and moisture around the plant). The more primitive mosses and liverworts lack vascular tissue and are, therefore, very limited in size.

Ferns do not produce flowers. They reproduce by spores, which are usually brown or green and normally formed on the underside of the fronds. For some gardeners the lack of flowers might be seen as an insurmountable problem, but the diversity of the frond shapes and the enormous variety of shades of green, sizes and textures is adequate compensation. (See pp.172–174 for details on the fern lifecycle.)

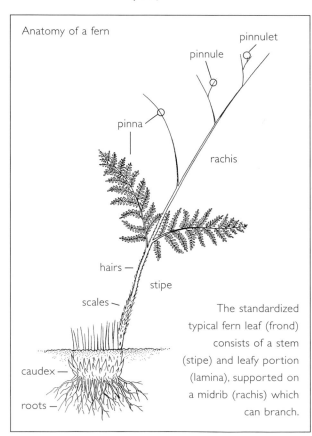

Anatomy of a fern

pinnulet

pinnule

pinna

rachis

hairs —

stipe

scales —

The standardized typical fern leaf (frond) consists of a stem (stipe) and leafy portion (lamina), supported on a midrib (rachis) which can branch.

caudex —

roots —

Whether in a mixed border or specialist fernery, ferns deserve wide use in the garden in their own right. For the more general gardener they have the great advantage of being second to none when it comes to adorning difficult shady corners, and virtually all gardens have such places, frequently embellished with nothing more than a dustbin or piles of junk.

A HISTORY OF FERN GROWING

Prior to the Victorian fern craze, ferns were rarely cultivated. They had little economic value and those considered to be useful medicinal herbs were harvested from the wild. In *Filices Britannicae* (1785) James Bolton provides a list of ferns for the hot house. Today, many ferns in his list are known to be perfectly hardy; the need for a hot house suggests fern growing was a rich man's hobby. Everything changed around 1842 with the appearance of *On the Growth of Plants in Closely Glazed Cases*, a little book written by Nathaniel Ward. He showed that even in grimy cities, plants could be grown in glazed cases without any damage from atmospheric pollution. This, coupled with the influence of books by George Francis and Edward Newman, started a fashion for collecting ferns as souvenirs of the countryside. By 1850 the craze was well underway, and throughout the 1860s and 1870s was sustained by a mass of books on the subject. Gradually, as the century approached its end, interest in ferns declined but, curiously, it was then that a few keen fern growers made a determined effort to form a society to study them. This society, called the North of England Pteridological Society, was founded in 1891. The following year it changed its name to British Pteridological Society, the name by which it is still known. (In the 1870s an attempt to form a fern society, also called the British Pteridological Society, had faltered and failed after five years. Very little is known about this group today.)

The authors of the many mid-Victorian books seem to have been the acknowledged fern experts – initially Edward Newman, soon followed by Thomas Moore and

Previous page: Ferns border a shady path in Rita Coughlin's garden at Lydiate Ash near Birmingham.

A impressive display of ferns in a dry border at Leinthall Starkes, Herefordshire.

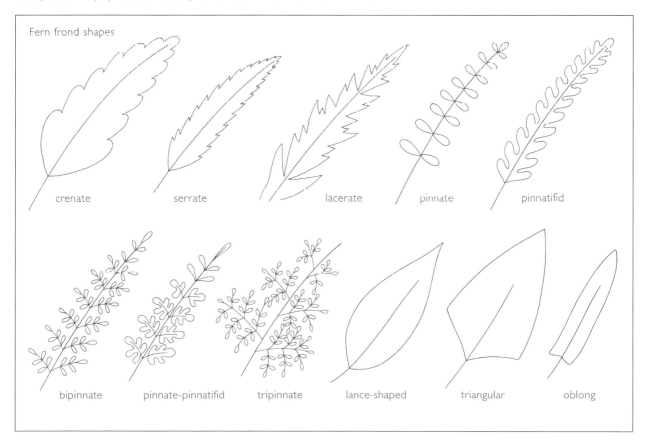

Fern frond shapes

crenate   serrate   lacerate   pinnate   pinnatifid

bipinnate   pinnate-pinnatifid   tripinnate   lance-shaped   triangular   oblong

Asplenium scolopendrium 'Crispum', alongside the summer house at Kyre.

Edward Lowe. Both Moore and Lowe took great interest in cultivars of British ferns that were being found by amateur collectors. Both named hundreds of forms — many not really worth the trouble. Nevertheless, plenty of good things were being discovered and brought into cultivation. Many are still well known, even after more than a hundred years, among them *Dryopteris filix-mas* 'Bollandiae', *Athyrium filix-femina* 'Victoriae', *Polystichum setiferum* 'Plumosum Bevis' and *Polypodium vulgare* 'Elegantissimum'.

As the century progressed Edward Lowe took up the lead role. His book *British Ferns* (1890) is still the most comprehensive book on fern cultivars ever published. A rich man living near Chepstow in Gwent, Wales, he was fascinated by the life cycle of ferns and conducted experiments to cross different taxa. Although these were successful, he had great difficulty getting his work accepted by the scientific community. It was only when he crossed two cultivars and produced an intermediate form that the importance of his work was recognized.

Lowe died in 1901 and the mantle fell to Charles

Druery who lived in Acton in West London and was a very successful fern grower. He was also a gifted writer, publishing a huge volume of material on ferns (and related matters) as well as three books. Druery's collection of plants was one of the best ever accumulated. When he died, he passed them on to William Cranfield of Enfield in Middlesex, a wealthy man who had plenty of space for cultivating ferns. Through the 1920s he established the best collections of the day, putting on magnificent exhibitions for the Royal Horticultural Society in London. Unfortunately, few of his plants were ever distributed to other growers and in many cases he had the only plants of a given cultivar. In old age, just after World War II, he decided to give his enormous fern collection, including many unique forms, to the RHS gardens at Wisley. It would seem that Wisley did not have the facilities to look after the collection, given all the post-war shortages, and struggled to maintain it. Today most have disappeared. If only Cranfield had been more inclined to distribute plants, more of the old treasures might still be in cultivation.

Fortunately, through the first three decades of the twentieth century, several other great fern growers also maintained good collections. Pre-eminent among these was Dr Frederick Stansfield who wrote many useful articles and grew his ferns well. Many of the most interesting ferns still in cultivation can be traced back to his collection.

In 1935 a young man suddenly took an interest in ferns. He was Jimmy Dyce, and it was to the great benefit of the British Pteridological Society that he came along when he did. Almost single-handed, he resurrected the society after the war and proceeded to build it up to the thriving organization that exists today. Jimmy held virtually every position within the society in his time, including being the first President Emeritus. He died in 1996, aged 91, still a leading member 61 years after he first joined.

One of Jimmy's great passions was to spread the interest in ferns as far and wide as he could. When he heard of interest in Australia, he established contact with Chris Goudey near Melbourne and helped the Fern Society of Victoria find its feet. This society has been a huge success and recently assisted with restoration of the huge Victorian fernery at Rippon Lea in Melbourne.

Jimmy also became involved in fern growing in the USA. The American Fern Society had been set up in 1893 after only a few years of fern interest (as far as I can discover, the first North American book on ferns was not published until around 1870). This society seemed to be more interested in the science of ferns and their distribution than in their culture. Ferns were obviously grown but I have never come across any reference to a specialist fern nursery in existence early in the twentieth century. It was not until around 1980 that two nurseries got underway. One of these, 'Fancy Fronds', was set up in Seattle and run by Judith Jones who made contact with Jimmy. A strong friendship developed between them, Jimmy doing all he could to help Judith set up a flourishing business. It is a strange coincidence that the only other specialist fern nursery in the USA, 'Foliage Gardens' run by Sue and Harry Olsen, is also in Seattle.

Working parallel to Jimmy for much of the same period was the nursery run in the southern English Lake District by Reginald Kaye. Although Reg was not deeply involved in the society, his nursery faithfully offered selections of ferns every year when virtually no other nurseries were trading in them. By offering many good things from his private garden, Reg helped carry the flame for fern growing for many years. He died in 1992 but his daughter-in-law and grandson continue to run his nursery.

Around 1970 ferns started to become more popular again in Britain. Jimmy Dyce's enthusiasm, and his encouragement of Hazel Key of Fibrex Nurseries, lead to another fern nursery emerging. Working in tandem with Ray and Rita Coughlin, Fibrex offered a good selection of garden-worthy species and cultivars Today there are several newer fern nurseries (see Appendix V, p.186). My own nursery, Rickard's Hardy Ferns, was begun in 1989. It has progressed much more quickly than I expected, and, like Fibrex and Reginald Kaye Ltd., now exhibits at many of the major flower shows. Today's gardeners have no excuse for not finding ferns for virtually every garden situation.

The future for fern growing is very rosy. Certainly here in Britain there is an ever-increasing awareness of ferns. His Royal Highness The Prince of Wales likes ferns and has created several ferneries in his garden near Tetbury in Gloucestershire, and across the world more and more ferneries are being created or restored.

FERN HUNTING

One hundred years ago fern hunting meant fern collecting; today this is illegal in most countries and should be discouraged. However, hunting ferns for photographs or simply to record distribution can give enormous pleasure. Both the American Fern Society and the British Pteridological Society arrange meetings specifically for this purpose. The great benefit of these forays is that even if the ferns prove elusive the scenery and company will be first class.

Just occasionally when fern hunting, a variant of potential garden merit may be found. What to do then is a problem. Collection is possible but only after the owner of the land has been consulted. Purists may prefer

Springtime croziers of *Polystichum yunnanense* compete easily with natural vegetation at Kyre Park.

to see variants left alone for ever, but I would counter that if left in the wild, variants rarely persist. They are more likely to survive if distributed in cultivation. An example of this is *Dryopteris filix-mas* 'Bollandiae' found in Kent, England in 1857 by a Mrs Bolland. The fern was collected and is still in cultivation, but has never been refound in the wild since. Recently, the *Dryopteris* expert, Christopher Fraser-Jenkins, was shown a specimen. He immediately thought it could well be a hybrid between *Dryopteris aemula* and *D. filix-mas*. Research will be needed to test his theory, but at least it is possible to do this research all these years later because Mrs Bolland collected the plant. There are many other similar cases of old clones of ferns still in cultivation that may one day prove useful to research.

In the old days when collecting was legal, if not always forgivable, the collectors would resort to clever tactics to capture their prizes. Charles Druery in *British Ferns and Their Varieties* (1910) wrote some wonderful notes on this subject. I reprint a short section here:

'... Of course it occasionally happens that the successful hunter is confronted with difficulties which will tax his inventive powers to overcome ... a very desirable harts tongue was noticed just over the arch spanning a Devonshire stream, and only just within reach of a trowel lashed to a stick. If dislodged it would inevitably fall into the rapid stream below and be lost. The problem was solved by the fortunate presence of an umbrella, which being opened and suspended under the arch by a string, eventually received the prize when dislodged. A second similar bridge difficulty with a variety of *Polypodium vulgare* was met differently: the umbrella could not be used as the wall was sheer, but by means of a loose slip knot of string, the fronds were lassoed, and when the root was dislodged, the plant was drawn up and bagged in the normal way.'

Druery was only after potential new cultivars, not species, and did little or no environmental damage. Unfortunately, however, before him, at the height of the Victorian fern craze, fern collecting was common on a large scale. Plant-hunting was a social thing, especially among the ladies, and baskets of ferns were gathered indiscriminately. Sometimes, with rare ferns such as woodsias, every plant found was collected, making some plants extinct in some localities. Despite this we can say

A cooling pergola of ferns is shaded by overhanging clematis and ivies at Lydiate Ash, near Birmingham.

that no fern species has become extinct in Britain since records began. Even near London, rarish conspicuous ferns, such as *Osmunda regalis*, are reappearing and are possibly nearly as common today as they were before the Victorian fern craze. Today our rarest ferns, including the woodsias, are protected by law in Britain – not only must they not be collected but the collection of spores is also illegal.

Not all plant hunters of the past wanted to collect their finds; however, their dedication to the cause was sometimes quite remarkable. Robert Lloyd Praeger recounts how on one occasion he became so engrossed in the flora of an Irish bog that darkness fell and he could not find his way home. It was a very isolated spot but luckily a cottage light was visible so he decided to walk towards it in a straight line. This entailed wading chest deep in freezing water. What a pleasure!

There is, of course, another form of fern hunting, which entails building up a collection from nurseries, friends, old gardens, and so on. Whole plants can be acquired or only propagating material. In many ways it is better to start with spores of a cultivar as you may then succeed in raising something completely new. Unfortunately, the rarest cultivars all need to be collected as divisions from an original crown. Often they are slow to grow to a divisible size, and are, therefore, very difficult to obtain. It makes hunting ferns all the more rewarding when you succeed.

FERNS AND THE DECORATIVE ARTS

The delicately attractive shapes of fern fronds were particularly admired during the nineteenth century and widely used to decorate everyday items, particularly in the English-speaking world. This interest, together with the love of the plants themselves, later became known as the Victorian fern craze, mentioned earlier. It ran from about 1845 to about 1880.

Many artefacts from this period have survived but are often overlooked. Building stones may be carved in the form of a fern frond, or the furniture and carvings in churches may represent ferns, for example the corbels at St Michael's Church, Farway in Devon. Fern decoration on gravestones, such as those in the churchyard at Lynton in North Devon, were popular. It was also common on household items. The iron works at Coalbrookdale in Shropshire, England produced three models of cast-iron garden seats with fern motifs. One, 'Fern and Blackberry' (*photo p.17*), is not uncommon, but the other two mod-

elled on the royal fern, *Osmunda regalis*, are extremely rare. Even umbrella stands were cast with fern patterns.

More noticeable, perhaps, are the many types of decorated china and pottery. Some potters made plates with ferns painted on them or with the shape of the fern moulded into the design. One of the earliest was William Brownfield whose fern pottery appeared from 1859 onwards. He produced jugs with raised patterns of rather stylized ferns. The fern segments could have been from many different species, and he used other plant parts, including wheat ears and acanthus, to complete the design. The jugs were, nevertheless, very elegant. Even more spectacular, and slightly more common, was the beautiful range of pottery produced by the Dudston factory at Stoke-on-Trent from 1860. Here, three-dimensional models of selected species were arranged in a frieze around a whole range of items including jugs, sugar basins and cheese dishes. The quality of this work is so excellent that the species of fern can often be determined. Among them are *Asplenium ceterach*, *Ophioglossum vulgatum* and *Botrychium lunaria*. The workmanship approaches the classical nature printing achieved with such style in some early Victorian books.

In 1870 H. Adams & Co. of Longton produced plates made from moulds into which fern fronds had been pressed. Accuracy in the moulding was not as great as the Dudston method but the plates were overpainted in very bright and accurate colours, again allowing identification of many of the species depicted. Produced from about 1880 to 1950, and quite common, but often overlooked, is the porcelain manufactured at the Royal Worcester factory where fronds of the hart's tongue fern were cleverly moulded into jugs, sugar bowls, and so on. They were usually white, but occasionally yellow or blue examples turn up.

Another set of plates I came upon were made by Wedgwood using fern transfers taken from Anne Pratt's book *The Ferns of Great Britain and their Allies* (1855). Although no doubt cheaply produced, the set is of great beauty – and even useful diagnostically!

Between about 1870 and 1900 a small group of companies in Scotland decorated wooden boxes with fern designs stencilled using a form of spatterwork. Groups of dried fronds were fixed to the wood and the paint was applied; once the background was sufficiently covered some fronds were removed and more paint was applied, more fronds removed and more paint applied, and so on, until an almost three-dimensional effect was created.

Coalbrookdale 'Fern and Blackberry' seat on Rickard's Hardy Ferns display at the Chelsea Flower Show in 1997.

Collectively this kind of product became known as Mauchline Ware. The items decorated range from needle boxes, fans and cigar cases to larger boxes.

Glassware did not escape adornment with ferns. However, the fern fronds were rarely convincingly modelled on glass. Designs supposedly of maidenhair ferns could equally well have been based on meadow rue; those with pinnate fronds could be pea leaves, and so on. Although possibly less attactive to the purist, these items are, nevertheless, still collectable and are probably the most readily available examples of fern-decorated ware.

Silverware seems to have suffered the same fate as glassware; where ferny motifs have been used, their design is stylized and rarely certainly based on a fern. Just occasionally, however, unique items of historic importance turn up. I was fortunate to be offered a complete set of medals won by E. J. Lowe, the great fern grower of the nineteenth century. He virtually cleared the board at the Royal Horticultural Society's exhibition of British ferns in 1892. The medals were beautifully mounted in a purpose-built display case – obviously he was very proud of his achievements (see also *Fern Growing*, 1895, E. J. Lowe).

In the past, lace work and crochet were popular pastimes for ladies, individual items of great beauty being produced, usually as one-off creations. Even today the talent is not dead; as recently as 1996 I was given a beautiful montage of 19 fern fronds embroidered by a dear friend, Bridget Graham. The fronds were all collected from her own garden in Cornwall and form a wonderful souvenir of happy times.

All the items mentioned so far were produced in Britain. However, fern mania spread well beyond this, in particular to New Zealand, where much fern-related material was produced. There was even a shop called 'Fern Shop' in Auckland in about 1880. It was run by Eric Craig who sold pressed ferns in books, on cards and in boxes; he also produced spatterwork boxes not so dissimilar to those produced as Mauchline Ware in Scotland (see also Goulding, 1977). Craig was not alone. Others joined the fern sales scene but two craftsman stand above all the others. These were the Seufferts, father and son. The older Seuffert was a central European *émigré* to New Zealand in 1861. He was an outstanding craftsman producing beautiful items of marquetry, such as desks and wooden book covers. The motifs were very often accurate images of fern fronds or even views of tree ferns from a distance. His work was carried on by his son (see Judd, 1990). These are now highly collectable and almost considered New Zealand national treasures.

This is only a brief account. The range of material of this kind is huge, and I am forever seeing or hearing of something new. It is great fun hunting antique shops and antique fairs to see what exists. Even on today's products, ferns are almost inescapable – modern ferny plates can be found and I recently bought a fern-pattern toilet mat!

FERN BOOKS

Fern books have been produced in such huge numbers over the years that it may seem unnecessary to produce another now. However, knowledge is always growing and new species and cultivars that need describing are continually being brought into cultivation. Furthermore, most of the excellent books from the past are no longer available and in any case the nomenclature is out of date, making their use today often rather difficult.

The first book on British ferns was written and engraved by James Bolton in 1785. It is a beautiful book. Many of the engravings are of such good quality that they are still acceptable today. For example his illustration of *Polystichum lonchitis* was used in Hutchinson and Thomas's *Welsh Ferns*, published in 1996. From 1785 up to 1900, some 400 or 500 books on ferns have been written in English (see Hall and Rickard).

After Bolton, the next book to appear in Britain was *An Analysis of the British Ferns and their Allies* by George Francis in 1837. This neat little book was extremely well timed as it lit the fuse on the embrionic fern craze. It was soon followed by Edward Newman's *History of British Ferns* (1840, 1844, 1854). This was a larger work and is still useful today; the historical accounts of fern discoveries are fascinating. Thomas Moore overlapped with Newman and copied from him, much to Newman's disgust. Nevertheless, after a shaky start, Moore produced some excellent books peaking with the production of *The Ferns of Great Britain and Ireland*, 1855. The folio illustrations in this book were all made by Bradbury using the nature-printing technique in which impressions are made of freshly harvested plant material. Their quality is superb; they are accurate to every detail and beautiful to boot! You can even feel the impression of the fern on the paper. In my opinion, Bradbury's nature prints were never surpassed. However, later books improved our knowledge, notably E. J. Lowe's *British Ferns* (1890), which included 1861 cultivars of British ferns and is still the most reliable reference list today. Charles Druery wrote three books, the best being *British Ferns and their Varieties* in 1910. This included the rather drab, but very useful nature prints produced in the 1870s by Colonel Jones.

After Druery there was a long gap before Reginald Kaye's *Hardy Ferns* appeared in 1968. This wonderful book was based on the author's intimate knowledge of the plants. He included an interesting list of hardy exotic ferns, short by today's standards, but for its time very comprehensive. Subsequently, Richard Rush produced his slim volume *A Guide to Hardy Ferns* in 1984. This is little more than a well-researched list but it added hugely to our knowledge of hardy ferns and what might be worth trying in temperate gardens. Most recently John Mickel wrote the very good *Ferns for American Gardens*, 1994. This lists a very comprehensive range of species and cultivars. Although it was based largely on American gardens, Europe was not ignored. Several photographs were taken in British gardens, including my own.

All the above books have been consulted in preparing this account, plus many more (see Appendix VI, Further Reading, p.187). Technical floras of distant lands are an invaluable source, but translation of foreign languages can be a problem. Even rather technical works, such as *New Species Syndrome in Indian Pteridology* by Fraser-Jenkins (1997), are invaluable as they help to ensure the most up-to-date name is used (although it is often a matter of opinion as to which is correct).

2 Choosing and Using Ferns

Ferns are amazingly accommodating and are fairly easy to grow in a wide range of situations. Virtually every garden has several areas that are very suitable for them: the corner where the dustbin stands is often a good start. Choices can be made according to what will do well or look good in any particular site. This chapter outlines what ferns need to thrive, together with some suggestions for planting attractive combinations.

CULTURAL CONSIDERATIONS

Site

It is commonly believed that all ferns like boggy conditions. Certainly, there are ferns that enjoy or even need very wet conditions, but well over half the species described in this book have no such requirement and many would die in such a situation. Reflection on where ferns grow in the wild reinforces this point. Not many

This border at Leinthall Starkes, Herefordshire includes the dead fronds of polypods in early summer.

ferns are found in boggy terrain, particularly not in north-west Europe. Where there are ferns, *Athyrium filix-femina* is usually common but otherwise other species are uncommon, such as *Osmunda regalis*, *Thelypteris palustris* or the very rare *Dryopteris cristata*. On the other hand, many species are found on old walls (aspleniums, male ferns, even bracken) where the supply of water is sparse and intermittent, and to succeed here they must be well adapted to occasional droughts. (Given that they are rather primitive, it is interesting that ferns can survive on walls better than virtually any other class of plant.)

In damper parts of the temperate world where ferns abound, they are usually found in well-drained sites. For example, in south-west England ferns such as *Polystichum setiferum*, *Asplenium scolopendrium*, *Asplenium trichomanes* and various species of *Dryopteris*, are luxuriant on roadside banks and are often the dominant plant in such habitats. These banks consist of stones and debris that have been cleared off the surrounding land over many years. The result is a site with good drainage and a fertile

growing medium that has developed over the centuries. Ferns love these conditions and are more likely to thrive here than in wetter places. While investigating what species grow in certain areas I have often found exciting lengths of banks along lanes with interesting-looking expanses of woodland behind. However, upon delving into the woods I am invariably disappointed at the poor range of species, often just confined to one or two *Dryopteris* – which are equally happy in both dryish or wettish sites. This is particularly the case where the ground is flat and poorly drained.

Banks

In gardens most ferns love a moist yet well-drained site. The average garden border fits the bill well, especially if it is shady and out of the wind. Even more perfect is a slight slope where conditions mimic those of a roadside bank as described above. Establishment may require a little extra care in such a position but, once they are growing well, the ferns can be wonderfully successful. A problem that may occur before the plants are fully established is erosion of the soil by rain or heavy watering. This will remove the topsoil and expose some of the plant's roots, with the result that the plant becomes insecure in its position. It is, therefore, a good idea to plant into a depression in the bank. As rain falls, soil from above will gradually wash down onto the fern rootstock and will eventually fill the depression and firm in the plant.

Dry areas

Some ferns are hardy but cannot tolerate winter wet such as is prevalent in the cool-temperate climate of the British Isles. Notable examples of this are species of *Cheilanthes* and *Pellaea*, which are best grown in an alpine house. A few species will grow outdoors in central England if provided with very good drainage and some overhead protection to the crown to keep it dryish over winter. Species in this category include: *Cheilanthes tomentosa*, *C. alabamensis*, *C. marantae* and *Pellaea ovata*.

There are a number of ferns that are happy in dryish conditions. By dryish I do not mean dust dry but, rather, slightly moist, certainly not boggy. Most are suited to dryish woodland. These include *Adiantum aleuticum*, *A. pedatum*, *A. venustum*, *A. fimbriatum*, *A.* × *mairisii*, and all other hardy adiantums, *Arachniodes standishii*, *Asple-*

The water garden at Savill Gardens, Windsor Great Park, features *Osmunda regalis* among other water-loving plants.

nium scolopendrium and cultivars, *Coniogramma japonica*, *Cyrtomium fortunei* and other cyrtomiums, most *Dry-opteris*, *Paesia scaberula*, *Polypodium australe*, *P. interjectum*, *P. vulgare*, and all other polypodiums, *Polystichum* species and *Polystichum setiferum* cultivars.

Ferns for rockeries

All the ferns for dry conditions can be grown in rock-eries. The following are also good: *Asplenium trichomanes* and cultivars, *Cystopteris fragilis* and other cystopteris, *Davallia mariesii*, *Woodsia obtusa* and *W. polystichoides*.

Bogs

Of course, there are ferns that prefer damp and boggy spots and, unfortunately, most of us do not have such a site. However, all is not lost – I have found a way to create

Frost adorning the margins of fronds of *Polystichum setiferum* 'Plumoso-multilobum'.

An attractive waterfall planting at Kyre Park, Worcestershire.

the ideal conditions for wet-loving ferns. First, excavate an area to a depth of about 15cm (6in), then lay old compost bags, slightly overlapping, in the bottom of the depression and replace the garden soil, perhaps improved with peat or well-rotted compost. This produces ideal conditions into which to plant moisture-loving ferns.

My garden at Leinthall Starkes in Herefordshire was on a fairly steep slope and it was well drained, especially where the underlying rubbly Wenlock limestone had been exposed. In an excavated, flattish area my compost-bag bog enabled me to grow *Osmunda* species and cultivars and other wet-loving ferns very happily. The only problem I encountered was during very dry periods, and not for the reason you might suspect. During such weather I tended to concentrate on watering other parts of the garden and neglected this area as it was usually wet enough. Unfortunately, there suddenly came a point when the soil dried out, and then, of course, the plants were in trouble as they could not seek water deeper because of the polythene layer. Urgent application of water soon saw them growing away again. I have realised that I must water my 'bog garden' about three weeks into a drought and from then on weekly until the rains come again. Apart from that one hiccup, I never had any other problems.

I get quite a lot of enquiries at my nursery for plants to be placed alongside water features in small gardens. Sometimes the adjoining soil is, indeed, wet, but more often than not the water feature is made of plastic or cement and adjacent soil is pretty dry, and therefore not suitable for water plants. Be prepared for this and plant accordingly. Another occasional enquiry is for plants that can stand inundation. The obvious solution here is *Osmunda regalis*. On Dartmoor, this fern grows on the banks of the rivers and occasionally gets completely flooded. At one point on the River Dart it has formed a colony right across the river, making a sort of weir that periodically gets washed away.

Ferns for very wet conditions

Athyrium species and *Athyrium filix-femina* cultivars, *Dryopteris cristata*, *Matteuccia struthiopteris*, *Onoclea sensibilis*, *Osmunda* species and *Osmunda regalis* cultivars, *Thelypteris palustris*, *Todea barbara*, *Woodwardia areolata* and *W. virginica*.

Ferns for moderately wet conditions

All those for wet condtions as well as the following: *Blechnum spicant* and other blechnums, *Equisetum hyemale*, *Gymnocarpium dryopteris*, *Oreopteris limbosperma* and cultivars, and *Phegopteris connectilis*.

Polypodium australe 'Cambricum' is an ideal fern for growing in a sunny spot.

Sun or shade?

Ferns generally prefer shade, particularly during the hottest times of the day: it is best to avoid planting in sites that receive full sun between noon and 3.00pm. Although some ferns can put up with such exposure, they will be somewhat less luxuriant. Many species of dryopteris, especially *Dryopteris affinis* and its cultivars, can, however, do well in sunny spots. In fact nearly all ferns that like reasonably good drainage will endure full sun (although they are better out of it during the midday peak (*Asplenium scolopendrium* cultivars are an exception, see below).

Even wet-loving ferns can be happy in sun if they are provided with adequate water: *Osmunda regalis* thrives in full sun at the RHS garden at Wisley where it is planted on the edges of lakes and water courses. The soft tree fern *Dicksonia antarctica* does well in a sunny site but has shorter leaves.

Full sun can be damaging to the thin-textured cultivars of the *Asplenium scolopendrium* Crispum Group. The leaves become unnaturally yellow, and brown blotchy burn marks can appear during the season. 'Golden Queen', a rather rare form in the Crispum Group, is naturally streaked yellow – the character is enhanced if it is planted in a bright spot but it is still best kept out of direct sun during the midday period. Fronds of any fern that has been grown in a cool shady site are almost certain to burn badly if they are suddenly exposed to sun; subsequent fronds will be healthy if sufficient water is provided.

The worst site for growing ferns is a south-facing sunny bank. However, although few of the normal range of garden ferns will thrive here, the desert ferns *Cheilanthes* and *Pellaea* are worth considering as long as they can be given good drainage and protection from overwinter wet.

Wind exposure

Like full sun, wind exposure is best avoided. Delicate fern fronds can be snapped and distorted by wind, defeating the object of growing them in the first place. Young fronds that are blown about can snag on each other, turning black at the tips and reducing the beauty of the frond when fully unfurled. One of the worst ferns for a windy site is *Adiantum aleuticum*: its fronds are fan-shaped and top heavy, readily catching the wind and snapping very easily. However, small leathery-fronded species, such as *Asplenium*, and leathery epiphytic microsoriums are rarely affected by wind.

Size

Hardy ferns range from tiny aspleniums or filmy ferns, only a centimetre or two high, to giant osmundas, up to 2m (6ft) tall, or tree ferns of almost unlimited height. A brief guide to the sizes of readily available species and

Small fern species, *Asplenium ruta-muraria* (left) and *A. trichomanes* (right), on a wall in North Herefordshire.

Handsome examples of *Cyathea dealbata* in a sheltered coastal garden in County Kerry, Ireland.

cultivars follows. More details can be found in An A–Z of Ferns (pp.42–169).

Up to 15cm (6in)
Asplenium trichomanes and cultivars, *Adiantum aleuticum* 'Subpumilum'.

15–30cm (6–12in)
Adiantum venustum, *Asplenium scolopendrium* 'Laceratum Kaye', *A. scolopendrium* Ramo-marginatum group, *Athyrium niponicum* 'Pictum', *Dryopteris affinis* 'Crispa Gracilis', *Polystichum setiferum* 'Congestum'.

30–60cm (12–24in)
Adiantum aleuticum, *Asplenium scolopendrium* cultivars (many), *Athyrium* (many), *Dryopteris* (many).

60–90cm (24–36in)
Osmunda claytoniana, *O. cinnamomea*, *Polystichum munitum*.

90–150cm (36–60in)
Dryopteris filix-mas 'Barnesii', *D. wallichiana*, *Matteuccia struthiopteris*, *Osmunda regalis* and cultivars.

Soil pH

pH is a measurement of acidity: pH 7 is neutral, with higher numbers progressively more alkaline and lower numbers progressively more acidic. A plant that likes lime is termed calcicole. Lime-haters are calcifuge.

It is a popular misconception that all ferns like acid soil. Some do, but the number is surprisingly small – most of the popular garden ferns are either calcicole or totally indifferent to all but very extreme soil pH. In practice, I find that the few true lime-haters can be grown satisfactorily in limy gardens by importing an ericaceous compost. If you are gardening on pure chalk, it is probably best to prepare a special bed for calcifuge; the chalk substrate can be shut out by lining a small area with polythene.

When I get the chance, one of my favourite pastimes is to stroll around towns and villages in the north of England in areas where fern cultivars were widely grown around 100 years ago. I am on the lookout for ferns growing in front gardens. There is a clear pattern in the types of ferns to be found in particular areas. In acid regions one only ever finds well-established clumps of dryopteris, athyrium, osmunda, and so on, while in limy areas polystichums and hart's tongues, as well as more dryopteris, are more likely. This indicates that ferns in the wrong soil will dwindle with time if neglected. In a modern garden this need not happen if the plants are loved — removal of competing weeds helps, as does adding lime, where necessary, or, for lime-haters, adding peat.

Ferns that prefer acid soil

Those marked ★ particularly prefer acid conditions.

Acid soil-loving fern *Blechnum chilense* at Savill Gardens, Windsor Great Park.

More details are given in An A–Z of Ferns (pp.42–169). Although this seems quite a long list it does not contain very many widely grown garden plants (the list of calcicoles given below has many more popular species).

Asplenium septentrionale and several other aspleniums★, *Blechnum* (all species)★, *Cheilanthes* (some), *Cryptogramma crispa*★, *Doodia* (most)★, *Gymnocarpium dryopteris*, *Oreopteris limbosperma*★, *Osmunda regalis*, *Paesia scaberula*, *Pellaea* (some), *Phegopteris connectilis*, *Polypodium vulgare*, *Pteridium aquilinum*, *Woodsia* (some), *Woodwardia virginica*★.

Note: Although *Osmunda regalis* may *prefer* acid soil, it is far from crucial. At Sizergh Castle in the north of England the National Collection of *Osmunda* is planted out in a large rockery created from water-washed limestone. Natural streams run through the garden and the water is presumably alkaline. Certainly, I have had no trouble with any species of osmunda in my garden on Wenlock limestone, or at my current nursery where the water is so limy that a glassful left overnight carries a scum of lime by morning.

Ferns that prefer alkaline soil

Those marked ★ particularly prefer alkaline conditions. More details are given in An A–Z of Ferns (pp.42–169).

Asplenium scolopendrium and cultivars, and many other

Asplenium species★, *Cystopteris fragilis* and most other species★, *Dryopteris submontana*★, *Equisetum* (most species), *Gymnocarpium robertianum*★, *Polystichum aculeatum*, *P. setiferum* and cultivars, *Polypodium australe*★.

Note: *Asplenium scolopendrium* tends to do rather badly in very acid gardens. Perhaps the best fern growers I have ever known, the late Ray Coughlin, a much missed great friend, and his widow Rita of Bromsgrove, could not get it to luxuriate in their acid, sandy garden, yet other lime-loving species, such as *Polypodium australe* and *Polystichum setiferum*, flourished. Added lime helped, but the *Asplenium scolopendrium* were never the quality of the couple's other ferns.

Ferns indifferent to soil pH

Adiantum (most), *Cyrtomium*, *Dryopteris* (most).

Soil type

Soil type affects soil moisture. Depending on the type of soil, the efficiency of its drainage varies and can influence the choice of species to grow. Drainage is usually more important than pH.

Sandy soils are free draining and usually need to be improved with added fibre in the form of peat, coir, leaf mould or well-rotted garden compost. All these improve water retention without making the ground too wet. The same organic materials can be added to very heavy soils, as they open up the soil structure and prevent waterlogging.

I am frequently asked if ferns will grow in heavy clay. The answer is yes – they love it. There is always some moisture available in clay, even in serious drought when cracks appear on the surface. The blocks of apparently dry soil are protecting the remaining moisture, and established ferns are able to reach it.

Although I have no experience of growing ferns on peaty soil I am sure it would suit them well. Again the addition of well-rotted compost would probably improve the structure.

Fertilizers

Ferns do benefit from fertilizer, but not as much as many other classes of plants. In the open garden it is not really necessary but can be added to achieve greater luxuriance. The old fern books recommend bonemeal for lime-loving species. I have used it but have never seen any real benefit. (A word of caution: use gloves with bonemeal.) Animal manure is a popular fertilizer. However, it is wise to make sure nothing too strong is used as

this can encourage excessive foliar growth at the expense of the roots, which is not good news as the fronds will be weak and easily affected by drought. I recommend only well-rotted horse manure, and preferably that which is three or four years old. Recently, I have heard stories of seaweed fertilizers giving stunning results. I have never tried them but I plan to in the future.

Feeding container plants

Pot-grown ferns require feeding. In my nursery, I use slow-release granules each spring as this enables me to feed each pot sufficiently once a year. When I am potting on young plants I always add granules to the mix, but if you are potting on in autumn, it is wise to cut back on the amount of feed given.

Slow-release granules are very convenient, though expensive, but I suspect the old-fashioned liquid feeds are more reliable. In a situation where only a few ferns are grown I think I would opt for regular liquid feeding through the growing months. Commercially, urea is sometimes used pre-mixed in the compost. This is fine in spring and summer but in the cold temperatures of winter the excessive nitrogen can be lethal.

Propagation

When I am propagating cuttings (ie. bulbils), I prefer to use no fertilizer until good growth of roots is visible. If fed too early, the leaves will grow but not the roots, and the young bulbil will not thrive. Unrooted tree fern trunks are somewhat similar. Again I do not feed them until the trunk has rooted well into the compost.

AESTHETIC CONSIDERATIONS

Species for ground cover

Most ferns have erect rhizomes that stay where you put them, but a few do have spreading rhizomes or stolons and are able to colonize quite large areas. Notable examples are: *Equisetum*, *Gymnocarpium dryopteris*, *Matteuccia struthiopteris*, *Onoclea sensibilis*, *Phegopteris connectilis*, *Polypodium*, *Thelypteris palustris*.

Matteuccia struthiopteris spreads by stolons. The rhizomes are erect, in time making each crown into a small tree fern. New crowns appear at random. If they grow where they are not wanted, they are easily removed and can then be given away, swapped or otherwise disposed of. *Onoclea sensibilis* and *Thelypteris palustris* both spread quite rapidly but the rhizomes are near the surface so their spread is usually fairly easily kept in check. *Gymnocarpium*

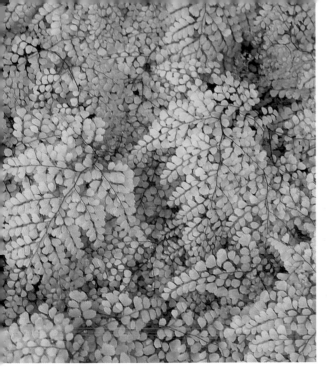

Adiantum venustum is one of the best species for ground cover and can be evergreen during mild winters.

dryopteris spreads near the surface and can become difficult to eradicate if allowed to become entangled with other plants. There is an example of this beautiful fern that has colonized large areas at Hergest Croft gardens near Kington in Herefordshire, England. Other species of *Gymnocarpium* spread in much the same way. *Phegopteris connectilis* spreads rather like *G. dryopteris*.

All *Equisetum* are extremely invasive, but many are very pretty and worthy garden plants. To grow them safely I always recommend planting them in a pot plunged in the bed just out of sight, but not so deep as to allow the rhizomes to escape! Polypodiums can spread and in time form good-sized clumps. It is as well not to plant different polypodiums close to each other as in time they become intertwined and then difficult to separate – I know, I've done it!

Most spreading ferns are deciduous. The polypodiums are the exception and are probably the best candidates in most situations. Spread can be speeded up by cutting a clump into many small pieces and planting them out 15cm (6in) from each other. In a couple of seasons the pieces should have joined up, rapidly increasing the clump size. If a larger clump is required the operation can be repeated again, and again.

Shape

To many people a fern is simply a plant that produces bracken-like fronds typically with much-divided lacy leaves. This is, of course, true of many species and

cultivars, but in reality the range of form available to gardeners is staggering. When my nursery puts on a display at flower shows, especially at the Chelsea Flower Show, we can use up to 200 different types of ferns. As well as simple lance-shaped, lacy fronds there are crested forms with attractive tassels at their tips, more feathery forms where the lacy texture is amplified and fronds where the blade is entire (not cut at all). These latter, uncut fronds are usually leathery and quite reflective, contrasting beautifully with the archetypal lacy forms. Frond shape is not the only variable: the addition of a trunk, as with the tree ferns, adds a completely different dimension.

Colour

Ferns are green, or are they? The majority are green, of course, but what a range of green! Forty shades is surely not an exaggeration.

In addition to shades of green there is reflectiveness: some fronds are glossy, such as those of *Asplenium scolopendrium* and *Blechnum colensoi*, while others, like those of *Blechnum wattsii*, are matt-green. The two types side by side can give quite a contrast. The hairs on the

Asplenium scolopendrium 'Ramosum' is a good example of a hardy fern with reflective leaves.

fronds of ferns such as *Polystichum polyblepharum* and *Dicksonia antarctica* can greatly enhance the fern's overall appearance, especially in spring when fronds are unfurling. Similarly scales on the rachis and stipe can also be beautiful. *Polystichum proliferum* and *Cyathea australis* are examples of ferns that are enhanced by their scaly fronds. Coloured scales are even better. The black-scaled new fronds of *Dryopteris neorosthornii* or the brown scales of some forms of *Dryopteris wallichiana* have quite an impact. In some species, such as the aptly named rustyback fern *(Asplenium ceterach)*, the back of the frond may be completely covered in brown scales.

Coloured fronds

Many Asian species have fronds in colours other than green. *Athyrium niponicum* 'Pictum' is a well-established deciduous favourite with grey fronds that have a mauve central section. *Athyrium otophorum* can be even more striking. Its fronds are yellow-green with a bright red rachis and main veins, while another lady fern, *A. vidalii*, has a dark red rachis and veins and a green lamina. Another Asian species, *Adiantum aleuticum* 'Japonicum', has staggeringly beautiful red fronds in spring. Other adiantums share the same character, albeit less strikingly, including *A. venustum* and *A. fimbriatum*.

Osmunda regalis 'Purpurascens' has red fronds in spring

Asplenium ceterach – the underside of the fronds is covered with brown scales, which gives the plant the name 'rustyback'.

Long golden hairs beard the croziers of *Polystichum polyblepharum* and the young fronds are glossy yellow-green.

The white underside of the fronds of *Cyathea dealbata* is the inspiration for the national emblem of New Zealand.

The fronds of *Dryopteris erythrosora* are red in spring, gradually changing to green as the season moves into summer.

Startling colours on fronds of *Athyrium niponicum* 'Pictum' make this a truly eye-catching specimen.

while the rachis and other midribs stay red throughout the season. *O. regalis* var. *spectabilis* can also be reddish in spring but eventually turns green. Within the native populations in western Europe, red-tinged forms of *O. regalis* can be found, especially towards the south and west. The late Philip Coke found a beautiful form in Eire many years ago. It is red in spring with a persistently red rachis and midribs and now bears his name. Red in osmunda occurs in other species, including *O. lancea* and *O. gracilis*.

Dryopteris erythrosora is a tough plant with bright red new fronds in spring. These turn bronze within a week or two, becoming green a month or so later. This species has the happy knack of continuing to produce new red fronds through most of the season. However, on very young plants the colour is often absent – do not despair: it will develop. In addition to this flushing of red *D. erythrosora* rings the changes through winter. It is evergreen in all but the severest winters and the overwintering fronds turn an attractive yellow. While *D. erythrosora* has triangular, bipinnate fronds, *D. lepidopoda* has lanceolate pinnate-pinnatifid fronds that are also red in spring.

Another species flushing red then bronze is *Woodwardia unigemmata*. Here the fronds can be 2m (6ft) – a spectacular sight in spring. The related genera of *Blechnum* and

Doodia also contain species that flush red in spring.

Ferns grown in sunny situations can sometimes be a rather sickly yellow, especially the Crispum forms of *Asplenium scolopendrium*. This is admired by some but I must admit, with one or two exceptions, I prefer the healthy, true, deeper green. There are forms of Crispum that are naturally striped at random with broad yellowish green bands between the normal green areas. 'Golden Queen' and 'Variegatum Bolton' are two such cultivars. This effect is best brought out in dappled sun, preferably not full sun around midday as some leaf scorch may occur. In deep shade the variegation may not develop. These are rare, much sought-after cultivars.

Dryopteris dickinsii and *D. juxtaposita* are among a selection of ferns that are often a pale green approaching

Pleasing associations of *Matteuccia struthiopteris* with *Tropaeolum speciosum* and hostas at Lydiate Ash.

yellowish green. There is even a yellow-flecked form of *Dryopteris filix-mas* called 'Lux-lunae' – unfortunately this is rare and may even be extinct.

Autumn colour can be attractive. *Osmunda regalis* 'Philip Coke' goes a beautiful butter-yellow for a few days each autumn, and, of course, in the depths of winter frost can pick out the shape of evergreen ferns in white crystals.

When choosing ferns, there is rarely much need to consider clashing colours; most shades are not strong and they all seem to fit in together well – at least they do to my untrained eye.

Choosing plants to grow with ferns

As something of a fern specialist I am not, perhaps, the best person to ask which plants mix well with ferns. However, I do grow quite a number of other plants and I find many very pleasing.

Stumpery on Rickard's Hardy Ferns' stand at Chelsea Flower Show 1998. The wood sets off the tracery of the fern fronds.

Ferns, being predominently shade-loving, mix well with many woodland herbaceous perennials. Various species of *Trillium* (toad lilies) are beautiful companions, as are the Martagon lily (*Lilium martagon*) and similar lily species. *Erythronium* (dog's tooth violet) is another favourite. In fact virtually all woodland bulbous plants are suitable, especially those that emerge early in the season, before the new fern fronds unfurl. I am very keen on all the very collectable species and forms of snowdrops. They mix well with *Polypodium australe* and its cultivars as both are in fine fettle in late winter. However, the persistence and post-flowering elongation of the snowdrop leaves is not always welcome. Hellebores come into the same category – beautiful when they flower but with overpowering summer foliage unless plenty of space is allowed. Hostas are obvious candidates for mixed plantings, especially with the feathery forms of dryopteris and polystichum. They are not so good with hart's tongue fern (*Asplenium scolopendrium*) as they are rather too similar. When growing *Polypodium australe* and any of its wonderful cultivars, bear in mind they die down during late spring and early summer, and choose accompanying plants that peform well during their rest period.

Ferns are beautiful with grasses and bamboos (so long as they are not the invasive kinds). I once saw a particularly attractive border at Burford House gardens in Shropshire where various grasses were planted with *Polystichum setiferum* 'Plumosum Bevis' and *P. setiferum* 'Plumoso-multilobum'. I was very impressed at how well the two types of plants complemented each other.

In damper areas where larger ferns like osmunda are being grown, candelabra primulas, *Gunnera manicata*, irises and other water-margin plants are perfect natural partners.

Stumperies

The concept of stumperies was promoted in the nineteenth century, particularly as a setting for ferns and as an alternative to a rockery where rock was not obtainable. Basically, it was suggested that tree stumps with a length of trunk still attached should be planted upside down in the ground with the root mass looking like a small dead shrub. This sounded rather unattractive and I dismissed the idea as being not to my taste. Subsequently, I exhibited ferns at many flower shows, and, presented with the problem of how to hide the plant pots, resorted to using old stumps and branches. It actually looks great! I now use the wood even if it is not essential for cover. I love the way the various shades of brown and the rough shapes of the wood set off the greens of the ferns and their delicate forms.

It is very easy to develop a stumpery in the garden. Make an apparently haphazard arrangement of irregularly shaped pieces of wood or tree stumps ('so that the interference of art shall never be detected': Repton) and plant the ferns in between. The larger the pieces of wood the better; slender branches are not so effective.

The only stumpery I have seen in a public garden is at Biddulph Grange in Staffordshire, England. It was made by James Bateman in the mid-nineteenth century. Originally the stumps were piled high enough to arch over the paths, although this is no longer the case; the ferns are still thriving. A truly wonderful stumpery has been created at Highgrove in Gloucestershire by His Royal Highness, the Prince of Wales. Densely planted with ferns and hostas, it is a sensational sight with a stump arch set off by two rustic temples. Such is the brilliance of the structure and planting that I have known it to inspire non-fern lovers to start growing ferns.

I believe there is a place for both stumperies and rockeries in modern gardens. Rockeries are an excellent backdrop for mountain plants, while stumperies come into their own in woodland situations.

Rockeries

Many ferns can be classed as alpines, that is small enough to be kept in small greenhouses or grown on rockeries. There are many, many plants that complement them in such situations. Among my favourites are lewisias,

The delicate little fern *Asplenium trichomanes* 'Ramo-cristatum' will enhance any rock garden.

saxifrages and primulas. Specialist alpine growers will have their own preferences. All those I have seen blend well with fern plantings.

Plants overhead

In a woodland garden the canopy planting is important. It must not be too dense, or too little moisture will be available for the ferns. Rhododendrons and other large shrubs are fine, although I prefer to plant the ferns between, rather than under them. Large overhead trees are perfect. As long as the trees are well spaced and the roots are at a reasonable depth, ferns thrive. Oak, hawthorn, birch and many ornamental trees are suitable, although I am wary of suckering species like flowering cherries. Ferns will grow under such trees but the suckers and the surface roots inevitably take more than their fair share of the soil moisture.

Beech trees are a special case: few plants grow under mature beeches. My nursery is close to the largest-girthed fern-leaved beech in Britain. As there were no weeds under it I used the space to heel in a wide selection of ferns. All of the species that like good drainage, especially the polypodiums, did well as long as they were planted around the periphery of the umbrage. Of course, the dark summer foliage and sparse rain penetration harmed them little and in autumn, when the leaf canopy dropped, the new polypodium fronds emerged.

Yew trees also deserve special mention. Again weed-free underneath, they are a tempting place to plant ferns, and, surprisingly, they have done very well for me, so long as the ferns are not positioned too near the trunk. In the periphery of the umbrage is, again, fine. My soil is heavy clay, which could be significant; on lighter soils planting under beech or yew may be less successful.

Plants to avoid

Some years ago I was tactfully advised not to use *Maianthemum bifolium* in my borders. Seduced by the charm of the little plant, I ignored the advice. I now have it running through much of my garden and through the rootstocks of some of my ferns. I think it is there forever! Another troublesome mistake was ivies. Quick-growing, attractive and green – an essential plus point for a fern lover – they are easily obtained in many varieties and make wonderful ground cover. Wonderful, that is, if they would stay between the ferns but, unfortunately, they do not. Once established they take over. I almost lost some choice ferns to ivy strangulation.

3 Special Cases

Most ferns can easily be grown in the open garden with just a little commonsense, but tree ferns, desert ferns and filmy ferns are a bit more difficult.

TREE FERNS

Few plants have such general appeal as tree ferns. Even non-gardeners, and certainly gardening non-fern lovers, take notice of tree ferns and want to grow them.

What is a tree fern?

A tree fern is more or less any other fern with large fronds, except that, in time, it produces a trunk. The trunk may be up to 18m (60ft) tall. It consists of a central caudex, a hardy woody stem with conducting tissue, surrounded by a mass of old leaf bases, fibre and roots. It is not true to say that the trunk is all root: it certainly contains roots but it is the woody caudex that gives it its strength. I once chainsawed through a dead trunk. The saw went through the peripheral tissue like butter, but when it reached the caudex it really struggled and for a while I thought it might not cut it through cleanly.

There are over 600 different species of tree fern. Although most are in the genus *Cyathea*, the most widely grown in cultivation are various species from the relatively small genus *Dicksonia*, particularly *Dicksonia antarctica*. *Cibotium* and *Lophosoria* are two other small related genera. The genus *Cyathea* has been split by some into a number of smaller genera including *Cnemidaria* and *Sphaeropteris* but I prefer to ignore these and keep them all in *Cyathea*. Species from some other genera, notably *Blechnum* also produce trunks, but these are not true tree ferns. Even hardy European species sometimes produce a 'trunk'; it is not unusual to see *Dryopteris affinis* with a stump a few centimetres high. Unfortunately, as the stump gets taller with age, the roots dry out and the plant eventually dies.

Horticulturally, *D. antarctica* has many advantages over almost all the other species. It is nearly hardy in the cool temperate climates, such as that of the British Isles. It is incredibly easy to grow. It is able to remain alive while being transported from Australia, which takes seven weeks in a container ship. Most remarkable of all it can survive being sawn off at ground level as a mature tree up to 6m (20ft) in height. The severed plant has no roots apart from those on the trunk. In due course the trunk is planted on the other side of the world, it produces new fronds in 4–6 weeks and within a year has rooted into its new growing medium! How many other trees would survive such abuse? I suspect none.

Many other tree fern species are listed in An A–Z of Ferns (pp.42–169) but none has the proven ability to survive this sort of treatment. Although a few others are being imported into Britain as trunked specimens, all come with at least a few roots attached. It is possible that *Dicksonia fibrosa* would survive the same sawn-off treatment, but I prefer not to be the one to take the chance. Certainly in New Zealand, some *D. squarrosa* grow when a severed trunk is planted as a fence post, but only a smallish proportion of the trunks produce fronds, and I suspect even fewer produce roots and become properly established. This is far inferior to *D. antarctica*. The success rate with the thousands of trunks I have imported on my nursery is something like 99 percent, and the failures have been down to mistakes by the growers over here.

Most tree ferns need much the same cultivation techniques as described below for *D. antarctica,* except that many are far less hardy and need to be kept under glass in cool climates (see Winter Protection, p.35).

Cultivation of Dicksonia antarctica

If the specimen is purchased as a newly imported log, I recommend soaking the base of the trunk for a few minutes prior to planting. If it is to be planted out in the garden, select a shady spot, out of the wind. Some compromise is perfectly acceptable in the absence of such a site, but as the site gets further from ideal, the plant tends to produce shorter fronds. Plant the log so that as little trunk as possible is buried, while ensuring that it is stable and will not topple over easily. As tree ferns are normally priced according to the length of trunk, burying unnecessary trunk is effectively burying money. Once the trunk is firmly in position, water it copiously. I direct the full force of a hose all over and all around the trunk from about 10cm (4in) below the top down to ground level. Some growers advocate filling the crown with water; I am not keen on this practice. If the weather is cold and damp the crown might sit uncomfortably wet, perhaps encouraging rot. In summer I am sure it would not be a problem but it is not a habit to get into.

Keep the log watered daily if possible, especially in more exposed sites, until the new leaves have emerged and expanded. If the odd day is missed it is not a serious problem, but a well-watered plant does produce longer fronds and is generally better set up for the next season, too. I have noticed my long-established plants are not so good as they were when they were really loved and watered daily: due to general commitments they now only get watered 3–4 times a year. They are still attractive but the fronds are now only 1.5–2m (5–6ft) long instead of 2.5m (9ft). I do not normally feed my dicksonias

Some examples of mixed species of tree fern at Rickard's Hardy Ferns, Kyre Park.

when they are planted in the garden. They seem to manage with plenty of water and the basic soil nutrients.

Pot specimens

If preferred, the log can be planted in a pot. Again, plant it as shallow as possible, but remember, when picking up the pot, that the log will fall out if not held upright. Water copiously and within six months the log should have rooted and become secure. Initially, I like to select a pot as small as possible for the log. There are several reasons for this: because the plant needs to be watered so much over the first few months, the soil inevitably gets very wet and a smaller pot has a better chance of drying out a little between waterings; the unrooted log is very difficult to secure in a large pot unless it is planted unacceptably deep; and smaller pots are easier to move around and are more economical on composts.

After one full year in the small pot (normally the next spring), the plant should have produced roots that will be

appearing out of the drainage holes. When this happens it is time to pot it on. At this stage I feed my plants for the first time. I avoid any feeding for the first year as I want the log to root into the compost. If it is fed too much nitrogen, there is a risk that a lot of foliage will be produced with little or no root, possibly stressing the plant if it is allowed to dry out at all. (Feeding with a high potash/low nitrogen product to encourage root growth may be fine but in my experience is not necessary.) Once roots are evident I am happy to feed with a general-purpose fertilizer.

Winter protection

Unfortunately no tree fern is totally hardy in the temperature experienced by most of the British Isles (zone 8). Recent winters have been very mild and virtually all *Dicksonia antarctica* have thrived outdoors, whether protected or not. Some growers feel that *D. antarctica* is fully hardy in Britain. However, please do not be lulled into a feeling of false security. Hard winters can be a problem and very hard winters fatal unless sensible precautions are taken. Recent losses over winter due to the weather have been almost nil, but remember that Britain, like most parts of the world, can get rogue winters, and losses in such seasons can be devastating. I remember touring Cornwall trying to find a 60–90cm (2–3ft) specimen in the mid-1980s, just after a severe winter. None of the plants I saw that had trunks shorter than 1.2m (4ft) was alive. True, they had not been protected but the way all the shorter plants were wiped out has convinced me that they were less hardy (very short, trunkless plants were fine as they were protected under snow). I can only guess why shorter plants seem less hardy. The temperature can be lower near the ground – hence ground frost – also the air flow around a short plant may be less, making drying out slower. I have wondered if the reason that there are no long-standing plantings of *D. antarctica* outside the very mildest gardens is the lack of availability of large specimens, which could survive in the colder areas. The recent spate of imports of large trunks has changed this and we may see evidence of wider hardiness of these much larger specimens.

Australians usually expect *D. antarctica* to be hardy in Britain. In Australia temperatures as low as −13°C (8°F) occur in tree fern areas. This is encouraging evidence in the hardiness debate but you must remember that even Tasmania is 10 degrees nearer the equator than is central England. Clearly the length of daylight in mid-winter is much longer, allowing more time to get temperatures above freezing most, if not all, days. Certainly, here in central England, I feel it is the all-day frosts, or even all-week frosts, that do the damage. In Papua New Guinea some species of cyathea live at around 3500m (11,500ft). Here they experience frost on many nights, but rarely as low as −9°C (15°F). Research has shown that the tissue at the trunk apex is sufficiently well insulated not to freeze before daytime warming occurs again.

There are three strategies for providing winter protection for tree ferns: keeping them in a conservatory all year round; overwintering small plants in a protected environment; and protecting larger plants outdoors *in situ*.

Growing in a conservatory

The safest way to grow tree ferns is to keep them all in a conservatory all year round. In a sunny conservatory they must be watered abundantly in hot weather during the growing period. They also need water from time to time in winter, especially if the conservatory is heated. In a shady conservatory, management is easier but plenty of water is still needed. In Britain *Cyathea australis*, *Dicksonia antarctica* and *D. fibrosa* should not need any heat over winter. Some other species, including *Cyathea dealbata*, *C. dregei*, *C. smithii* and *Dicksonia squarrosa* and most of the other tree ferns in An A–Z of Ferns (pp.42–169) prefer the minimum temperature to be at or above freezing.

Overwintering in a protected environment

Alternatively, plants of *C. australis*, *D. antarctica* and *D. fibrosa* with less than 60cm (2ft) of trunk, are best overwintered in a protected environment. As mentioned above, smaller plants are less hardy than anything taller. The cut-off point of 60cm (2ft) is arbitrary but, in my experience, reasonable. Fortunately, shorter plants are also lighter and not too difficult to move around. Many growers have them as a patio feature from spring to autumn, or plunge the pot in the garden so that it looks as though it is planted out, then move it inside in autumn.

Protecting plants *in situ*

Larger plants of the three hardiest species can be left out over winter but, in my opinion, need protecting in zone 8 or colder. Over about 15 years I have developed the following strategy in what is probably the coldest area of lowland England. The lowest temperature recorded during this period was −15°C (5°F). The plants were well protected (as described below) and I have had no losses. It seems to me that it is the meristem (the bud tissue in the crown) that is vital for the continued success of the plant, so from late October to mid-April I protect this area of the plant. This is done at the end of the growing season so there are no new fronds waiting to unfold.

The ring of fronds at the top of the trunk forms a funnel that leads down into the trunk very nearly as low as the meristem. This funnel will readily collect water. To prevent this from happening I stuff it with straw to about 15cm (6in) above the top of the trunk. This keeps the meristem warmer and keeps out the worst of the winter wet, greatly reducing the risk of a block of ice forming in the crown. In a mild winter this is sufficient protection for large plants of 1.2m (4ft) or taller. For shorter plants, in addition to the straw I wrap an insulating material around the top of the trunk. I use a belt of polystyrene plant trays, tied together and cushioned from the trunk with more straw – the straw is stuffed behind the trays and keeps them tight. I also tie a circular piece of polystyrene over the crown, which helps divert rain water away from the meristem. In this way the top of the trunk is fully boxed in against the cold, and to some extent the wet. If particularly severe weather is forecast, further layers of insulation, perhaps sacking or straw bales, can be positioned around the trunk.

This *Cyathea australis* in a logging-devastated forest will soon be bulldozed into a huge bonfire with the rest of the debris.

Many people have experimented successfully using garden fleece instead of polystyrene for protection, but as recent winters have been very mild I remain somewhat cautious. Another favourite material with some people is bubble wrap. I am not keen on it as I think it could well lead to the crown sweating and then possibly rotting. I have heard of tops of tree ferns being completely wrapped in polythene, leaves and all. I think this is potentially dangerous and the ideal breeding ground for rots.

All the above may be irrelevant to anyone gardening in or near the heart of large cities or near western coasts. Frosts tend to be rare in such places, allowing *D. antarctica* at least to be grown with much less need for protection.

I always hope that a new species will come into cultivation that is hardier than *D. antarctica*. At the moment, none is proven better, but *Cyathea australis* and *Dicksonia fibrosa* are interesting and, surprisingly, *D. sellowiana* from South America also looks promising. Superficially very similar to *D. antarctica*, it has done very well over three winters in Hereford.

Provenance of Dicksonia antarctica

There has been much discussion over the relative hardiness of *D. antarctica* sourced from different regions. It is often referred to as the Tasmanian tree fern, but I am

informed from Australia that no plants harvested in Tasmania may be legally exported out of Australia. It is, therefore, odds-on that virtually all plants in cultivation elsewhere in the world came from Victoria or possibly New South Wales or even, many years ago, from South Australia, where it is now apparently extinct. Tasmanian plants may be hardier than mainland·plants, but so far as I am aware there is no evidence of any difference emerging where populations from the two areas have been studied. Traditionally in horticulture, plants from cold areas are thought to be hardier, so it will be interesting to see if any evidence to support this emerges in the future.

Environmental impact

Some concern has been expressed over the wholesale harvest of tree ferns from the forests of Australia (and New Zealand). I recently visited the harvesting sites in the Otway Ranges to the south-west of Melbourne and came away convinced that tree fern harvesting from the wild is sustainable and is having no significant environmental effect. How can this be? The answer is that forestry is the main, indeed, virtually only industry, in the tree fern areas. When areas of forest are felled for timber, all plants in the understories are completely destroyed. Huge machinery removes the commercially valuable wood and then bulldozers push all unwanted debris, including many tree ferns, into huge piles which are then burned. The areas are immediately reseeded with eucalyptus species which need light to germinate. No vegetation is allowed to survive as this would prevent the crop from establishing. I can confirm that eucalyptus forests are harvested every 60 or so years; I counted the annual rings on the largest stumps. In that time *D. antarctica* and *C. australis* have plenty of time to recolonise the forest floor.

Forestry felling is not clear felling in the sense that hundreds of acres are totally cleared. The state laws insist that all waterways have an undamaged buffer zone either side. For rivers the band is wide, but even for damp ditches along spring lines an area of something like 50m (160ft) is left untouched. In practice, therefore, felled areas are penetrated by fingers of virgin forest so when the land is left alone after the eucalyptus trees are resown, the natural forest species are within easy colonization range, allowing the forest to again appear totally natural by the time it is felled 60 years later. It should be noted that where coniferous plantations replace the semi-natural eucalyptus, the harvesting interval is much

shorter and the tree ferns usually also shorter. They are thinner as well, as they are slightly drawn up by the lower light levels. It is said that they are often poorer quality.

The fern cutters, who harvest the tree ferns are, therefore, salvaging a waste product of the timber industry. Their job is arduous. They are given only short notice of where the next felling operation will take place and they must get in to the designated area and remove as many of the tree ferns as possible in a short time. This is not easy! The forests are usually trackless and the edges of the areas difficult to define. Plus the cutters must be careful not to cut into the buffer areas around water courses. I spent a few hours with a team while the timber fellers were only about a hundred metres away. It was quite an experience as huge eucalyptus trees were falling ominously close. Of course, not all the tree ferns are salvaged. If by chance other species, such as *Cyathea cunninghamii*, are in an area to be cleared, the fern cutters cannot touch them by law. But they will be trashed just the same by the foresters. It is important to reiterate that forestry is the cornerstone of the local economy, the main employer in the region, and without it there would be serious depopulation – the foresters are only doing their job! But it remains that tree fern harvesting really is a salvage operation with no environmental impact in itself.

Choice of tree fern species
Outdoors

In cool temperate regions *Dicksonia antarctica* is the first choice. It is tough, relatively hardy and has been in cultivation long enough for a fair bit to be known about what it will or will not tolerate. Generally, it has done so well that I am asked by successful growers what other species they can try outdoors in zone 8. To my mind there are two choices.

The first is *Dicksonia fibrosa*. I have had this outdoors for 11 winters with no problems at all. The lowest temperature over this period was −12°C (10°F). The plants in question were well protected but not only did they survive: they also grew about 5cm (2in) of trunk a year – twice the amount of the best I have achieved with *D. antarctica*. The drawback with *D. fibrosa* is that it is superficially very similar to *D. antarctica*. It *is* a different species but even botanists have attempted to merge them together as one over the years. In the world of gardens this is disappointing to all but the specialist plantsman.

For something that is really quite different I recommend *Cyathea australis*. I have had a single plant of this species outdoors for two winters. So far so good. It should be at least as hardy as *D. antarctica* because it comes from the same general area of Australia. It is a plant of rather more open places than *D. antarctica*, and should, therefore, stand exposure and frost better. Its altitude limit is very similar to *D. antarctica* and may even go slightly higher, another plus factor. Overall, it may prove to be at least as hardy as *D. antarctica*. On the debit side it is apparently deciduous, even in Australia, whereas *D. antarctica* is often evergreen. To date, information on cultivation of *C. australis* in cool temperate regions is rather sparse, but the prospects of success are good and it would seem to be a suitable species for wider hardiness testing.

C. australis is fundamentally different from the two hardiest dicksonias. It is abundantly covered with scales on the croziers and stipes. The leaf bases are very spiny and are arranged in symmetrical patterns throughout the length of the trunk. The common name, rough tree fern, refers to the vicious spines on the persistent leaf bases. Gloves are recommended for handling large specimens! The fronds are broader and more divided than those of

Desert fern, *Cheilanthes tomentosa*, in Clive and Doreen Brotherton's garden near Birmingham.

the dicksonias and the frond stipes are long. Fronds also tend to be a paler green. Overall it is very distinct and comes closest to filling the need for a different type of tree fern.

For anyone lucky enough to live in an area where frosts are rare, there are other species that can be considered. I have heard of plants of *Cyathea dealbata, C. smithii, Dicksonia squarrosa* and *D. sellowiana* doing well. As mentioned above, *D. sellowiana* may prove to be as hardy as *D. antarctica* but information is currently limited.

DESERT FERNS

The term may seem a contradiction, but by desert ferns I mean those that can survive the dry periods experienced annually in various parts of the world – southwest USA, Mexico, western South Africa, the periphery of the Australian desert, the Mediterranean region and other dryish areas. Normally these ferns are either in the genera *Pellaea* or *Cheilanthes*. Species from other genera grow in the same areas, but these two are best adapted to dry conditions.

Only a few of these ferns are common in cultivation but many are beautiful and deserve to be better known. Unfortunately, few can stand a cold wet winter, but if treated like alpines and grown in an alpine house virtually all are, in fact, hardy down to around −10°C (14°F).

Cultivation

For their successful culture they need a free-draining compost. One part loam-based compost and one part sharp grit works well. Some species are lime-hating, while others like lime, but this compost seems to work well for both groups (the odd amount of lime in the loam-based compost does not seem to have any detrimental effect on the lime-hating species). During the growing season the plants need to be kept very well watered – deserts are presumably wet during the growing season! It is best to avoid getting any water on the foliage. When resting they need little water. Most species are deciduous or, at best, become untidy over winter. Do not give in to the temptation to remove the old fronds too soon; it can be harmful to the plant. It is best to wait until the new season's fronds are underway before tidying off the old ones.

FILMY FERNS

Filmy ferns are a beautiful group of ferns with thin-textured fronds, often only one cell thick. The fronds are so thin that a finger passing behind them is clearly visible.

They flourish in areas of high humidity and are rarely suitable for the open garden. However, because of their semi-transparent beauty and their glossy, damp-looking surface, they are much loved by enthusiasts. Most species are in the family Hymenophyllaceae and include two principal genera, *Hymenophyllum* and *Trichomanes*. Both these large genera have recently been subdivided by botanists, introducing quite a few new names. However, in most cases everyone will know what you are referring to if you stick to the two mentioned above. There are also one or two other genera which contain some filmy ferns. The genus *Leptopteris* has several species, most notably *Leptopteris superba*, the Prince of Wales feather. This large fern is native to New Zealand and requires the same management as the true filmy ferns. There is a filmy fern called *Cystopteris membranifolia* that occurs in Mexico, where it grows by waterfalls. It survived for several years in my garden before neglect got the better of it.

Cultivation

The requirement for high humidity rules filmy ferns out for outdoor culture in most gardens. If you are lucky enough to have a very humid corner, typically with a fast-running stream, there are some species worth trying that are likely to be hardy in zone 8 or 7. The three species native to the British Isles and Europe, *Trichomanes speciosum*, *Hymenophyllum tunbrigense* and *H. wilsonii,* are all worth a try but they are difficult to come by and should never be collected from the wild. Slightly more readily available are some of the Australasian species, including *Hymenophyllum flabellatum* and *Trichomanes venosum* (*Polyphlebium venosum*), which are being imported as chance epiphytes on the trunks of Australian and New Zealand tree ferns. They can be left *in situ* to take their chances, or they can be cut off and grown on in a suitable environment. If left *in situ*, remember to plant the tree fern with the filmy fern in the shade, usually on the northern side.

I do not know if any growers have had any long-term success with filmy ferns outdoors on tree fern trunks but I would like to hear of any successes. I have removed one or two species from *D. antarctica* and transferred them to a protected environment. I cut them out on little slabs of tree fern fibre using a sharp penknife. The pieces are about 4cm (1½in) deep into trunk and 20cm (8in) square.

The high humidity these filmy ferns require is best achieved in a closed glass case. The concept of growing

Filmy fern (*Hymenophyllum* species) growing on mossy ground in a coastal garden in County Kerry, Ireland.

ferns in cases was introduced to the world in 1842 by Nathaniel Ward. Beautifully elaborate Wardian cases were constructed during the Victorian period, but today most of these have disappeared. I now use an old fish tank with grit in the base covered with a shallow layer of an ericaceous compost – most filmy ferns are calcifuge. The ferns are either planted into the soil as rooted plants or the slabs of tree fern trunk are laid on the surface or leant against the side of the tank. Misting with water is essential after planting but, if the tank is covered, further watering will rarely be necessary. The tank should be placed away from direct sunlight.

I have a small trunk of *D. antarctica* that is covered with *Trichomanes venosum*. It is remarkably tolerant of relatively dry atmosphere. I have exhibited it at several flower shows, including Chelsea, where it has had to survive exposure for up to a week away from its humid home. It must be one of the best candidates for trying in the open garden.

Part Two The Plants

4 An A–Z of Ferns

This A–Z includes ferns that are good garden plants, or cold greenhouse plants in cool temperate regions. Some may need more protection but are worth growing because they are of special interest. The overwhelming majority have either been grown in my garden in central England or in my unheated polytunnels. There are also some that I have not grown: they were either overlooked, too rare or are new introductions. Many of the plants are not readily available from nurseries: however, spores of the rare and unusual are often available from specialist societies. Many of the best cultivars are sterile and often obtained from other enthusiasts by exchange or gift; it is therefore a very good idea to join a society to see these rarer gems, and perhaps one day own them.

NAMING OF CULTIVARS

Before 1959 cultivars could be named at the whim of any individual as long as they were published in a book, a nursery catalogue, a magazine, a journal, or any similar publication. This led to cases of names becoming a little unwieldy. The International Code of Nomenclature for Cultivated Plants (first edition 1953) was, therefore, established to try to bring some worldwide conformity to nomenclature of cultivated plants. In summary, the rules now state that a cultivar named after 1 January 1959 must be named in a living language (ie. not Latin).

This sounds very sensible and straightforward but it has meant shedding old naming conventions and breaking continuity with old literature. For example *Athyrium filix-femina* 'Plumosum Axminster' is an old cultivar. If a new form is raised that is similar, but distinct, it cannot now be named, for example, 'Plumosum Cristatum Coke', as this is a newly created name and 'plumosum' and 'cristatum' are words from a dead language, viz. Latin. A compromise has, therefore, been proposed. This allows for the creation of 'cultivar-groups'. The cultivar-group epithet is not an essential part of the name, and may be based on an accepted pre-existing Latin-form cultivar epithet. It can also be used in tandem with a new non-Latin cultivar epithet to allow the affinities of the new cultivar to be readily understood. To follow through the above example:

Athyrium filix-femina 'Plumosum Cristatum Coke' is unacceptable. *Athyrium filix-femina* (Plumosum Group) 'Philip Coke' is acceptable. The Plumosum Group can be shed, thus *Athyrium filix-femina* 'Philip Coke' is also acceptable and would be the correct name.

Polypodium australe 'Semilacerum Carew Lane' is unacceptable, whereas *Polypodium australe* (Semilacerum Group) 'Carew Lane' is acceptable and *Polypodium australe* 'Carew Lane' is also acceptable.

Where a completely new break occurs there is not necessarily any need to refer to any previously established group of cultivars. (For further reading on this subject, see Barnes, Peter, *Pteridologist* 1,5. 1988.)

Some cultivar names are fairly long and it has long been acceptable to hyphenate them to make them easier to read. Recently, however, there has been a move to remove the hyphen. I feel this to be a retrograde step so I have retained the hyphens for names in this book, eg. 'Plumoso-multilobum' rather than 'Plumosomultilobum'.

CLASSIFICATION OF CULTIVARS

The first clear attempt to classify cultivars was completed by Dr F.W. Stansfield during the 1880s. This scheme was accepted by E.J. Lowe and published in *British Ferns* (1890). It stood unaltered until 1968 when Reginald Kaye modified it in his book *Hardy Ferns*. It was revamped by Jimmy Dyce (Dyce, 1987) and I have slightly revised the system in the version given below. Not all types of cultivar are represented in every species. Some forms are common to most species, eg. 'Cristatum', while others may be restricted virtually to a single species, eg. 'Setigerum' in *Athyrium filix-femina*. Many other terms are used to describe cultivars (see Dyce, 1988) but those explained here are the commonest and should allow many if not all cultivars to be identified to a basic level.

There are two main divisions: A classifies the fern according to the shape of the frond and B classifies it according to the form of the pinnae. A third, smaller division contains lesser types.

Previous page: *Onychium japonicum* has the common name 'carrot fern', the distinctive fronds looking rather like carrot leaves.

Division A: Variation in shape (skeleton) of frond

Group 1 Cristatum – repeated terminal division or cresting

a) Capitatum – at frond apex only.

b) Cristatum – at pinnae tips, with or without apical cresting.

c) Percristatum – at pinnae and pinnule tips, with or without apical cresting.

d) Grandiceps – crest broader than frond.

Group 2 Ramosum – major skeletal division

a) Ramosum – main leaf stipe (stipe and/or rachis) divides once or repeatedly.

b) Cruciatum – secondary leaf rachis (pinnae) divides one or more times at junctions with main stipe.

c) Brachiatum – basal pinnae elongate to resemble separate fronds.

Group 3 Other skeletal changes

a) Angustatum – pinnae greatly reduced in length with narrowed frond.

b) Deltatum – pinnae elongated progressively towards frond base to create deltoid shape.

c) Parvum – frond normal in shape but greatly reduced in size.

d) Congestum – spacing between pinnae and pinnules reduced causing overlapping of leafy parts, often combined with brittleness.

e) Revolvens or Reflexum – pinnae and/or pinnules reflexed, giving frond and/or pinnae a tubular appearance.

f) Depauperatum – pinnae and/or pinnules reduced, irregular or missing.

Division B: Variation in degree and form of dissection of frond lamina or parts thereof

Group 1 Dissectum – margins incised or indented.

a) Dentatum – pinnae or pinnules with shallow regular teeth. Further subdivided into Crenatum (teeth rounded) or Serratum (teeth saw-like).

b) Setigerum – pinnules indented deeply into narrow segments with pointed teeth or bristles.

c) Laciniatum – frond, pinnae or pinnules torn deeply into narrow segments or irregularly pointed lobes.

d) Incisum – pinnae or pinnules deeply and irregularly indented.

Group 2 Decompositum – pinnules subdivided into pinnule-like parts.

a) Plumosum – pinnules large and divided one or more times giving feathery appearance; with some exceptions sori absent or scanty. In *Asplenium scolopendrium* the plumose form appears as a thin-textured crisped frond.

b) Tripinnatum – pinnules enlarged and divided into distinct pinnulets, or merely lobed (throughout whole frond).

c) Subtripinnatum – pinnules enlarged and divided into distinct pinnulets, or merely lobed (restricted to parts of frond).

Group 3 Divisum – pinnules divided; restricted to *Polystichum setiferum*.

a) Acutilobum – pinnules narrow, undivided or sharply serrate, very pointed; sharply serrate or undivided but basal lobes distinct, completely or almost separate, narrow, sharply pointed; texture hard; glossy.

b) Multilobum – pinnules enlarged, very divided, final segments wide and foliose; texture soft; not glossy, pale to mid-green. (i) Multilobum – pinnae divided up to three times. (ii) Plumoso-multilobum – pinnae more enlarged, final segments pinnule-shaped, densely massed and overlapping, building up into a frond thickness of 2cm (¾in) or more.

c) Divisilobum – pinnules enlarged, very divided, final segments very narrow, often glossy and dark green. (i) Divisilobum – pinnae divided up to three times, final segments elongated and pointed, texture hard to semi-soft, glossy. (ii) Plumoso-divisilobum – pinnae more enlarged, final segments tend to be slightly wider and softer, semi-glossy; pinnae wide and very overlapping.

d) Pulcherrimum – lower pinnules (and rarely the upper ones) greatly extended, slender, sickle-shaped, deeply divided; points run out into slender twisted threads, capable of producing prothalli, texture soft.

e) Conspicuolobum – pinnules round, undivided; basal lobes separate and distinct, very round; texture soft.

Group 4 Foliosum – leafy.

a) Foliosum – pinnules wide and leafy, not divided, often overlapping.

b) Rotundatum – pinnules broad and rounded.

Division C: Other variations

Group 1 Rugosum – blade surfaces leathery and uneven, restricted to *Asplenium scolopendrium*.

a) Marginatum – fleshy ridges on under and/or upper frond surfaces, parallel to midrib, usually marginal; often combined with Muricatum.

b) Muricatum – frond surfaces rough and leathery, covered with short hard excrescences.

Group 2 Other pinnule characters.

a) Crispatum – pinnules twisted or crisped.

b) Linearum – pinnules very narrow and undivided.

c) Variegatum – changes in colour.

EUROPEAN PLANT HARDINESS ZONE MAP

The hardiness zone map of Europe is based on one prepared by the Royal Horticultural Society. The zones are
defined by the average annual minimum temperatures
experienced by the area in question. Plants that are hardy
in a particular zone may usually also be grown in all
zones warmer than it; for example, a plant that is hardy
in zone 6, should survive in zones 7 and warmer. However, the zone system is only a guide. Zone boundaries
can only be approximate on such a small scale map.
Microclimates within each area may mean you can grow
plants from a warmer zone, or conversely, some plants
hardy in your zone may not survive in your garden. This
is particularly true towards the upper and lower limits of
each zone. (See also Hardiness p.46.)

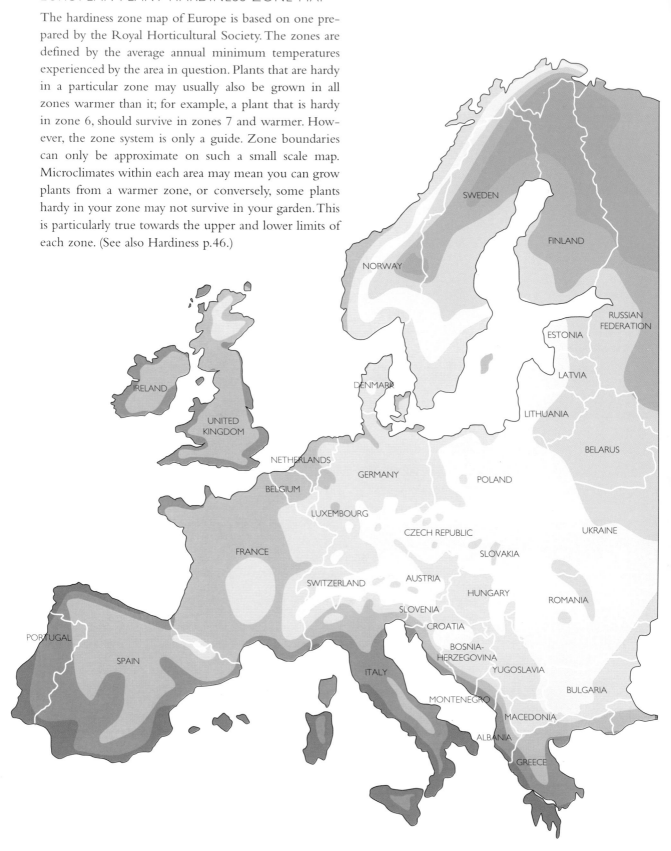

USA PLANT HARDINESS ZONE MAP

The USA hardiness zone map shows the hardiness zone system developed by the United States Department of Agriculture. The map works in the same way as the European one (see opposite).

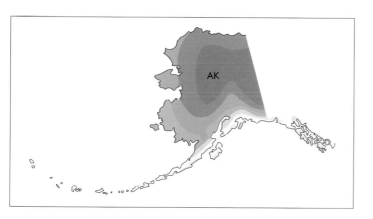

		Fahrenheit	Celsius
Zone 1		below -50°	below -46°
Zone 2		-50° to -40°	-46° to -40°
Zone 3		-40° to -30°	-40° to -34°
Zone 4		-30° to -20°	-34° to -29°
Zone 5		-20° to -10°	-29° to -23°
Zone 6		-10° to 0°	-23° to -18°
Zone 7		0° to 10°	-18° to -12°
Zone 8		10° to 20°	-12° to -7°
Zone 9		20° to 30°	-7° to -1°
Zone 10		30° to 40°	-1° to 4°
Zone 11		above 40°	above 4°

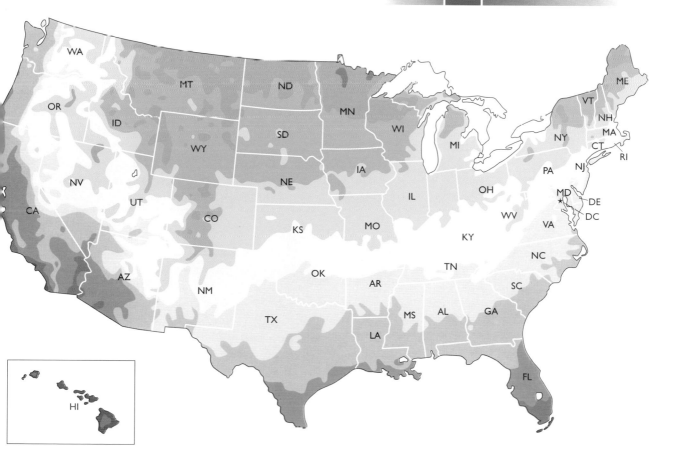

GUIDE TO ENTRIES

Where appropriate, the following information is given for each entry in the A–Z.

Synonym – other Latin names in common use.

Common name – given only when it is a name in common use.

Country or region of origin.

Height (H) – this is the frond length, and is obviously very dependent on growing conditions. In luxuriant conditions the given dimensions will be exceeded. Where a second figure is given this is frond width.

Deciduous (D), evergreen (E) or wintergreen (W) – Deciduous ferns lose their fronds and more or less disappear over winter. Evergreen ferns are green all year, but may begin to look tatty by spring. There are two kinds of wintergreen ferns – those that stay green most of the winter but are usually tatty by midwinter as the fronds collapse under light snow or in strong winds; or *Polypodium australe* and its cultivars, which send up new fronds in mid- to late summer and die down again in mid- to late spring.

Site preference –

Dry: use a very well-drained compost including liberal amounts of grit. Usually in a well-ventilated spot, often in full sun. Often in an alpine house.

Dry/Wet: a well-drained site in shade. Typically woodland but often created artificially in gardens along the north walls of houses and fences.

Wet/Dry: damp site in shade. As for dry/wet but 'on the wet side' most of the year.

Wet: waterside or bog plantings. Not usually inundated but some species, eg. *Osmunda regalis* can withstand severe flooding in winter. Many of these species will tolerate full sun as long as they always have a plentiful supply of water.

Hardiness – Hardiness zones are given for each species. These zones were worked out by the United States Department of Agriculture and are based on an estimate of the average annual minimum temperature. They are at best a rough guide to the climate at a given site; temperatures can vary enormously within a single garden, let alone a region. Particularly severe winters or mild winters will alter the zone rating. For example, here in central England the past two winters have been relatively mild, with my garden just squeezing into zone 9, but my average for the previous ten years puts me firmly in zone 8; a cold winter in 1981 meant we slipped into zone 5 or even 4.

It is particularly difficult to equate minimum temperatures between essentially dry continental climates and wet oceanic ones; many plants will tolerate lower temperatures in dry conditions: for example, few of the *Cheilanthes* species listed here will survive if they are grown outside in a wet, zone 8 climate, but they are hardy in the same area when grown in a dry, well-ventilated greenhouse.

All ferns included in this book should be hardy in southern African and southern Australia.

One hardiness zone is usually given per species. The fern is normally hardy in that zone and in most warmer (higher number) zones. The zone given for each species is the coldest it is likely to survive and some protection overwinter is often advisable. If your zone is one number higher than that given, then the plant should not need any cosseting. When experimenting with ferns of unknown hardiness, think positive. It is useful to remember that although a plant may not naturally occur in cold regions, it is not necessarily cold-sensitive. I have grown ferns from Mexico, Jamaica, India, Australia and so on outdoors for years. Where zone 8 is given as the coldest zone for a species, this is often based on my experience in my own garden. In fact, if the fern is tried in lower temperatures it may well survive. Experimentation is well worthwhile.

Key distinguishing features – If possible, differences between species and cultivars have been restricted to easily recognized characters; sometimes, however, a hand lens will be useful. There is often a jizz unique to each taxon which cannot easily be put into words. Hopefully illustrations will help here. Technical terms have been kept to a minimum but are occasionally used for the sake of brevity. The glossary (p.180) explains their meaning.

ADIANTUM (maidenhair ferns)

This is one of the most beautiful of all the fern genera. It is a huge genus with, unfortunately, only relatively few hardy or half hardy species. All species listed are worth acquiring, and a little trouble taken to protect half hardy species can be very rewarding. No doubt, in time, more hardy species suitable for sheltered niches, even in quite cold gardens, will be discovered. In *A Guide to Hardy Ferns* Richard Rush lists a few other species worth trying if they become available.

Maidenhair ferns are very distinctive. The pinnules are borne on thin, shiny black stems. The pinnae themselves are usually oblong or fan-shaped. Characteristically the

Adiantum aleuticum in a mixed fern planting at Leinthall Starkes, Herefordshire.

spores are produced in a sorus formed by a fold along the distal edge of the pinnule. Maidenhair ferns are not normally fussy about soil type; certainly many species actually prefer lime.

A. aethiopicum (common maidenhair of Australia)
Australia, New Zealand, Africa, H15cm (6in), D, Dry/Wet, Zone 9, possibly 8. Fronds mainly bipinnate, triangular. A creeping plant with small, rounded pinnules. 'Possibly semi-hardy' Rush, 1984. In Australia this fern grows on dryish banks above streams in woodland and can survive severe drought. It is native quite well south including Victoria. In England, it has survived overwinter in unheated polytunnels with temperatures down to −10°C (14°F).

A. aleuticum (Aleutian maidenhair)
Western coast of North America, Japan, H30–60cm (12–24in), D, Dry/Wet, avoid windy sites, Zone 3. Fronds pale green, pedate (erect stipe divides into a fan of finger-like sections), each 'finger' further divided into a series of triangular segments (pinnules). Eventually forms a clump. Like 'Japonicum' (below) new fronds are occasionally slightly flushed with pink. This is such a deservedly popular fern that various wild collections have been named unofficially. For example "Patrick Creek" and "Perry Creek" are both attractive plants but not sufficiently distinct to warrant varietal status. (*A. pedatum*, below, is very similar to *A. aleuticum*. It comes from the east coast of North America.)

'Japonicum' (Japanese maidenhair) Japan, H30-45cm (12-18in), Zone 8. Sometimes referred to as "Asiatic forms", this differs from the typical plant by having rosy-pink foliage with contrasting black stipes in spring. There is some doubt over whether this is correctly placed under *A. aleuticum* or *A. pedatum*. Originating from the Pacific fringes, it is remote from the east coast of North

Adiantum aleuticum 'Subpumilum', a beautiful dwarf fern that will enhance rock garden, border or stone trough.

America, and therefore more logically allied to *A. aleuticum*, but curiously there is sometimes a relationship between the floras of Japan and the east coast of America. DNA analysis in the future will reveal its true identity. This form is less reliable in the garden: it seems to need more shelter and is probably less hardy.

'Imbricatum' H15–30cm (6–12in). Intermediate between the typical plant and 'Subpumilum'. Comes more or less true from spores.

'Laciniatum' *(Plate V)* H30–60cm (12–24in). Each pinnule is deeply lacerated giving the whole plant a very wispy appearance. Comes true from spores. Rare.

'Subpumilum' (dwarf maidenhair) H7–15cm (3–6in), D, W in a mild winter. Differs from the typical plant in being much smaller, with overlapping pinnae and being more tolerant of wind. Ideal for borders, stone troughs or rock gardens. In the wild this form is rare, only known from a handful of sites in the Pacific north-west of America. It grows in proximity to the typical plant along

with plants of all intermediate sizes, see 'Imbricatum' (above). In horticulture it, nevertheless, comes true from spores.

'Tasselatum' has crested tips. It has occasionally occurred in sowings at Fancy Fronds Nursery in Seattle. Unfortunately, it is not a constant form and sometimes reverts.

A. capillus-veneris (true maidenhair)
Europe, including south-west British Isles, H30–38cm (12–15in), D, Dry/Wet, Zone 9, possibly 8. Fronds bipinnate, each pinnule rounded with a crenate margin on sterile fronds. If fertile, the sori are formed from the reflexed edge of pinnules. Typically the sorus is elongated, not circular. (The very similar tender species *A. cuneatum* has circular sori.) It is found in many parts of the world and is the only British native maidenhair. In Britain it is a maritime species recorded from a few sites along the south and west coasts, plus, curiously, some inland sites on sheltered walls. In the wild the plant luxuriates in areas where water runs over lime-bearing rock; tufa is often formed on site. The running water may help to protect against low winter temperatures; despite the frequent presence of running water the plants are never waterlogged. It is not reliably hardy in central Britain, but it succeeded for me in a sheltered, well-drained site, although the fronds were very small and late in appearing. During the nineteenth century many cultivars were in cultivation. However, many were only slightly different from the parent type and most are now extinct.

'Cornubiense' (Cornish maidenhair) H30cm (12in). A variety found originally in Cornwall. A beautiful fern with deeply lacerated pinnules. Probably not fully hardy but has survived –9°C (16°F) with me. Thought to be extinct, this cultivar resurfaced in horticulture in Australia.

'Daphnites' H20cm (8in). An old cultivar raised by Lowe in 1870 from spores given him by Sir Joseph Hooker. The plant is erect and the pinnae so crowded and confluent as to give the appearance of cresting. This plant is so distinct and its provenance so curious that I wonder if it might be a form of a different, yet allied, species.

A. davidi *(Plate V)*
Himalaya, H15cm (6in), D, Dry/Wet, Zone 8. Superficially similar to *A. venustum* (below) but differs in having deeply serrated pinnule margins. Fronds pink in spring turning green more gradually than *A. venustum*.

A. fimbriatum
Himalaya, H15cm (6in), D, Dry/Wet, Zone 8. Recent introduction which has proved hardy in central England.

Fronds bi- to tripinnate, lance-shaped. Pinnules small and finely toothed along outer margins. An interesting new possibility for a sheltered niche.

A. formosum
East Asia, Australia, H22cm (9in), D, Dry/Wet, Zone 8. Fronds triangular, bipinnate, very handsome. They are produced from deeply creeping underground rhizomes. The depth at which the rhizomes creep seems to be the key to the fern's unexpected hardiness, but plant it in a protected site, eg. under a stone. Plants appear late in the season but in time a good clump can develop. Propagate by spores or division.

A. hispidulum (rosy maidenhair)
Australia, H30cm (12in), D, Dry/Wet, Zone 9. Reported as hardy by Reginald Kaye. I have never tried it outside but it is occasionally available commercially and should be worth trying in sheltered gardens. Fronds pedately divided, pink when young but maturing to very dark green.

The very handsome *Adiantum formosum* is a surprisingly hardy maidenhair fern from Australia.

A. jordanii (Californian maidenhair)
Western USA, H30cm .(12in), D, Dry/Wet, Zone 8. Fronds narrowly triangular, usually bipinnate. Day length seems to determine when it produces new fronds: it flushes in early spring and again in autumn, and I have never seen fronds produced in summer, even when well watered. Although perfectly hardy the sporadic production of fronds makes this rather more difficult to grow than other maidenhair ferns.

A. × mairisii (Mairis's hybrid maidenhair)
H38cm (15in), D, Dry, Zone 8. Fronds bipinnate with rounded pinnules on a shiny black rachis and midrib. This hybrid fern was raised at the nursery of Mairis and Co before 1885. It was named by Thomas Moore, who thought the parentage might be *A. capillus-veneris* and *A. cuneatum*. Over a hundred years later this parentage still seems possible as modern chromosome counts are consistent with Moore's theory. (See Richard Rush, *Bulletin of the British Pteridological Society*, 1983, p.261.) The fern resembles *A. capillus-veneris* in general form but is more erect with slightly smaller pinnules and has greater vigour; it is, therefore, a far better garden plant. Its

greatest asset is its hardiness – I have grown it outdoors for decades; my only concession to slight tenderness is to plant it among stones. In time it spreads beyond any protection and thrives. It remains rare in cultivation, but it has a spreading habit and can be divided periodically to increase stock.

A. pedatum (eastern maidenhair)
Eastern North America, H45–60cm (18–24in), D, Dry, Zone 3, avoid windy sites. True *A. pedatum* is very uncommon in cultivation, at least in Europe; plants supplied as *A. pedatum* are usually *A. aleuticum*. The two species were separated by Paris in 1991 (Rhodora, vol. 93, pp.105-122). It is difficult to define the differences between *A. pedatum* and *A. aleuticum* as both have pedate fronds with shiny black-brown rachis and midribs, but mature plants seen side by side are clearly different. As a guide, *A. pedatum* has larger pinnules with rounded crenulate lobes; each pinnule is held in the same plane as the frond, ie. flat. In *A. aleuticum* the pinnules are smaller with angular denticulate lobes and each pinnule is twisted out of the plane of the frond. In *A. pedatum* each frond has more branches, and is usually a paler green. In a well-lit site the fronds of *A. pedatum* arch laxly while those of *A. aleuticum* tend to be more stiffly erect. At shows where both species are on display *A. pedatum* wins in terms of general appreciation. Propagate by spores.

Asiatic forms H30–45cm (12–18in). This description crops up in cultivation. New fronds are pink. Plants I have seen are forms of *A. aleuticum* 'Japonicum' (above).

'Miss Sharples' H30–45cm (12–18in). The origin of this name is rather amusing. The original plant was given to the well-known nurseryman Reginald Kaye many years ago by a Miss Sharples. Not unreasonably, he labelled it 'Miss Sharples' so he could remember its provenance. Unknown to him another nurseryman collected spores, assumed 'Miss Sharples' was its correct name and sold plants under that name. The name has stuck.

Until recently I thought 'Miss Sharples' was a form of *A. aleuticum*. However, at the time it appeared and before, the North American maidenhair fern offered by British nurseries was probably exclusively *A. pedatum*. Photographs in Perry's catalogues in the 1950s are clearly *A. pedatum*. *A. aleuticum* was introduced more recently – possibly by Judith Jones, proprietor of the nursery Fancy Fronds in Seattle. Dutch nurseries got hold of it and introduced it in quantity. 'Miss Sharples' history dates from before Judith Jones's introductions and, given its much larger pinnules and paler frond colour, I now won-

der if it is in fact a form of *A. pedatum*. It differs from the type plant in having conspicuously lobed pinnules.

A. poiretii (Mexican maidenhair)
Central and South America, Africa, H20cm (8in), D, Dry/Wet, Zone 8. Fronds narrowly triangular, bipinnate, not unlike *A. capillus-veneris* but smaller. Often Mexican plants have a beautiful yellow indusium covering the sori. I grew this for many years in a limestone quarry garden; it was late to reappear each spring, but it survived – until I moved house!

A. × tracyi
Pacific north-west America, H22–38cm (9–15in), D, Dry/Wet, Zone 3. A hybrid between *A. aleuticum* and *A. jordanii*. Rarely available because it is sterile, but easy to grow. It more closely resembles *A. aleuticum* but differs from it in not having regularly divided pedate fronds. Propagate by division.

A. venustum (Himalayan maidenhair) *(Plate V)*
H22–38cm (9–15in), D, Dry, Zone 5. Deciduous but can remain green through some winters. Croziers of new fronds are pink. They emerge in early spring and withstand late frosts with ease. Fronds rapidly turn dull green. Dryish to moist shade or semi-shade. Rhizomes creep near soil surface and produce tripinnate, narrowly triangular fronds. Gradually spreads to give excellent groundcover. Best propagated by division but ensure sections of rhizome are not buried too deeply and that they are firmly fixed – freshly planted-out rhizomes of *A. venustum* make excellent bird-nesting material.

ANOGRAMMA

A small genus with one hardy species.

A. leptophylla (annual fern)
South-west Europe, North Africa, H5–12cm (2–5in), D, Wet/Dry, Zone 9. Fronds narrowly lance-shaped to triangular, usually bipinnate. An annual fern that comes freely from spores. It can be grown in a pot in an unheated greenhouse, where it should reappear annually. In the garden it needs a warm spot and reasonable humidity. It is certainly frost hardy but I have never grown it outdoors.

ARACHNIODES

An attractive genus closely related to *Polystichum* and *Dryopteris*. The sorus is kidney-shaped, as in *Dryopteris*, but the pinnules terminate in bristles and the frond texture is often leathery, rather like *Polystichum*. There are many species other than those listed here that are not in

The arching fronds of *Arachniodes standishii*, the 'upside-down fern' from East Asia.

general cultivation but could be well worth trying. Some species were formerly placed in *Leptorumohra* or *Polystichopsis*.

A. aristata
South-east Asia, Australasia, H30cm (12in), but up to 90cm (3ft) in warmer climates, E, Dry/Wet, Zone 7, possibly 6. Needs a sheltered site inland in Britain. Glossy triangular, bipinnate to tripinnate fronds, the lowest pair of pinnules on the basal pinnae are greatly elongated. Rarely cultivated but it is hardy in a sheltered, moist, but not boggy site.

A. denticulata
Jamaica, Mexico, H15cm (6in), larger in warmer climates, D, Dry/Wet, Zone 8. A beautifully dissected fern. Fronds tripinnate, triangular with a long stipe. Pinnules quite narrow giving the frond an airy appearance. Despite its provenance, it has been hardy with me for many years; the new fronds are, however, late appearing.

Protect the crown from winter damp with straw. The ability to cultivate a plant from the West Indies outside in the relatively cold climate of central Britain encourages experimentation with other unlikely subjects.

A. simplicior, syn. A. aristata 'Variegata'
Japan, China, H30cm (12in), E, Dry/Wet, Zone 7. Very handsome fern with broadly triangular, bipinnate, hard-textured fronds. They are glossy green with prominent yellowish areas either side of the midrib. Hardy here for many years.

A. standishii, formerly Polystichopsis standishii (upside-down fern)
Japan, Korea, H45–60cm (18–24in), W, Dry/Wet, Zone 5. Fronds ovate, tripinnate, pale green. Spores produced mainly towards base of frond. The ovate frond is quite different from most members of the genus.

A. webbianum
Madiera, H38cm (15in), D, Dry/Wet, Zone 9, possibly 8. Larger-growing species somewhat similar to *A. aristata* but with more open bi- to tripinnate fronds. Hardy in Gloucestershire for many years.

ASPLENIUM

Asplenium is a very large genus with plants all over the world of greatly varying appearance and greatly differing cultural requirements. All species have a rather leathery feel to the fronds and all have elongated sori. This list includes a selection of species; many others are known but they are either of little garden merit or very similar in appearance to included species. *A. scolopendrium* has in the past been placed in its own genus, *Phyllitis*, but modern concensus has sunk it into *Asplenium*. Culturally it is easier to grow than most small asplenia from temperate regions. Tropical and warm temperate species, such as *A. bulbiferum*, are excluded from this work.

A. adiantum-nigrum (black spleenwort)
Europe, including British Isles, Asia, North America, North Africa, H7–38m (3–15in), E, Dry/Wet, Zone 4. Fronds leathery, triangular, bi- to tripinnate. The common name is derived from the black rachis – particularly on the underside. Difficult to cultivate in pots as it is easily overwatered, but usually easy in the garden if given good drainage. The subspecies *corrunense*, from serpentine

The rare hybrid *Asplenium* × *alternifolium* growing on a stone wall in France.

rock in Britain, approaches *A. cuneifolium* (below) but is not strongly triangular and is tetraploid.

A. adulterinum
Central Europe, Scandinavia on serpentine rock, H7–12cm (3–5in E, Dry/Wet, Zone 6. Similar to *A. trichomanes* except the midrib is green at the tip and dark brown at the base. Although now behaving as a true species it is known to be derived from the hybrid between *A. trichomanes* and *A. viride*. Cultivate in a free-draining mix. Serpentine rock is helpful but not essential for establishment.

A. × alternifolium (alternate-leaved spleenwort)
Europe, including British Isles, North America, H5–15cm (2–6in), E, Dry/Wet, Zone 5. Calcifuge. Extremely rare, but very pretty little fern. Fronds pinnate, perhaps bipinnate at base. Pinnules lance-shaped, attached at 45 degrees to the rachis. Fronds and midribs green. A sterile hybrid between *A. trichomanes* subsp. *trichomanes* and *A. septentrionale*. Grows well on an acid scree bed.

A. ceterach, syn. *Ceterach officinarum* (rustyback fern)
Europe, including British Isles, Asia, North Africa, H8–20cm (3–8in), E, Dry/Wet, Zone 5. Fronds pinnatifid with triangular lobes. Underside of pinnae covered with brown scales. In drought the fronds curl up and appear dead, only to reopen with addition of moisture. Usually found growing on sunny rocks or walls. Unfortunately difficult to grow, it must have very good drainage in sun or light shade. Preferably with some lime in the mix. Rarely commercially available.

'Crenatum' Triangular lobes themselves crenately lobed. Crenations tend to appear in well-grown plants. Rare in cultivation but particularly common in the wild in western Eire.

'Cristatum' Tips of fronds crested. In cultivation but very rare.

A. csikii, formerly *A. trichomanes* subsp. *pachyrachis*, *A. trichomanes* var. *harovii*, *A. trichomanes* 'Subaequale'
Europe, including British Isles, H10–15cm (4–6in), E, Dry/Wet, Zone 5. Recent work by Johannes Vogel at the Natural History Museum, London has shown this to be a distinct species. It differs most conspicuously from *A. trichomanes* in having lobed, overlapping pinnae and blue-green fronds. In the wild it is almost confined to limestone rocks and walls, typically living in tiny caves out of direct rainfall. It can be cultivated in a free-draining calcareous mixture. Ideal in an alpine house. It is a tetraploid.

Asplenium csiki 'Trogyense' in South Wales, still growing where it was first discovered in 1872.

'Trogyense' Discovered by a Mr Pierce in 1872 in South Wales. It is a particularly well-developed form with deeply crenate pinnae margins.

'Velum' Discovered by Lowe growing among 'Trogyense' in 1890. It differs from 'Trogyense' in that the lower basal lobe of each pinna projects nearly at right angles to the remainder of the pinna, almost like a curtain.

A. cuneifolium
Central Europe, 15–20cm (6–8in), E, Dry/Wet, Zone 4. Fronds strongly triangular, bi- or tripinnate. Diploid. In the wild it grows only on serpentine rock, so it is a good idea to include some ground-up serpentine in the mix in cultivation. Not to be confused with the very similar *A. adiantum-nigrum* subsp. *corrunense* (above) which is also found on serpentine.

A. dareoides
South America, H7–10cm (3–4in), E, Dry/Wet, Zone 5. Very hardy in Britain. Fronds tripinnate and roundly triangular with slightly rounded segments. A beautiful creeping fern, easily grown in a shady border with good drainage.

A. × ebenoides
Eastern USA, H15–20cm (6–8in), E, Dry/Wet, Zone 6. A fertile hybrid between *A. platyneuron* and *A. rhizophyllus*. Fronds suberect, pinnate with variable shaped pinnae, usually triangular. Will root from the tip of some leaves.

Quite intermediate between the parents. Cultivate in a well-drained site or an alpine house.

A. fissum
Central Europe, H7–25cm (3–10in), D, Dry/Wet, Zone 6. Fronds erect, lance-shaped or narrowly triangular, bipinnate. Pinnules fan-shaped, divided into linear segments. In nature, a plant of calcareous screes and rock crevices. Difficult in cultivation, needing a stony, calcareous mix, perhaps best in an alpine house.

A. flabellifolium (necklace fern)
Australia, New Zealand, H7–15cm (3–6in), E, Dry/Wet, Zone 9, possibly 8. Fronds pinnate with green rachis. Bulbils, formed near the tip, grow into new plants, allowing a colony to develop. Probably hardy in a sheltered, well-drained spot, otherwise fine in an alpine house. Grows on rocks and screes in the wild.

A. fontanum (fountain spleenwort)
Central Europe, Asia (Himalaya), H7–30cm (3–12in), E, Dry/Wet, Zone 5. The common name is derived from the fountain-like growth. Fronds narrowly lance-shaped with the longest pinnae normally about two-thirds the length of the frond from the base, bipinnate-pinnatifid. Naturally found on limestone rocks. It is particularly common in the French sub-Alps on shady, dryish rocks and walls. In the garden it likes well-drained calcareous soil. Unfortunately slugs love it. Fine in an alpine house.

A. foreziense
Europe, mainly central France, H7–22cm (3–9in), E, Dry/Wet, Zone 5. Fronds lance-shaped but less markedly so than *A. fontanum* with the longest pinnae about one-third the length of the frond from the base, bipinnate, leathery. Confined to acid rocks and walls (see also *A. obovatum* subsp. *lanceolatum*); in cultivation needs acid, well-drained soil and protection from slugs.

A. hemionitis
Portugal, Azores, H7–25cm (3–10in), E, Dry/Wet, Zone 9. Fronds palmately 3- or 5-lobed, each lobe entire. Not widely in cultivation but surviving in a shelter in a garden in Glasgow, Scotland. Needs acidic conditions, good drainage and a humid site.

A. hybridum
Croatia, H7–15cm (3–6in), E, Dry/Wet, Zone 8, possibly 7. Derived from the hybrid between *A. ceterach* and *A. sagittatum* and restricted to an offshore island in the northern Adriatic. Fronds triangular and entire, but lobed. Difficult to cultivate, but sufficiently distinctive to make the effort worthwhile, probably best in an alpine house in a coarse mix.

PLATE I
Asplenium scolopendrium I

'Crispum Fimbriatum Bolton'

'Undulatum Muricatum' *(see also Plate II)*

'Crispum Moly'

'Spirale'

Crispum Group (narrow form)

All fronds shown approximately half size

'Crispum Fimbriatum'

'Crispum Speciosum
Moly'

'Golden Queen'

'Crispum Bolton's
Nobile'

'Crispum Variegatum
Bolton'

A. incisum
Japan, H7–25cm (3–10in), E, Dry/Wet, Zone 8, possibly 9. Fronds narrowly lance-shaped, being broadest two-thirds of length from base, bipinnate. Pinnules lobed; pinnae triangular. Stipe short with very small basal pinnae. Hardy in my unheated polytunnel, should do well in well-drained site in a sheltered garden.

A. jahandiezii
France, H5–7 × 1cm (2–3 × ½in), E, Dry, Zone 5. Fronds linear, pinnate, leathery. Pinnae almost round, distal margin serrated. In nature confined to a single gorge where it is quite common in rock crevices. I know of one plant that was in cultivation in an alpine house for about 25 years in a calcareous stony mix, watered rarely. A beautiful species quite unlike any other.

A. lepidum
Central Europe H2.5–5cm (1–2in), D, Dry, Zone 5. Fronds bipinnate; pinnules fan-shaped, few. Texture thin, slightly translucent. A native of deep, humid limestone gorges. Difficult in cultivation, it needs a stony, calcareous mix and a very sheltered site.

A. marinum (sea spleenwort)
West Europe, including British Isles, H7–22cm (3–9in), E, Dry/Wet, Zone 9. Fronds narrowly lance-shaped, very leathery, pinnate, dark glossy green. Fronds almost 60cm (24in) long have recently been reported from Rathlin Island, Northern Ireland. In nature it is usually found on acid or limestone sea cliffs, also on walls but almost always near the sea. Difficult to cultivate but I have seen well-grown plants in horticulture. It does not seem to need sea salt but it does not like severe frosts. Must have shelter from prolonged low humidity, ideal in a glazed case if not too wet.

A. monanthes (single sorus spleenwort) *(Plate V)*
North America, H12–25cm (5–10in), E, Dry/Wet, Zone 7. Fronds pinnate with black rachis. Superficially similar to *A. trichomanes* but with more erect fronds and usually only one sorus on each pinnule. Pinnules oblong appearing to droop either side of the rachis. Hardy in a protected site, eg. beside stones with good drainage and a cool root run underneath, or in an alpine house.

A. obovatum subsp. lanceolatum, syn. *A. lanceolatum*, *A. billotii*
West Europe, including British Isles, H7–22cm (3–9in), E, Dry/Wet, Zone 8. Fronds lance-shaped, bipinnate, leathery. Locally common on acid rocks and walls in south-west Britain and Wales. In the garden it needs acid conditions, very good drainage and protection from

slugs. Differs from the very similar *A. foreziense* in having deeper, more narrowly toothed pinnules.

A. onopteris
South and west Europe, including Eire, H7–30cm (3–12in), E, Dry/Wet, Zone 8. Fronds strongly triangular, tripinnate – resembles a very finely cut *A. adiantum-nigrum*. Very hardy with me, despite preferring a Mediterranean climate in the wild. Does well in a reasonably well-drained, half-shaded border.

A. petrarchae
Mediterranean Europe and Africa, H5–7cm (2–3in), E, Dry, Zone 9. Fronds lance-shaped, pinnate. Pinnae covered in glandular hairs, almost circular, incised around tip. Grows in shady crevices in sunny outcrops of limestone where the roots can be fairly cool but the fronds are often in full sun. In the garden it needs a warm, sunny spot with a stony limestone mix. Avoid water direct to the crown if possible.

A. platyneuron (ebony spleenwort)
North America, H12–38cm (5–15in), E, Dry/Wet, Zone 5. Fronds pinnate with dark brown rachis. Sterile fronds spreading, fertile fronds more erect. Pinnae narrowly triangular and alternate along the rachis. Superficially similar to *A. trichomanes* but pinnae shape and growth form is distinctive. Tolerant of a wide range of pH but must have good drainage.

A. rhizophyllus, syn. *Camptosorus rhizophyllus* (walking fern)
North America, H7–15cm (3–6in), E, Dry/Wet, Zone 5. Fronds pinnate, simple, slender, broadest at base. Bulbils produced at frond tips root to become new plants. In the wild found on or near limestone rocks. Colonies soon develop in cultivation but must have a well-drained mix and must not dry out. Very tasty to slugs. Beware of too much moisture over winter.

A. ruta-muraria (wall rue)
Northern hemisphere, including British Isles, H5–15cm (2–6in), E, Dry/Wet, Zone 4. Fronds triangular, bipinnate, leathery, dull green. Although very common it is almost impossible to cultivate. Sometimes becomes established on garden rock, otherwise the best chance of success is with spores.

A. scolopendrium, syn. *Phyllitis scolopendrium*, *Scolopendrium vulgare* (hart's tongue fern)
Europe, including British Isles, H45–60cm (18–24in), E, Dry/Wet, Zone 5. Fronds strap-shaped, entire. Clump-forming, excellent as a contrast to the more feathery types of fern. Prefers lime in soil; this is not essential but

plants are less luxuriant in very acid conditions. Best in full or semi-shade as bright midday sun can burn brown lesions into the fronds. There are related species around the northern hemisphere. Occasionally in wet seasons or in particularly wet sites, the fungus disease *Milesina scolopendrii* can infect fronds. The symptoms are brown lesions, not unlike sunburn, but they differ in producing a few white powdery spores in the centre of the lesion on the lower surface. The disease can be kept in check by removing infected fronds and by cleaning up established plants in the spring just before the new fronds emerge. If preferred, a rust-active systemic fungicide may be applied. In North America, var. *americanum* looks similar (it has double the number of chromosomes) but it is not such a strong grower; *A. lindenii* from Mexico may be the same taxon. *Phyllitis* (*Asplenium*) *japonicum* looks similar but may be genetically distinct. The robust character of the European hart's tongue fern makes it one of the very best garden plants. Fortunately there are many cultivars in cultivation. All are fertile, except the best forms of 'Crispum', and all are worth growing.

'Cornutum' H30cm (12in). Terminal part of the frond lamina is missing and the midrib is continued as a short horn. Not a great beauty.

Crispum Group *(Plate I)* H30–60cm (12–24in). Fronds

A narrow, undulate form of *Asplenium scolopendrium*, approaching 'Crispum'.

sterile, green and deeply goffered – from the side they resemble an Elizabethan ruff. The Crispum Group of cultivars are the plumose form (see p.43) and the cream of the hart's tongues. Being sterile they are rarely propagated, but may be divided or propagated from leaf bases (pp.175–177). In 1650–51 Bauhin and Cherler described *Phyllitis crispa* in *Historia Plantarum Universalis*: this was probably a true Crispum, one of the earliest fern varieties mentioned in print. Over the years around one hundred cultivars in this group have been named. Unfortunately most are now lost or no longer recognized. Surviving forms are listed below.

'Crispum Bolton's Nobile' *(Plate I)* H45cm (18in). Found on Warton Crag in North Lancashire around 1900 and grown by H. Bolton, although he may not have been the finder. It is the boldest form known. The fronds are often 10cm (4in) wide. The goffering is not as tight as in some forms but it is a beautiful fern.

Crispum Cristatum Group H30–60cm (12–24in). Sporelings of 'Crispum Moly' are often branched or crested. Some forms are very attractive but others look a little 'over the top'.

'Crispum Fimbriatum' *(Plate I)* H30–45cm (12–18in). The original cultivar in this group was 'Crispum Fimbriatum Stansfield', unfortunately long extinct or lost. Surviving illustrations show fronds beautifully crisped with extremely deeply and finely lacerated margins. I suspect that this level of development was only ever achieved in optimum conditions under glass and maybe some of the lesser forms in cultivation today might achieve similar distinction if suitably cultivated. 'Crispum Fimbriatum' is worth growing in the open garden, the serrated margin making it stand out from other crispums. These plants are sparingly fertile and could arguably be placed under the Undulatum Group.

'Crispum Fimbriatum Bolton' *(Plate I)* H30cm (12in). Raised by Robert Bolton c1915. A crested, fimbriate form. A true crispum, being sterile. The fronds are narrow. A very neat little plant.

'Crispum Moly' *(Plate I)* H45–60cm (18–24in). A fertile form, I believe more correctly classed in the Undulatum Group (below). The frond tapers to a sharp point.

'Crispum Robinson' or "Robinson's broad form" H50 × 9cm (20 × 3½in). Found by Mr Robinson in North Lancashire pre-1890. This is a problematic cultivar. Plants grown under this name in collections are not as broad as I would expect, being more like 'Crispum Speciosum Moly'.

PLATE II
Asplenium scolopendrium 2

'Laceratum
Kaye'

'Undulatum
Muricatum'
(see also Plate I)

Sagittato-
cristatum
Group

'Peraferens'

Ramo-marginatum
Group

Fimbriatum
Group

Muricatum
Group
(dwarf form)

All fronds shown approximately half size

'Ramosum'

Ramo-cristatum
Group

Ramo-cristatum Group
(from near Shirenewton)

'Marginatum'

'Cristatum'

'Drummondiae'

'Crispum Speciosum Moly' *(Plate I)* H60cm (24in). Possibly a sporeling of 'Crispum Moly', perhaps originally raised by Moly at Charmouth in Dorset in the 1870s. The goffering is very tight and deep, in good light some yellow striping develops from the midrib to the frond margin. A tall upright fern. A very similar form was recently found near Cheddar, Somerset by C. and M. Potts. Other early tall forms of crispum, now lost, include 'Crispum Stablerae' and 'Crispum Keall'.

'Drummondiae' *(Plate II)* H30–45cm (12–18in). Very rare. Found by a Miss Drummond in 1861 near Falmouth in Cornwall. It is a fimbriate, crested crispum, but is sparsely fertile. The plant in cultivation today may be the original clone or progeny. Well grown in close conditions, it is a beautiful plant with lax fronds, wonderful in a hanging basket. In the open the fimbriations do not develop fully and the fronds remain more or less erect. Very rarely, bulbils develop on the upper surface of the frond and new plants can be raised from them. Additionally, new plants can be raised by aposporous growths from the tips of the fimbriations.

'Golden Queen', syn. 'Crispum Golden Queen' *(Plate I)* H30–38cm (12–15in). A true crispum with deeply goffered fronds, irregularly variegated yellow. The variegation may cover a 7–10cm (3–4in) section of a frond or may be just a few stripes running from the midrib to the margin. It develops much more conspicuously in sun, but too much sun can burn the yellow areas, which turn brown by late season. For this reason it is best grown in semi-shade. In deep shade it remains green. This rare cultivar is grown to perfection at Stancombe Park near Wootton-under-Edge in Gloucestershire. The rare 'Crispum Variegatum Bolton' *(Plate I)* is virtually indistinguishable from 'Golden Queen'.

'Kaye's Superb' H38–45cm (15–18in). Raised from 'Crispum Moly' by Reginald Kaye in the 1970s or 1980s. It is a beautiful form, very similar to 'Speciosum' but not apparently so strong growing. Another cultivar raised by Kaye at the same time was 'Kaye's Splendour'. This was a magnificent form with the fronds broadest in the middle, but unfortunately the original plant died before it could be multiplied. However, it may reappear in future sowings of 'Crispum Moly'.

'Sagittato-crispum' H45cm (18in). A form of crispum with small sagittate projections at the base of the frond, giving the frond base the shape of an arrowhead. They are obvious on detached fronds but are not noticeable on an established plant.

'Cristatum' *(Plate II)* H38cm (15in). Fronds crested at tip. Although the crest at the tip of the frond is wider than the lamina, the term 'Grandiceps', which usually describes this feature, is rarely used in *A. scolopendrium*. (Very heavily crested forms are named 'Capitatum' and 'Coronatum'.) Good forms of 'Cristatum' are uncommon in the wild. Usually the cresting at the tip is weak, being little more than branched ends, which often disappear under all but the most favourable conditions. Alternatively, the cresting develops with the maturity of the plant and the frond splits repeatedly lower down becoming 'Ramo-cristatum' (below).

Fimbriatum Group *(Plate II)* H30cm (12in). Fronds slightly narrowed with margins finely but deeply serrate. Closely related to 'Marginatum' from which it differs by lacking a slim wing of tissue running the length of the fronds on the underside, either side of the midrib. This may have originated from 'Fissum-latum' or 'Fissile' both found by Mr Elworthy in the mid-nineteenth century.

'Laceratum Kaye', syn. 'Kaye's Lacerated' *(Plate II)* H20–30cm (8–12in). Fronds almost triangular, broadest towards base, margins deeply lacerated. Slightly variable from spores. This attractive cultivar was discovered growing on the stone walls at Kaye's nursery in Silverdale, North Lancashire. Jimmy Dyce always maintained he saw it first but I suspect Reg already knew it was there. Discovered in 1952 or 1953, it was described as 'Laceratum' found by Reginald Kaye, an acceptable name at that time; however, the name was not specifically published as 'Laceratum Kaye' until after 1959. The name I have used is, therefore, arguably unacceptable under the International Code of Nomenclature for Cultivated Plants. The recommended name is 'Kaye's Lacerated', which I dislike.

'Marginatum' *(Plate II)* H38cm (15in). Perhaps the most common cultivar of *A. scolopendrium* occurring in the wild. A day's fern hunting in the Devon/Dorset borders will usually turn up a plant in this group. Typically the underside of the frond has a wing of tissue running more or less its entire length near the margin on its undersurface. The margin is also crenately lobed. Sometimes the wing of tissue is lacking but the name 'Marginatum' is still applied if the margin is lobed. The rarer form 'Supralineatum' has the wing of tissue on the upper surface. Sometimes, in 'Suprasoriferum', the sporangia creep around the frond margin onto the upper surface.

Muricatum Group *(Plate II)* H38–45cm (15–18in). The upper surface of the frond carries rows of pimples, in contrast to the glossy, reflective fronds of normal cultivars of the hart's tongue. From spores, therefore, variable. Many forms of this group have been raised over the years and we still have the gene pool to re-raise most, if not all again. Of greatest interest is 'Undulatum Muricatum' *(Plate I)*, raised by Lowe in the later half of the nineteeth century. As the name suggests, the frond is undulating and muricate (rough-surfaced). I gathered spores of this cultivar from the grounds of Shirenewton Hall – Lowe's garden. At the British Pteridological Society Centenary Fern Show at Pebworth in 1991 a dwarf, tightly crisped form of 'Undulatum Muricatum', raised by long-standing society member Alf Hoare, won the Best in Show award out of about 250 plants.

'Peraferens' *(Plate II)* H10–20cm (4–8in). An extraordinary cultivar, similar to 'Cornutum' but with the horned frond tip enclosed in a small pocket or pouch.

Ramo-cristatum Group (see also 'Cristatum') *(Plate II)* H38cm (15in). Fronds branch repeatedly from near the base. All terminals crested. Strictly speaking more common than 'Cristatum'. Good forms are still being found every few years in the wild. I found one I call 'Feizor' in a limestone pavement in Yorkshire in 1972. Another find was in the vicinity of Lowe's home at Shirenewton. If the frond branches but the tip is not truly crested, the cultivar is 'Ramosum' *(Plate II)*.

Ramo-marginatum Group *(Plate II)* H30cm (12in). Fronds dark green, branch repeatedly from base to the tip of the frond, fan-shaped with narrow segments, the width of divisions varies from plant to plant. Strictly speaking marginate forms should have a wing of tissue running the length of the underside of the frond on either side of the midrib. In practice, it is often missing. Included in this group are quite a large number of old forms not now recognized by name. However, careful study of existing material could easily result in the rediscovery of these and the selection of new distinct cultivars. The original form was raised by fern enthusiast Abraham Clapham of Scarborough around 1860. It reappears occasionally in modern spore sowings and is worth looking out for. Another of Clapham's selections, 'Keratoides', with an irregularly lacerated frond branching from near the base, also belongs in this group. (The frond shown on Plate II approaches 'Keratoides'.) 'Cervicornu' is similar except the branching is nearer the tip of the frond. The form 'Treble', raised by Fibrex Nurseries, was an unusual sparsely branched form with broader segments. It could now be extinct.

'Reniforme' H15cm (6in). All fronds orbicular. Unfor-

Asplenium scolopendrium 'Sagittato-projectum Sclater' was recently rediscovered in the Bolton collection.

tunately, this form is not stable and usually reverts to normal after a few seasons.

Sagittato-cristatum Group *(Plate II)* H20–30cm (8–12in). Fronds crested with arrowhead-shaped lobes at base. In the best examples of this group, the lobes at the base of the frond enlarge into a pair of lateral arms, which may be 10–12cm (4–5in) long and each terminate in a fan-shaped crest. The main part of the frond is broad and undulating and itself terminates in a broad crest. 'Alto', distributed by Fibrex Nurseries, was a dwarf form.

'Sagittato-projectum Sclater' H30cm (12in). An old cultivar which turned up recently in the Jim Lord collection (an offshoot of the Bolton collection). The fronds are arrow-shaped at the base; the rest of the frond is lacerated with a small flat crest at the top.

'Spirale' *(Plate I)* H12cm (5in). Thick-textured fronds twisted in a spiral. An old Victorian cultivar – similar

PLATE III
Athyrium filix-femina I

'Plumosum Drueryi'

'Plumosum
Superbum
Druery'

'Plumosum
Divaricatum'

'Plumosum Axminster'

'Kalothrix'

'Clarissima
Bolton'

'Philip Coke'

forms have been re-raised several times since, most recently by Dominic Kaye (grandson of Reginald Kaye) whose form 'Corkscrew' is 30–38cm (12–15in) tall.

Undulatum Group *(Plate II)* H30–38cm (12–15in). Frond margin deeply waved. Usually fertile. For simplicity I advocate that all undulate, thick-textured, fertile forms of *A. scolopendrium* are placed here and all undulate, thin-textured, sterile forms are treated as part of the Crispum Group. This was the strategy used by Lowe in the 1860s. There are one or two fertile crispums eg. 'Crispum Moly'; I suggest they are better grouped here. 'Crispum Moly', being fertile, is an excellent source of new forms of true crispums. A selection from the Undulatum Group distributed from Holland is poor and hardy deserving of the name. I list these, rather unkindly, as wavy forms. An attractive narrow form is shown on p.57.

'Variegatum' H30–50cm (12–20in). Yellow or white bands randomly running from the midrib to the edge of the frond. Many forms of 'Variegatum' have been raised, but often they are purely a product of the environment in which they grow – usually bright sunlight. Philip Coke grew many beautiful yellow forms in his garden at Stinchcombe in the Cotswolds but most plants seemed to lose the variegations when grown elsewhere. Philip even raised a variegated form of 'Undulato-muricatum' which has remained variegated with me.

A. seelosii
Central Europe, Pyrenees, H2.5–5cm (1–2in), E, Dry,

Zone 5. Fronds ternate (divided into three narrow segments), fleshy. Difficult to cutivate, needs a calcareous, stony mix, probably best in an alpine house to protect it from excessive winter wet. The central European form is hairy; that from the Pyrenees, subsp. *glabrum*, lacks hairs.

A. septentrionale (forked spleenwort)
Central Europe, including British Isles, North America, Asia, H5–15cm (2–6in), E, Dry, Zone 4. A native of acid rocks and walls. Fronds narrowly linear, completely lacking pinnae but with one or two forks towards the tip. A well-established plant can look like a tuft of grass, but it is nevertheless a fascinating and attractive fern. Rare in Britain but common in acidic rock areas of Central Europe, especially in the Massif Central of France. Around the eastern Black Sea the population has only half the number of chromosomes and is called subsp. *caucasica*. There are no cultivars.

A. trichomanes (maidenhair spleenwort) *(Plate V)*
Cosmopolitan, including British Isles, H7–20cm (3–8in), E, Dry/Wet, Zone 3. A beautiful little fern with simple pinnate fronds. Pinnae usually spherical or short oblong. Rachis shiny dark brown or black. There are many subspecies, all are extremely difficult to separate on vegetative characters but for the record the two commonest are subsp. *trichomanes* and subsp. *quadrivalens*. subsp. *trichomanes* is diploid and grows on acid or lime-free rocks and walls. Pinnae are almost round, usually smaller than subsp. *quadrivalens*. Rarer in the wild and rare in cultivation. Subsp. *quadrivalens* is tetraploid and prefers calcareous rocks or mortared walls. Pinnae almost rectangular, often quite large. As far as I know all cultivars in cultivation are this subspecies. Occasionally the two subspecies hybridize producing an intermediate form, nothosubspecies *lusaticum*, which can be H30–38cm (12–15in) long. All forms need good drainage especially over winter in pots. All are fine in a shady border or more particularly in a rock garden.

'Incisum Moule' *(Plate V)* H12cm (5in), E, Dry. Like the type plant except the pinnae are prettily incised. Fertile and comes true from spores. Introduced by Moule, a fern nurseryman living in Ilfracombe, Devon in the nineteenth century. Recently, a crested form was raised by Stuart Williams. I have named it after him *(Plate V)*.

'Greenfield' **(Incisum Group)** H15cm (6in), E, Dry. Sterile, much more finely incised than 'Incisum Moule', this is the true plumose form of the species. Very rare, found by Percy Greenfield in Somerset in 1961. For many decades this plant was cultivated by Kaye at his

The forked fronds of the unusual fern, *Asplenium septentrionale*, on a wall in mid-Wales.

nursery in North Lancashire; it may still be there. I include it because several similar forms have been found over the past 150 years. The very best was 'Incisum-Claphamii', for which it is worth keeping an eye open. Propagation by division, although one day it may be possible to propagate with tissue culture. No true Incisum has been recorded in Britain since 1961 but Michel Boudrie has come across 2 or 3 plants of a similar form in France in the last few years.

'Ramo-cristatum' *(Plate V)* H7–15cm (3–6in). Fronds branch with each terminal crested. 'Cristatum', where only the tip of the frond is crested, is uncommon. Comes true from spores and persists in several localities in the wild where it was known in the nineteenth century.

A. viride (green spleenwort) *(Plate V)*
Britain, Europe, North America, Asia, H10–15cm (4–6in), E, Dry/Wet, Zone 3. Fronds simply pinnate, similar to *A. trichomanes* except the midrib is entirely green. Pinnules orbicular with crenately lobed margins. A very pretty fern of shady niches in lime-rich mountainous areas. Cultivate in a free-draining calcareous mix, ideally among limestone rocks in a shady spot, either in the garden or an alpine house. Apparently short-lived, this fern has the irritating habit of suddenly dying, just when it appears to be well established.

'Ramosum' H10–15cm (4–6in). A form with some fronds forking near the tip, frequently occurring in the wild. The type specimen used by Linnaeus when he named the species was branching and he named the specimen *A. trichomanes ramosum*. For a time this was adopted as the correct Latin name for the species; fortunately common sense has prevailed and the species is once again known as *A. viride*.

ATHYRIUM

A large genus of deciduous ferns that have shortly linear sori with a slight bend at one end, often described as J-shaped. *Athyrium* is closely related to several other genera, eg. *Deparia*, *Diplazium*, *Lunathyrium* and *Cornopteris*, and some species seem to be moved around from genus to genus in horticulture. The best species for the garden is *A. filix-femina*. It is robust and grows well in damp shade. There are many species native to Eastern Asia that are hardy in Britain and deserve to be more widely grown. Unfortunately, they are difficult to name. However, once good books on Chinese, Himalayan and Japanese ferns appear in English, hopefully, it will be possible to get to grips with the problem.

A. distentifolium, syn. *A. alpestre* (alpine lady fern, alpine polypody)
Europe, including Scotland, Asia, H60–75cm (24–30in), D, Wet/Dry, Zone 5. Common at high altitudes on acid mountains. A distinct variety, var. *americanum*, grows in North America. Very similar to *A. filix-femina* but lacks an indusium (the sorus is naked), and has a slightly less delicately divided frond. The lack of indusium is a rare feature in *Athyrium*; all ferns with naked sori were originally grouped in the genus *Polypodium* – hence the common name alpine polypody, but the obvious close relationship with other athyriums has quite correctly placed it here. Grows well in the garden, irrespective of altitude, in a moist, shady spot. Happier in acid soils.

var. flexile, syn. *A. flexile* H15–30cm (6–12in), D, Wet/Dry. A very rare fern, known only from a few alpine corries in the north of Scotland. Handsome and distinct. Pinnae short with few rounded pinnules. Fronds lance-shaped, narrow, broadest near base, where they are often reflexed. Sori mainly produced at base of fronds. Ideal for damp borders, shady damp niches in rock gardens or an alpine house.

'Laciniatum' First raised by Stansfield's fern nursery in Lancashire in 1857. Recently re-raised by Heather McHaffie while researching var. *flexile*, from which it differs by having irregularly cut pinnules.

A. filix-femina (lady fern)
Northern hemisphere, including British Isles, H1–1.5m (3–5ft), D, Wet, Zone 3. Common in moist sites throughout the northern hemisphere, even spreading into Africa and tropical America. Fronds lance-shaped, very feathery, tripinnate. Dies down with first air frosts of autumn. Easily cultivated in cool, shaded, moist situations. Will grow in full sun if given plenty of moisture, eg. at pool margin. Usually more luxuriant on acid soils but still does well in alkaline sites. Propagate by division or spores, or rarely by bulbils – see *A. filix-femina* 'Plumosum Divaricatum', or apospory (see Propagation p.176) – see 'Clarissima'.

Over 300 cultivars have been described over the past 150 years. Cultivars raised from spores frequently appear similar to the parent but are not the same. This can lead to the incorrect application of the parent name to the sporelings; it is therefore better to use the group naming system explained above (p.43). This tendency not to come true from spores sometimes leads to the raising of a completely new cultivar or the re-raising of a 'lost' treasure (eg. 'Kalothrix', below).

'Acrocladon' *(Plate IV)* Found by Monkman at Castle

Howard in 1860. Fronds branch repeatedly from near the base, the plant resembling a ball. Very rare but grown for many decades by Reginald Kaye. Sparingly fertile; a few of the spore offspring resemble the parent, but some fine things have been raised – 'Unco-glomeratum' for example.

Capitatum Group H60cm (24in). Tip of fronds crested but pinnae uncrested. 'Coronatum' is a selected form.

'Caput Medusae' Raised by Mapplebeck. Fronds branch repeatedly with twisted segments, resembling Medusa's hair. I have never seen a convincing specimen of this fern but the name, if not the plant, is in cultivation.

'Clarissima Bolton' *(Plate III)* Found in Lancashire by Bolton and friend in 1893. Similar to 'Clarissima Jones' but smaller, slightly finer cut and somewhat inconstant. Like 'Clarissima Jones' this is aposporous but the offspring are usually depauperate.

'Clarissima Jones' Found in North Devon by the fern nurseryman Moule in 1868, this is probably the most sought-after cultivar of any fern. Fronds tripinnate with all divisions slim and elongated producing a very elegant airy frond, perhaps 60cm (24in) across. It looks delicate but in practice is remarkably robust. It does not produce spores, so propagation is by division, but unfortunately the crowns are slow to split; it is therefore rare and plants have recently changed hands for £250 each. On this variety apospory was first discovered. In the literature young plants raised are said to be indistinguishable from the parent, but folklore has it that they are depauperate. The few that I have raised have all been fine plants: the confusion may have arisen from the tendency of 'Clarissima Bolton' to produce depauperate offspring.

Corymbiferum Group As Cristatum Group except the terminal crest is bunched in several planes, ie. not a flat fan. Crest narrower than the rest of the frond.

'Congestum' As the type plant except the rachis and pinnae midribs are reduced in length and the leafy parts of the frond overlap. 'Congestum Cristatum' *(Plate IV)* is the crested form.

Cristatum Group *(Plate IV)* H60cm (24in). Tip of fronds and pinnae crested; crest flat, ie. in one plane. Individual plants vary. Crest at tip of frond narrower than rest of frond. See also Capitatum Group, Corymbiferum Group, Grandiceps Group and Percristatum Group for selected forms of the Cristatum Group.

Cruciatum Group H60cm (24in). Pinnae branch at their point of attachment to the rachis, opposite pairs of pinnae, therefore forming a string of crosses along the frond. Very unusual in the plant world and very attractive. Often referred to as 'Victoriae' in trade; in fact 'Victoriae' is the original member of this group and invariably a superior plant.

Fancy Fronds Group H15–20cm (6–8in), Wet/Dry. Raised by Judith Jones in her nursery Fancy Fronds in Seattle. These are dwarf lady ferns with fimbriate edges to the pinnae. Some are crested, some are plain.

'Fieldiae' *(Plate IV)* H60–90cm (24–36in). A form of Cruciatum Group. The true form is narrow-fronded, cruciate and more foliose than 'Victoriae'. Plants in general cultivation are spore-raised and, therefore, variable, but it is possible that the original clone still thrives in an out-of-the-way garden. First discovered in 1860, just pipping 'Victoriae' as the first cruciate lady fern found.

'Frizelliae' (tatting fern) *(Plate IV)* H15–22cm (6–9in), Wet/Dry. Pinnate. Found by Mrs Frizell in Co Wicklow, Eire in 1857. Pinnae reduced to circular lobes along each side of the midrib, resembling tatting (handmade lace). Fronds dwarf (22cm/9in) and uncrested in the typical form, but most plants in cultivation are spore-raised and can grow longer fronds and crest at the tips ('Frizelliae Cristatum'), or branch at any point along the rachis ('Frizelliae Ramosum'). In lesser forms some fronds may produce the occasional normal pinna. Because the pinnae are reduced to circular lobes 'Frizelliae' is less leafy than most lady ferns; it therefore loses less water in dry weather and can tolerate drier sites in the garden. Ideal in borders and rock gardens. Very pretty, very different.

'Gemmatum' H60cm (24in). Fronds narrow; pinnae and frond tips with bunched crests. Red-stemmed form is 'Gemmatum Bolton' *(Plate IV)*, green-stemmed form 'Gemmatum Barnes'. Few spore progeny are like parents, best propagated by division. Probably raised from 'Glomeratum', a similar form no longer in cultivation.

Grandiceps Group H60cm (24in). As Cristatum Group except the crest at the tip of the frond is broader than the rest of the frond.

'Kaye's Crisp', syn. 'Crispum Grandiceps Kaye' an unacceptable name, H30cm (12in). Selected by Reginald Kaye as a chance sporeling in 1948. A dwarf grandiceps (crest broader than the frond). Pinnae branching. Pinnules leafy. A very pretty little fern that was a favourite with Kaye.

'Kalothrix' *(Plate III)* Kalothrix literally means 'beautiful hair'. In this cultivar the tips of all the pinnae divisions are elongated into diaphanous, hair-like structures. All divisions are slender giving the plant an airy appearance.

It could be considered as a particular form of plumosum. Probably originally raised from 'Plumosum Horsfall' (now sadly probably extinct) and again more recently from 'Plumosum Penny'. Sparingly fertile but comes more or less true from spores. Two forms are currently in cultivation. One tends to revert in part to its plumose parent, the other is apparently constant.

'Longipinnulum' An old cultivar I rediscovered in East Devon in 1972. A crested form with pinnules rather longer than usual.

'Medio-deficiens', syn. *A. f.* 'Abasipinnulum' H60cm (24in). The original plant found at Wigton by Druery in 1884 is probably now extinct but forms with basal pinnules or basal pinnae missing are in cultivation. A fine form came as a chance sporeling in Jimmy Dyce's garden in Loughton, Essex. Fronds may be crested or plain.

'Minutissimum' H30–60cm (12–24in). A form I include with some reluctance. Plants under this name are imported from Holland. They are not necessarily minute and, in fact, tend to be rather variable in size, and they have no distinguishing feature apart from their supposed small size. Good plants do, however, form a clump around 30cm (12in) high which can be useful in garden design.

'Nudicaule Cristatum' H30–45cm (12–18in). First raised by Mapplebeck. Long bare stipe with a very large three-dimensional head. Strictly speaking it should be called 'Nudicaule Capitatum'. The form distributed by Reginald Kaye may be Mapplebeck's form, but it is known as 'Nudicaule Cristatum Kaye' *(Plate IV)*

Percristatum Group H60cm (24in). As Cristatum Group but tips of pinnules also crested.

Plumosum Group H60–150cm (24–60in). A beautiful group of cultivars. Tri-, quadri- or even quinquepinnate. The frond divisions are more leafy than usual: they overlap and give a very feathery frond, hence "plumosum". Unlike plumosum forms of most other ferns, the plumose forms of lady fern are usually fertile. They do not come true from spores but, with patience, many fine things can be raised. Many forms have been named and a few are still in cultivation – all are worth growing but all are rare. Whether or not all the named forms in cultivation are correctly named is open to debate.

'Philip Coke', syn. 'Plumosum Cristatum Coke' *(Plate III)*. Philip Coke raised many fine plumose lady ferns in the 1970s: the one named in his memory is especially good. It has finely dissected fronds with fingered crests. Very rare.

'Plumosum Axminster' *(Plate III)* Discovered in a boggy meadow near Axminster in Devon by J. Trott in 1863. Tripinnate, almost quadripinnate, not the most feathery form of plumosum but well worth growing. It comes tolerably true from spores: it is not possible to tell the original clone from good sporelings. Improved sports occur from time to time in spore sowings, most notably 'Plumosum Elegans Parsons'.

'Plumosum Barnes' Found in Westmorland in 1863 by Barnes. This is a true plumosum but less feathery than some. It is rarely fertile. Possibly extinct, although I have a plant under this name that came from Reginald Kaye many years ago.

'Plumosum Divaricatum' *(Plate III)* Discovered wild in Lancashire by W. Morris in 1872, probably the best plumose lady fern found in the wild. This plant is very rare but still in cultivation. The stipe is longer than in most lady ferns and the pinnules are narrow so there are spaces between them giving the frond an airy appearance (*divaricatum* means spread asunder or stretched apart). Some pinnules can also be missing, and it is, therefore, slightly depauperate. In 1883 Druery discovered bulbils on the underside of the frond; these he was able to grow into plants identical to the parent.

In 1986 Newey reported the discovery of bulbils on the fronds of 'Plumosum Superbum Druery' (uncrested form, see below). At the time I thought this was more correctly 'Plumosum Superbum Dissectum Druery', but subsequently wondered why the very observant Druery himself never apparently reported bulbils on any of the plumosums he raised. I am therefore forced to conclude that the plant we grow as 'Plumosum Superbum Dissectum Druery' is probably 'Plumosum Divaricatum'.

'Plumosum Drueryi' *(Plate III)* Sporeling of 'Plumosum Superbum Druery'. Possibly the most beautiful of the lady ferns. This fern is still in cultivation but very rare as it can only be propagated by division. When well grown it is quadripinnate, sometimes approaching quinquipinnate. Pinnae broad, overlapping one another. This fern is not crested although Druery himself illustrates a crested frond of 'Plumosum Superbum Druery' captioned in error as this cultivar on page 44 of *The Book of British Ferns* (1903). Each pinnule resembles a tiny frond. Druery gave a beautiful example to Queen Victoria; it may still survive in one of the Royal gardens.

'Plumosum Elegans Parsons' A finely cut sporeling raised from 'Plumosum Axminster' by Parsons around 1870. Now probably extinct but an important cultivar,

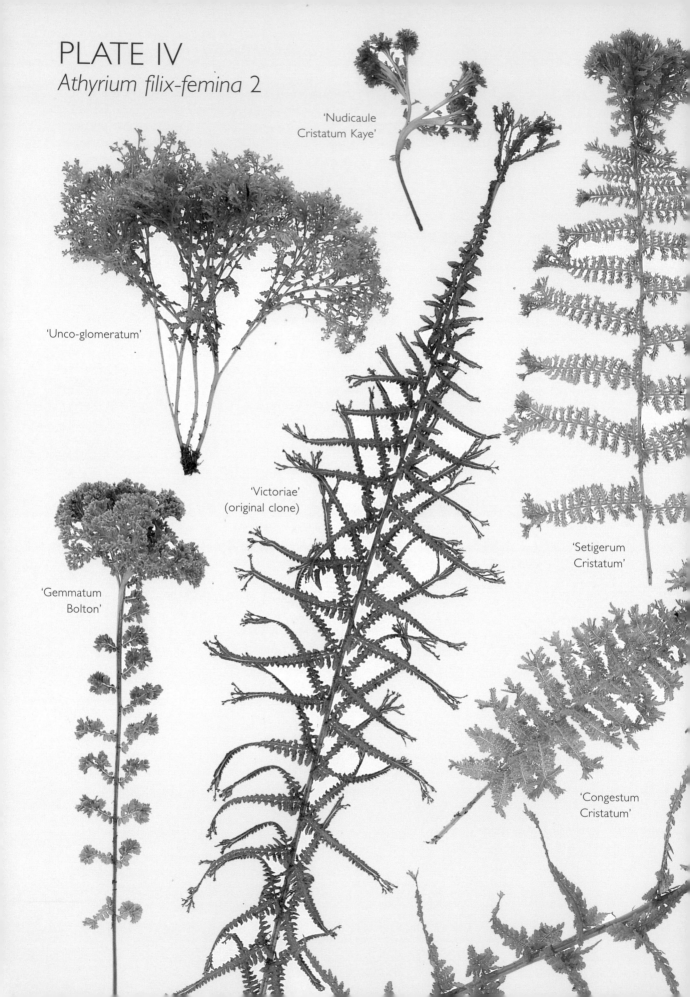

PLATE IV
Athyrium filix-femina 2

'Nudicaule
Cristatum Kaye'

'Unco-glomeratum'

'Victoriae'
(original clone)

'Gemmatum
Bolton'

'Setigerum
Cristatum'

'Congestum
Cristatum'

All fronds shown approximately half size

'Fieldiae'

'Acrocladon'

'Frizelliae'

'Cristatum
Group'

'Vernoniae'

included here as it was the source of the Druery group of plumosums – some of the finest ferns ever raised, two of which are still in cultivation.

'Plumosum Penny' Probably raised from 'Plumosum Horsfall' by Penny in Lancaster, introduced by Reginald Kaye in 1957. A very fine large plumosum, but one of the first ferns to die back in autumn.

'Plumosum Superbum Dissectum Druery' Raised from 'Plumosum Superbum Druery'. Ultimate divisions finely cut, reminiscent of 'Plumosum Elegans Parsons', its grandparent, from which it differs in having broader pinnae. Probably extinct, but included here as the cultivar 'Plumosum Divaricatum' may possibly belong here.

'Plumosum Superbum Druery' *(Plate III)* A very fine variety raised from 'Plumosum Elegans Parsons' by Druery in 1886. Frond tips and pinnae crested in flat fans. All frond parts foliose (not finely dissected). There are two plants in cultivation under this name: the crested form is correctly placed here. The other, uncrested form, is either 'Plumosum Superbum Dissectum Druery' or more probably 'Plumosum Divaricatum'.

'Reflexum' H60cm (24in). First found in 1858 in Westmorland by Clowes. Rediscovered by Jimmy Dyce in a garden in Craven, Yorkshire around 1990. Fronds normal except all divisions are slender and recurved (edges are down-turned).

'Revolvens' H60cm (24in). Originally found by Druery in 1891 in Strathblane, Scotland. I recently found a similar plant in Derbyshire. The pinnae are recurved, bending around behind the rachis, almost forming a tube.

'Setigerum' A group of cultivars with all tips bristly. From spores crested ('Setigerum Cristatum'; *Plate IV*), simple ('Setigerum') or congested ('Setigerum Congestum') forms can be raised – all very pretty. Can hybridize with other cultivars, for example with 'Victoriae' it forms 'Setigerum Victoriae'.

'Unco-glomeratum' *(Plate IV)* H10–15cm (4–6in). Progeny of 'Acrocladon' first raised by Stansfield in 1878. I re-raised this recently in a small crop of mixed sporelings of 'Acrocladon'. Fronds branch repeatedly from the base, all terminal divisions slender and diaphanous. In close conditions reputedly able to form prothalli at the tips, from which new fronds can be grown.

'Vernoniae' *(Plate IV)* H60cm (24in), D, Wet. As the type plant except each pinnulet is briefly stiped, crispy and elliptical with a laciniated margin, particularly towards the tip of the frond. A beautiful, feathery form.

Plants uncrested. Found by Mrs Vernon in the 1850s or 1860s. 'Vernoniae Cristatum' is a crested form of 'Vernoniae' first raised from 'Vernoniae' by Mr Jones in 1873. 'Vernoniae Corymbiferum', which has a very heavy crest, might reappear in sowings.

'Victoriae' *(Plate IV)* H90cm (36in), D, Wet. Found near Drymen in central Scotland in 1861 by a student named Cosh. It is percruciate, that is the pinnae are cruciate (cross-shaped) on the rachis and the pinnules are cruciate on the pinna axis. The original clone of this fern is very rare and changes hands at around £100 when available. It can be distinguished from other cruciate forms by its greater size (90cm/3ft-plus when mature) and its percruciate, airy frond form. It can only be propagated in true character by division. Unfortunately side crowns are produced infrequently, hence the rarity of the original clone. Good things can be raised from the spores but, as explained under Cruciatum Group (above), the sporelings will almost certainly differ from the parent in detail. Over the years many sporelings of 'Victoriae' have been selected and given names. Any of these could well reappear in sowings. The most remarkable form is 'Setigerum Victoriae', which is a hybrid between 'Setigerum' and 'Victoriae' and has beautifully setigerate (bristly) pinnules coupled with the cruciate pinnae. Originally raised by Birkenhead at the turn of the century, lost, and then re-raised by Ray Coughlin in the 1980s, it is still in cultivation.

A. niponicum **'Pictum'**, syn. *A. goeringianum* 'Pictum', *A. iseanum* 'Pictum' (Japanese painted fern) H30–38cm (12–15in), D, Wet. Zone 6. One of the most popular garden ferns. Fronds bipinnate, lance-shaped, greyish-green with mauve midribs; the mauve colour suffuses into the lamina. Fronds mostly horizontal (spreading). Easy to grow if given sufficient moisture. For many years my plant struggled in a dryish spot under trees. I moved it to a rockery where its roots could run through the moist soil under the stones and it thrived. There are several selected forms. The crested form is pretty with fronds and pinnae crested. There are also forms selected for their especially good colour. Occasionally green forms are offered. These come up in spore sowings with the purplish form. They are a natural form and are worth growing in their own right.

A. niponicum **hybrid** H45cm (18in), Wet/Dry. This is an erect, larger form of *A. niponicum* 'Pictum'. I have not tried to grow the spores, although they would certainly appear to be viable. Reputed to be a hybrid with

Athyrium otophorum is another attractively coloured fern species from Japan.

Athyrium filix-femina. This fern is well worth growing if available.

A. otophorum (eared lady fern)

Japan, H30–45cm (12–18in), D, Wet, Zone 5. Fronds bipinnate, lance-shaped, fresh green with reddish stipe and veins. A very striking plant adding colour to a fern garden. For a lady fern it retains its fronds unexpectedly long into autumn.

A. palustre

Japan, H30–45cm (12–18in), D, Wet/Dry, Zone 7. Very similar to A. niponicum 'Pictum', but with more erect fronds. It spreads more rapidly and is easily propagated from sections of rhizome.

A. proliferum

Eastern Asia, H60cm (24in), D, Wet/Dry, Zone 8. Reddish-tinted like so many Asian lady ferns. This one is distinguished by a bulbil produced about 7cm (3in) below the tip of the frond.

A. pycnocarpon, syn. Diplazium pycnocarpon (glade fern)

North America, H45cm (18in), D, Wet/Dry, Zone 5. Very distinctive fern with pinnate fronds. The pinnae are entire and well-spaced up the frond. Fertile fronds are produced later in the season; they are more erect and have slightly narrower pinnae. The rhizomes are short creeping, allowing a good colony to be formed in a few years. I grew this in a rather dry spot where it did tolerably well. I feel it could have been much taller in a moist site.

A. spinulosum, syn. A. subtriangulare

East Asia, H45cm (18in), D, Wet/Dry, Zone 8, possibly 7. Fronds dark green, triangular, bi- to tripinnate. Stipe reddish-brown, longer than lamina. Rhizomes creeping.

A. thelypteroides, syn. Diplazium acrostichoides (silvery glade fern)

North America, east Asia, H60–90cm (24–36in), D, Wet/Dry, Zone 5. Fronds pinnate-pinnatifid, broadly lance-shaped, fresh green; rachis and stipe also green. Pinna segments squared at the tip, somewhat like Dryopteris affinis. The silver colour of the frond underside is due to the silvery indusium covering the developing sporangia.

A. vidalii

Japan, H30–45cm (12–18in), D, Wet, Zone 6. Fronds

bipinnate, new fronds reddish, more open and taller than *A. niponicum*. Another Japanese species with some colour other than green.

BLECHNUM (hard ferns, water ferns)

Blechnum is a large genus of usually evergreen ferns, with the new foliage in spring often being pink. Some are well established as garden plants but many others deserve to be tried in temperate gardens. In the temperate regions of the northern hemisphere there are few native species, but there are many more in the tropics and southern temperate regions. All species prefer acidic soils, but most will do well as long as conditions are at least neutral (ie. pH 6.5 or less). Most species are dimorphic, that is sporing fronds differ from sterile fronds. Sporing fronds are usually more erect and longer with a narrower lamina. The sori are arranged along either side of the pinna vein, usually in a more or less continuous row. *Blechnum* are very similar to *Doodia*, except in *Doodia* the sori are arranged in 1 or 2 rows along either side of the midrib, and in *Blechnum* there is only one long continuous sorus along each side of the pinna segment.

B. auriculatum
South America, H15–30cm (6–12in), D, Wet/Dry, Zone 8. Perhaps not truly deciduous, but tatty and inconspicuous over winter. Sporing and sterile fronds similar: lance-shaped, pinnatifid. Pinnae 2.5–5cm (1–2in) long, tapering with an ear-like lobe at the base. Surprisingly hardy, slow creeping even in exposed sites in central England. Perhaps more tolerant of dry conditions than most other blechnums.

B. cartilagineum (gristle fern)
Australia, H30–90cm (12–36in), W, Wet/Dry, Zone 9. Fronds often pink when young, pinnate, narrowly triangular; fertile and non-fertile fronds similar. Pinnae broad at their bases. Frond texture tough, hence rather unattractive common name. Well suited to more open positions, being able to stand short droughts.

B. chambersii (lance water fern)
Australasia, H30cm (12in), W, Wet, Zone 9, or possibly 8. Vegetative fronds pinnatifid, lance-shaped, dark green. Fertile fronds similar except they are shorter and the pinnae are much narrower. In most situations the fronds are all flaccid, with the sporing ones muddled in with the vegetative ones. Needs wet conditions and good shelter; in nature it is a forest plant.

B. chilense
South America, H90–150cm (36–60in), E, Wet/Dry, Zone 7. Few popular garden plants can have been so frequently misnamed as this one. For many years it has been mistakenly known as *B. tabulare*, a small tree fern that grows in South Africa (at the summit of Table Mountain) and is not hardy. It is frequently confused with *B. magellanicum* (below), another South American species. More recently the correct name for this fern has been given as *B. cordatum*, but I believe this to be a similar, tropical species, and therefore wrong. Until the name stabilizes I prefer to stick with *B. chilense*, especially as it has become quite widely accepted. Despite all the names, it is a magnificent garden plant with bold, dark green, pinnatifid fronds, up to 22cm (9in) wide. The rhizomes creep slowly, forming a large clump in a few years; outlying crowns can appear 12–15cm (5–6in) from established clumps. In time the oldest crowns produce short trunks up to 15cm (6in) tall. Given sufficient moisture it can achieve frond lengths of 150cm (60in), even in central England.

B. colensoi
New Zealand, H30cm (12in), E, Wet/Dry, Zone 9. Fronds pinnatifid, 10–15cm (4–6in) wide, very dark green, almost black. Pinnae few and broad each with a sharp-pointed tip. Grows in dark, shady forest corners. 'Possibly hardy', Rush, 1984. I have not grown it outdoors, but it should do well in sheltered gardens, particularly in high rainfall areas.

B. discolor
New Zealand, H38cm (15in), W, Wet/Dry, Zone 8. Eventually a short-trunk forming species, even outdoors in Britain: the trunk can reach 15cm (6in) tall quite quickly. Fronds light green, pinnatifid, fairly narrow 5–7cm (2–3in) wide, erect in a shuttlecock. Side crowns are produced, forming a colony in time. Pinnae crowded on the rachis. The sporing fronds are very distinctive in the centre of the crown. Hardy with me for years in a dryish spot, but would do better in a moist site.

B. fluviatile (ray water fern)
New Zealand, H45cm (18in), E, Wet/Dry, Zone 6. Fronds 2.5–5cm (1–2in) wide, pale green, pinnate with short blunt segments. Sterile fronds spread out horizontally from the crown, surrounding erect sporing fronds. Brown scales along the rachis very noticeable. Hardy with me for years in a sheltered spot.

B. magellanicum
South America, H90cm (36in), E, Wet/Dry, Zone 8. Regretfully, I have never seen this fern but I am reliably informed it is in cultivation in Britain and it is distinct

from *B. chilense*. A photograph I have seen shows the fronds more spreading than in *B. chilense*, also Rush (1984) says stiff hairs at base of stipe, rather than broad scales, help to distinguish this species from *B. chilense*.

B. minus (soft water fern)

New Zealand, H30cm (12in), D, Dry/Wet, Zone 8. There are two taxa under this name: this one, from New Zealand, which is hardy, and a similar species from Australia, which is more difficult to establish (zone 9). Fronds broad, 10–15cm (4–6in), dark green, pinnatifid. Rhizomes creeping. New fronds pink. I have grown this for years in a peat bed under dwarf rhododendrons but Reginald Kaye grew it on his Westmorland limestone rocks: it thrived for both of us. Perhaps it is not strongly calcifuge or perhaps the lime in the limestone was not available to the fern. The Australian species under this name sometimes has stout, erect rhizomes, covered in brown leaf bases, which can be up to 60cm (24in) tall in wet acidic sites. I would expect plants of this size to be hardy in zone 8.

B. minus × B. wattsii

Australia, H30–45cm (12–18in), E, Wet/Dry, Zone 8?. Given hybrid vigour and both parents' temperate origins this fern may prove hardy: I have not grown it outside. Fronds pinnate, the pinnae dark green, 10–15cm (4–6in) broad and quite distant from each other. Midrib red-brown.

B. niponicum, syn. *Struthiopteris niponica*

Japan, H30cm (12in), E, Wet/Dry, Zone 8. A beautiful species closely allied to *B. spicant* but with bright pink new fronds. Pinnae pale green when mature. Some plants from the Pacific north-west of America show similarities to this species and may prove to be the same. Japanese form hardy in central England.

B. novae-zealandiae

New Zealand, H60–150cm (24–60in), W, Wet/Dry, Zone 7. A very handsome fern, common in New Zealand but only recently named. Fronds pinnate, 15–22cm (6–9in) broad, yellow-green, particularly when young. Pinnae broad, often overlapping. Seems hardy.

B. nudum (fishbone water fern)

Australia, H60cm (24in), E, Wet/Dry, Acid, Zone 9, possibly 8. Forms regular shuttlecocks of pinnatifid fronds. Pinnae long (5–7cm/2–3in) and tapering. Needs shade; can form large colonies in moist ground by streams but it is also good in a container. Larger plants can have slender trunks up to 60cm (24in) tall covered with black shiny leaf bases and are probably hardy in zone 8.

Blechnum nudum – a superb dwarf tree fern that is ideal for conservatories.

'Cristatum' H45cm (18in), is the crested form. The crests are simple and in the same plane as the frond – flat. Unusual and rare.

B. patersonii (strap water fern)

Australia, H30cm (12in), W, Wet/Dry, Zone 9, possibly 8. An unusual blechnum with fronds strap-shaped, 2cm (¾in) wide, pinkish when young, although some clones can be disappointingly green. In older plants some fronds develop a few broad pinnae. 'Perhaps hardy', Richard Rush, 1984. Doubtfully hardy in cold temperate areas but so striking that it is worth trying in warmer areas with an oceanic climate. Otherwise, cool greenhouse, needs shade with adjacent water.

B. penna-marina *(Plate V)*

New Zealand, Australia, South America H7–22cm (3–9in), E, Wet/Dry, Zone 5. Fronds pinnatifid, narrow (1cm/½in wide). Rhizomes creeping. Fertile fronds very erect and slightly longer than given sizes. Quite quickly forms a colony. Excellent as edging on peat block walls, as at Knightshayes in Devon. Can invade lawns and survive mowing! Nevertheless, it is not likely to be troublesomely invasive as the rhizomes are near the surface and easily removed where they are not wanted.

The species has been divided into several botanical subspecies. Two are commonly cultivated, both excellent garden plants with pinkish young fronds. There is a larger form, 15–22cm (6–9in) tall, probably subsp. *penna-marina*,

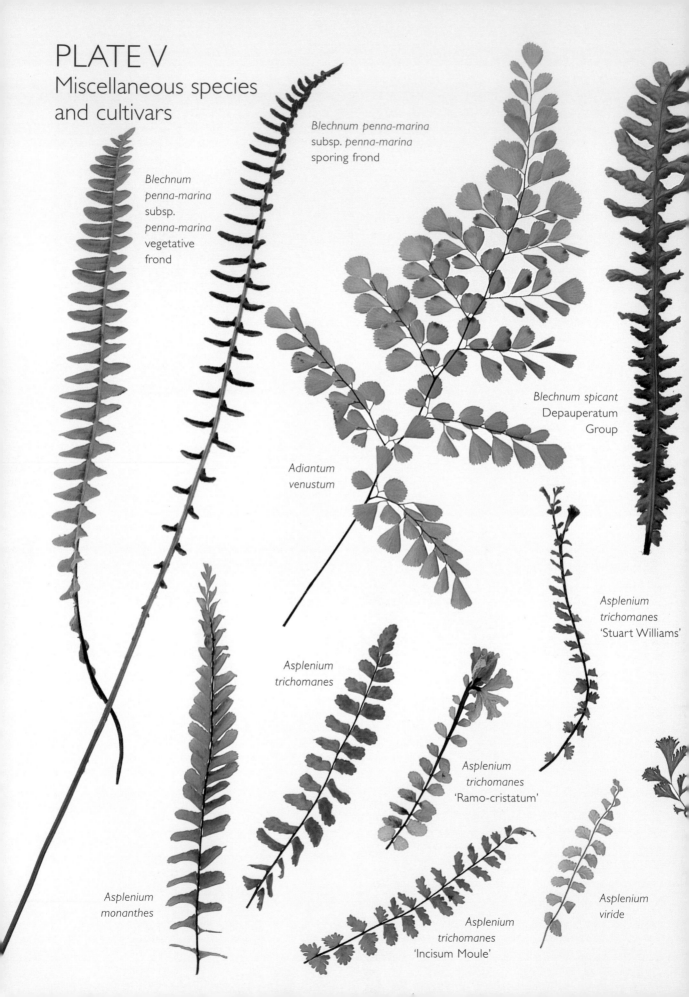

PLATE V
Miscellaneous species and cultivars

Blechnum penna-marina subsp. *penna-marina* sporing frond

Blechnum penna-marina subsp. *penna-marina* vegetative frond

Blechnum spicant Depauperatum Group

Adiantum venustum

Asplenium trichomanes 'Stuart Williams'

Asplenium trichomanes

Asplenium trichomanes 'Ramo-cristatum'

Asplenium monanthes

Asplenium trichomanes 'Incisum Moule'

Asplenium viride

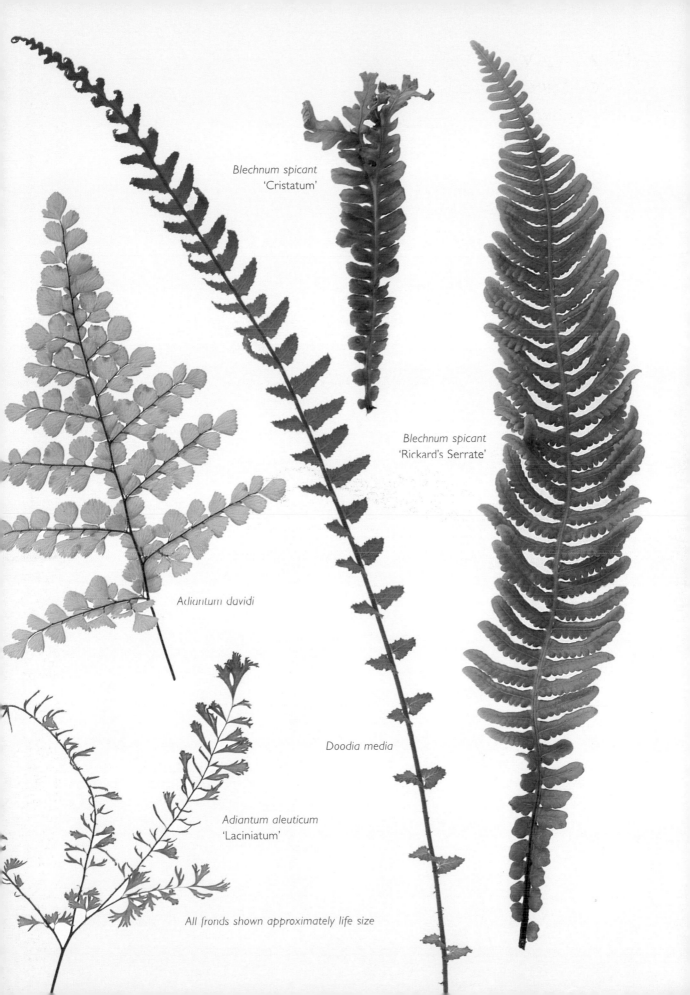

Blechnum spicant
'Cristatum'

Blechnum spicant
'Rickard's Serrate'

Adiantum davidi

Doodia media

Adiantum aleuticum
'Laciniatum'

All fronds shown approximately life size

with smooth green pinnae, and a shorter form, 7–15cm (3–6in) tall, probably subsp. *alpina*, with the pinnae more prominently veined and red-tinted. Both forms come from cold areas and have proved very hardy throughout Britain.

'Cristatum' is a crested cultivar of the shorter reddish form.

B. spicant

Most of the temperate northern hemisphere, including British Isles, H30–45cm (12–18in), E, Wet/Dry, Zone 4. Sterile fronds spreading, narrowly lance-shaped, 2.5–5cm (1–2in) wide, pinnatifid, glossy dark green. Sporing fronds erect with narrower pinnae. A beautiful evergreen fern for all-year-round appeal. Neutral to acid soil only.

'Anomalum' A curiosity with sporing fronds the same as the sterile vegetative fronds.

'Congestum' H6-10cm (2½–4in). A beautiful form recently brought into cultivation. Fronds congested, very neat.

'Crispo-minutissimum' H5cm (2in). Found wild in North Wales by Nigel Hall in 1979. Fronds very short, crisp and overlapping. According to Jimmy Dyce, then President of the British Pteridological Society, a first-rate treasure. Sadly this is probably extinct but it offers proof that, even today, exciting cultivars occur throughout the range of a given species.

'Crispum' H30cm (12in). This form came to me from Judith Jones, proprietor of Fancy Fronds fern nursery in Seattle, who selected it from sowings of wild spores originally collected in the Cascade Mountains. It is a very interesting find: the pinnae are twisted giving the whole plant a very crisp appearance. Fronds suberect.

'Cristatum' (Plate V) British Isles, H15cm (6in). A rare form of our native species with regularly crested frond tips. However, the pinnae are not crested, so perhaps this cultivar should be called 'Capitatum'; in well-grown plants the frond itself branches below the apex and could be called 'Ramo-cristatum'. During the 1970s I thought this cultivar extinct but I saw it in a collection in Perth, Scotland, then it turned up in Holland and Australia. The crests completely change the shape of the plant. Instead of the elegant star form of the species, 'Cristatum' is tight and ball-like. Very attractive in its own way. In the wild it is not uncommon to find plants with the odd frond forking. However, they are usually inconsistent and have little merit for gardens.

Blechnum penna-marina, a reddish form, probably subsp. alpina, which also has prominently veined pinnae.

Depauperatum Group (Plate V) H30cm (12in). I found this plant growing on a wall at Glenbeigh in Co. Kerry, Eire. As its name suggests, the pinnae are often missing, but it is not unattractive. Fronds are narrower than in the species and it has a very different appearance.

'Heterophyllum' British Isles, H15cm (6in). A curious fern. Fronds irregular, pinnatifid (approaching hart's tongue *Asplenium*): no two are quite the same. A very rare form, not reported since described by Druery in 1910, and it may even have been extinct by then. However, it was recently rediscovered wild in mid-Wales by Arthur Chater; plants are now in cultivation from the spores collected.

'Redwood Giant' A large form from California, introduced into Britain by Judith Jones.

'Rickard's Serrate' (Plate V) British Isles, H30–45cm (12–18in). (Named by John Mickel, in 1994, not me!) I found this plant growing wild in North Wales in 1972 on a British Pteridological Society excursion. Since then it has been widely grown from spores. Like the type plant, except that it is bipinnatifid (pinnae are lobed), especially on the basiscopic side. Pinnae slightly sickle shaped. Similar forms were grown in the nineteenth century as 'Serratum' or 'Semilacerum'. Richard Rush raised 'Bipinnatifidum Rush' from my original find. It may still be in cultivation. The pinnae were more regularly, but more shallowly lobed along both sides than in 'Rickard's Serrate'.

B. vulcanicum (wedge water fern)

Australia, New Zealand, H45cm (18in), W, Wet/Dry, Zone 9, possibly 8. Fronds pinnatifid, new fronds bronze-red. Bears a passing resemblance to *B. cartilagineum*, but, nevertheless, quite attractive. Pinnae narrowing towards tips, appearing distant from each other. Fronds narrowly triangular, 5–7cm (2–3in) wide. Needs a sheltered site, preferably in an oceanic climate zone.

B. wattsii (hard water fern)

Australia, H60cm (24in), E, Wet/Dry, Zone 9, possibly 8. Superficially resembles *B. chilense*, but pinnae are broader and fewer. Midribs red-brown, pinnae 10–15cm (4–6in) long. New fronds bronzy-pink. Native to the forests of *Dicksonia antarctica* in south-east Australia; given its vigorous growth rate, it may well prove hardy, even in central England.

CHEILANTHES (lip ferns, cloak ferns)

A large genus of ferns adapted to grow in rocky areas, often in deserts, where some humidity may linger. They are often covered with scales or hairs, particularly on the underside of the frond, to slow water loss by transpiration. In severe drought conditions many species roll up their fronds to help minimize water loss. The common names refer to the sorus formed from the folded lip of the pinnae. *Pellaea* is another genus well represented in dry regions.

All species of *Cheilanthes* listed are hardy in a cold greenhouse, well ventilated over winter, in central England. The zone figure given is an indication of where each species may survive outdoors if protected from winter wet. The largest concentration of species in horticulture comes from the south-western United States and northern Mexico where winters can be very cold. Other areas have not yet been thoroughly collected but additional species are sure to appear in cultivation in the future. These descriptions are, hopefully, accurate but critical botanists may not agree with the use of the term hair as opposed to scale: I have described each as I have seen them with a hand lens but with an electron microscope all may be scales.

Most species are given here as evergreen; in fact many fronds do shrivel over winter but only rarely do all fronds perish.

C. acrostica, syn. C. fragrans (Plate VI)

Europe, H10–20 × 2.5cm (4–8 × 1in), E, Dry, Zone 8. Fronds lance-shaped, tripinnate-pinnatifid, with triangular pinnae. Few tan scales along underside of main midribs of pinnae, also on rachis. Hardy outdoors in central England given good drainage and good light.

C. alabamensis (Plate VI)

USA, H22–30cm (9–12in), E, Dry, Zone 7. Fronds erect, lance-shaped to narrowly lance-shaped, bipinnate-pinnatifid, mid-green, lacking conspicuous scales on the lamina with few hair-like scales on the rachis. Stipe blackish. Hardy outdoors for several seasons in central England, although it does not get as tall as in an alpine house. There are several closely related species including *C. notholaenoides* and *C. cuculans*.

C. argentea (Plate VI)

Eastern Asia, H15–20cm (6–8in), E, Dry, Zone 5. Fronds spreading, pinnate-pinnatifid, triangular with the lowest basiscopic pair of pinnules elongated, making it almost pentagonal. Fronds green from above but the undersurface is covered with a beautiful white wax. There are no scales or hairs. Stipe shiny brown. Plants in cultivation which lack the white waxy undersurface may be minor variants, hybrids or a different species. Given its provenance, Mickel (1994) believes this should be hardy. It is

worth trying outdoors in a dryish site and protected for the duration of the winter.

C. aschenborniana

Mexico, USA, H15–30 × 5cm (6–12 × 2in), E, Dry, Zone 8. Fronds lance-shaped, erect, bipinnate-pinnatifid, whitish hairs on upper surface, covered with golden-brown shaggy scales below. Rachis brown also with shaggy scales.

C. austrotenuifolia (rock fern)

Australia, H25–38cm (10–15in), E, Dry, Zone 8. Fronds tripinnate, broadly triangular to ovate, on a long stipe. Rachis with scattered scales, no hairs. Rhizomes creeping, can form a good clump in time. Foliage flushes fresh green in spring. Not widely grown in Europe but hardy in an alpine house and possibly outdoors if given dry conditions.

C. beitelii (Plate VI)

Mexico, H30–45 × 3.5cm (12–18 × 1½in), E, Dry, Zone 9. Fronds narrow, lance-shaped, pinnate; pinnae round with deeply crenate lobes. Upper surface with few white stellate hairs, lower surface densely covered with cream-coloured hairs. Scales on midribs and stipe.

C. bonariensis (Plate VI)

North and central America, south to Chile and Argentina, H15–30 × 2cm (6–12 × ¾in), E, Dry, Zone 8. Fronds lance-shaped, pinnate-pinnatifid. Upper surface green with few inconspicuous hairs, underside covered with thick matted white, woolly hairs. Stipe dark brown with few white hairs. Apparently hardy in Seattle, USA.

C. candida (Plate VI)

Texas, Mexico, H30–45 × 15cm (12–18 × 6in), E, Dry, Zone 8. Fronds triangular, bipinnate-pinnatifid, few white hairs on upper surface, but lower surface mealy and covered with white hairs. White hairs also on rachis and stipe. Also few brown scales on stipe.

C. chusana

China, Japan, H15cm (6in), E, Dry, Zone 8. Fronds bipinnate on a scaly rachis. Rush (1984) says this is probably hardy. I have not seen it grown outdoors but it should be tried when available.

C. coriacea

Yemen, north-east Africa, 5–10cm (2–4in), E, Dry, Zone 8. Fronds triangular, pinnate-pinnatifid to bipinnatifid, slightly leathery. Upper surface naked, lower surface slightly hairy.

C. covillei

Southern USA, Mexico, H7cm (3in), E, Dry, Zone 7. Fronds dark green, tripinnate, narrowly triangular, 2cm

(¾in) wide, with white scales on upper surface. Dense broad fawn scales on lower surface.

C. cuculans, see *C. alabamensis*.

C. distans *(Plate VI)*
Australasia, H10–20 × 2.5cm (4–8 × 1in), E, Dry, Zone 8. Fronds lance-shaped, bipinnate-pinnatifid, very few hairs on top surface with few white scales beneath. Pinnae triangular. Relatively easy in my unheated polytunnel, could be a candidate for experimentation outdoors, even in central England.

C. eatonii *(Plate VI)*
South-west USA, Mexico, H30–50 × 5cm (12–20 × 2in), E, Dry, Zone 8. Fronds erect, pinnate-pinnatifid, upper surface covered with matted woolly white hairs. White hairs also on lower surface. Rachis with brown scales lying flat against it, as well as white hairs. Certainly the most sought-after species in the genus. Unfortunately, difficult outdoors in central England, but there have been some recent reports of success with past mild winters. The white foliage makes this one of the most eye-catching ferns on a show bench. **f. castanea** differs from the type by being less hairy, and possibly slightly hardier.

C. feei (slender lip fern)
USA, H15cm (6in), E, Dry, Zone 6. Fronds bipinnate covered with long whitish hairs especially on the under-surface. Rush (1984) believes this to be hardy; it certainly should be, given its natural distribution. Plants in cultivation under this name are often a different species.

C. fendleri
Southern USA, Mexico, H15–30 × 5cm (6–12 × 2in), E, Dry, Zone 6. Fronds narrowly triangular-lanceolate, tripinnate. Upper surface lacks scales but lower surface is covered with white or brown scales. Stipe brown. Hardy in Seattle, USA.

C. fragrans, see *C. acrostica*.

C. guanchica
Madeira, Canary Isles, H15–25cm (6–10in), E, Dry, Zone 8. Fronds erect, bipinnate-pinnatifid, lance-shaped with oblong segments. Fronds lack hairs but have a few scales on rachis and pinnae midribs.

C. humilis, syn. *C. sieberi*
New Zealand, H30–45cm (12–18in), E, Dry, Zone 8. Fronds erect, narrowly triangular, tripinnate. Pinnae triangular; pinnae and pinnules distant from each other, giving a very open frond. Lacking any conspicuous mealy covering. Rachis brown with few scales on stipe and midribs. Alpine house or outdoors only in warm, drier areas.

C. jamaicensis *(Plate VI)*
Jamaica, Mexico, H20–30cm (8–12in), E, Dry, Zone 8. Fronds tripinnate, narrowly triangular, bright green. Few white twisted scales on top surface of lamina, with plentiful white hairs on underside. Stipe scaly. Similar to *C. tomentosa* but less hairy and a brighter green.

C. kaulfussii (glandular lip fern) *(Plate VI)*
USA to South America, H15–30cm (6–12in), E, Dry, Zone 8. Fronds yellow-green, tripinnate-pinnatifid, triangular, but the basiscopic pinnules are extended, making it almost pentagonal. Stipe erect but laminae angled almost flat. A few white glandular hairs on top of lamina and abundant glandular hairs on underside and on the rachis and stipe. The common name is very appropriate. A pretty delicate fern.

C. lanosa *(Plate VI)*
Eastern USA, H15–30 × 2cm (6–12 × ¾in), E, Dry, Zone 5. Fronds green, spreading, lance-shaped, bipinnate-pinnatifid. Few straight white hairs on both surfaces; stipe sparingly hairy and thin. Potentially hardy in central England. Pinnules distant from each other. Plants in cultivation under this name are often *C. tomentosa*, which has greyer fronds, woolly hairs on both sides of lamina, pinnules closer together and a thicker stipe.

C. lendigera *(Plate VI)*
Southern USA into Central America, H15–45cm (6–18in), E, Dry, Zone 8. Fronds yellowish green, tripinnate, triangular, 10cm (4in) wide. White hairs few on upper surface but abundant and woolly on undersurface. Stipe and rachis brown but covered with white woolly hairs.

C. lindheimeri (fairy swords)
Southern USA, Mexico, H20–30 × 3.5cm (8–12 × 1½in), E, Dry, Zone 8. Fronds grey-green, narrowly triangular, bipinnate-pinnatifid; new fronds very silvery. Downy hairs on upper surface of frond, broad tan scales on underside and rachis. Stipe brown.

C. maderensis, formerly *Notholaena marantae*
Madeira, H15–30cm (6–12in), E, Dry, Zone 8. Fronds lance-shaped, pinnate-bipinnatifid. Tiny brown glands scattered on lower side of lamina. Rachis and pinnae midribs scaly beneath. Cold tolerant: survived several years outdoors in central England with straw and a slate over the crown in winter.

C. marantae, syn. *Notholaena marantae* *(Plate VI)*
Europe to Himalaya, Yemen, Ethiopia, H15–30cm (6–12in), E, Dry, Zone 7, possibly 6. Acid, rocky soil. Fronds pinnate-bipinnatifid with a thick carpet of brown

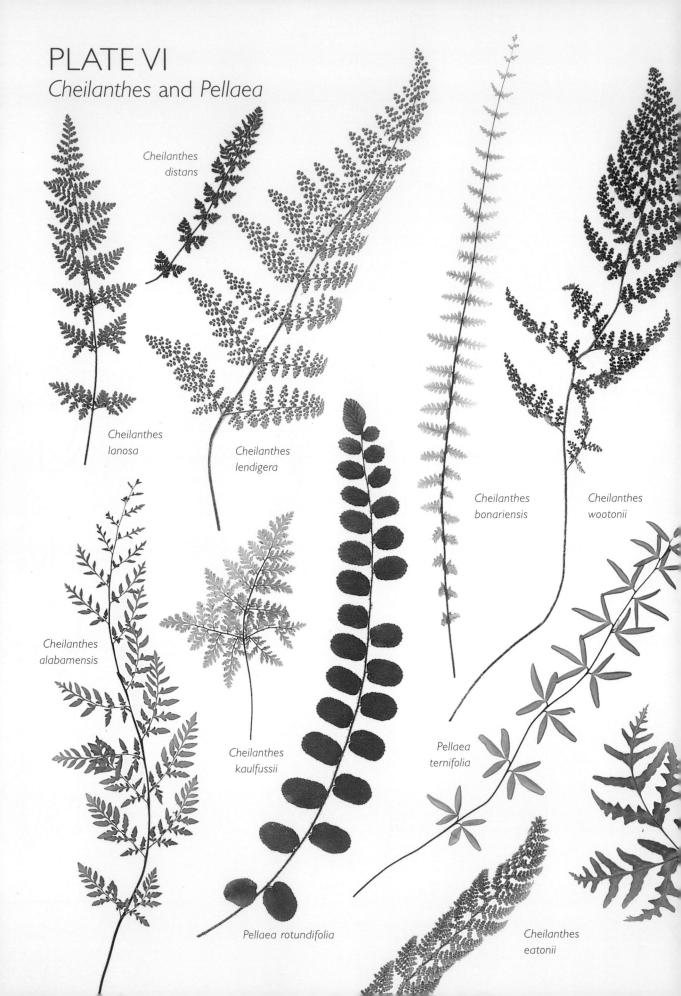

PLATE VI
Cheilanthes and *Pellaea*

Cheilanthes distans

Cheilanthes lanosa

Cheilanthes lendigera

Cheilanthes bonariensis

Cheilanthes wootonii

Cheilanthes alabamensis

Cheilanthes kaulfussii

Pellaea ternifolia

Pellaea rotundifolia

Cheilanthes eatonii

All fronds approximately life size

Cheilanthes candida

Cheilanthes jamaicensis

Cheilanthes siliquosa

Cheilanthes pruinata

Cheilanthes beitelii

Cheilanthes marantae

Cheilanthes tomentosa

Pellaea andromedifolia

Cheilanthes argentea

Cheilanthes acrostica

scales covering the undersurface. In central Europe it grows well in very cold areas and, with tender loving care, can be established outdoors in central England, but prolonged winter wet is a problem. Good in an alpine house. The form in the Himalaya is distinct and will probably need to be described as a different taxon.

C. myriophylla
Central and South America, H30–45cm (12–18in), E, Dry, Zone 8. Fronds lance-shaped-triangular, quadripinnate. Pinnae triangular. Ultimate divisions elliptic and rather small. Pale hairs on underside of lamina, scales on rachis, hairs flattened against mid-brown stipe. Not obviously covered with scales or hairs. A fern very popular for its very delicate appearance.

C. notholaenoides, see *C. alabamensis*.

C. platychlamys
Himalaya, H15cm (6in), E, Dry, Zone 8. Fronds triangular, pinnate-pinnatifid, powdery white meal scattered on upper surface, lower surface white all over. No conspicuous hairs or scales.

C. pruinata *(Plate VI)*
South America, H30–38 × 1cm (12–15 × ½in), E, Dry, Zone 8, possibly 7. Fronds erect, slender, pinnate-pinnatifid. Pinnae without scales or hairs, equilaterally triangular turned at right angles to the plane of the frond. Red-brown scales on rachis. One of the highest altitude ferns in the world, being recorded at over 4400m (14,000ft) in the Andes. Must be cold-hardy; I have not tried it outdoors but winter wet could be a problem.

C. siliquosa, syn. *Aspidotis densa* (Indian's dream) *(Plate VI)*
North-west America, H7–15cm (3–6in), E, Dry, Zone 7. Fronds triangular, tripinnate, all divisions elongated; sterile fronds have toothed margins. Very pretty. Fronds and brown stipe hairless. Thrived outdoors in central England for several years in a well-drained spot in shelter of a large stone. Otherwise requires an alpine house.

C. sinuata
USA, South America, H30cm (12in), E, Dry, Zone 8. Fronds narrow, pinnate-pinnatifid, silvery with a beautiful white-scaly felt covering the undersurface; there are a few inconspicuous scales on the upper surface. Rachis brown.

C. standleyi
USA, Mexico, H15–25 × 9cm (6–10 × 3½in), E, Dry, Zone 9. Fronds pentagonal, pinnate-pinnatifid on a stipe 10–20cm (4–8in) long. Top surface of lamina sparingly waxy. Undersurface densely covered with cream-coloured wax. Rachis waxy with few broad scales.

C. tomentosa *(Plate VI)*
South-eastern USA, H30–45cm (12–18in), E, Dry, Zone 6. Fronds grey-green, erect, narrowly lance-shaped, tripinnate-pinnatifid, with a few white hairs on the top surface and cream woolly hairs on undersurface. Fronds look slightly woolly. Pinnae triangular. A very pretty fern and the easiest cheilanthes to grow outdoors in central England. Given good drainage and protection from winter wet (straw held in place with a slate), it has thrived here for ten or more years. There is a form from the Santa Rita Mountains in cultivation. It is well worth growing, a neater plant with broader, leafier fronds.

C. vellea
Europe, H10–15 × 2.5cm (4–6 × 1in), E, Dry, Zone 8. The correct botanical name for this species is in dispute, opinions varying between *Cossentinia vellea* or *Notholaena lanuginosa*: I have kept it under *Cheilanthes* for convenience. Fronds lance-shaped, grey-green bipinnate, both upper and lower surfaces covered with downy hairs. Croziers silvery. Pale brown, thick hairs on rachis; stipe very short or absent. There is also a *C. vellea* described from Australia, a different species.

C. wootonii (bearded lip fern)
USA, Mexico, H15–20 × 5–6cm (6–10 × 2–2½in), E, Dry, Zone 8. Fronds grey-green, lance-shaped, tripinnate, leafy. Pinnulets round. Upper surface lacks scales but broad buff scales on underside of pinnae along midribs protrude beyond the pinna margin and are visible from above – hence 'bearded lip fern'. A very beautiful plant. Scales and hairs on broad rachis.

CIBOTIUM

A genus of tree ferns in the family Cyatheaceae. Some species do not produce trunks so typical of *Cyathea* but the two species listed here from Hawaii are trunk-forming and surprisingly cold-resistant. For other tree ferns see *Cyathea* and *Dicksonia*.

C. glaucum (hapu'u'ii)
Hawaii, H Trunk to 3m × to 30cm (10ft × to 1ft), Fronds 1–2m (3–6ft), E, Wet/Dry, Zone 9, or possibly 8. Fronds slightly glossy green above, grey-glaucous below, bipinnate-pinnatifid, triangular, on long stipe. Slim very dark brown broken line along either side of stipe. Pale hairs, not abundant, on stipe.

C. menziesii (hapu'u)
Hawaii, H trunk to 3m (10ft), fronds 1–2m (3–6ft), E, Wet/Dry, Zone 9, or possibly 8. Fronds slightly glossy surfaces, bipinnate-pinnatifid, triangular on a long stipe.

Dark hairs abundant on stipe. Needs protection over winter in central England (zone 8), but should do well in slightly warmer regions.

CONIOGRAMME (bamboo fern)

A small very distinct genus of several rather similar species from Eastern Asia, Africa and Mexico. Rarely cultivated in Britain. Fronds are bipinnate at the base when mature, pinnules are stalked, broad, entire tapering to a blunt point. The common name refers to the superficial resemblance of the pinnae to bamboo leaves. Sporangia are formed on the underside of the frond, tightly packed together in narrow rows running from the pinnule midrib to the pinnule margin. The sporangia are naked, ie. not covered with an indusium. (See also Khullar, 1994.)

Although no species is common in cultivation, there are three species usually considered to be fairly widely grown. Unfortunately, the similarity between them has lead to a blurring of the species lines. In horticulture correctly named plants are probably the exception rather than the rule. The following key distinctions may help true identification.

C. fraxinea
Himalaya, east Asia, not Japan, H30–60cm (12–24in), D, Dry/Wet, Zone 8. As *C. japonica* except veins open (not netted). The only cultivated species with a smooth margin to the pinnule: it may rarely be lobed, but it is never serrated.

C. intermedia
Himalaya, east Asia, not Japan, H30–60cm (12–24in), D, Dry/Wet, Zone 8. As above except veins open and pinna margin serrated.

C. japonica
Japan, east Asia, H30–60cm (12–24in), D, Dry/Wet, Zone 8, possibly 7. Fronds bipinnate when mature, veins anastomosing (netted within the pinnule). Pinnule margin acutely lobed.

'Flavomaculata' (syn. 'Variegata') is a variegated form. The variegation exists as golden bars arranged herringbone-fashion along the pinnules. Variegated forms are recorded in several other species.

Cossentinia vellea, see *Cheilanthes vellea*.

CRYPTOGRAMMA (parsley ferns)

A small genus of ferns confined to cool temperate regions of the northern hemisphere. Fronds divided much like parsley. Many crested lady fern cultivars (*Athyrium filix-femina*) are often likened to parsley but in *Cryptogramma* the fronds are not crested. In North America the common name rock brake refers to the habitat of these ferns among rocks, particularly as pioneer stabilizers of screes. Difficult to grow, but worth trying. All species are rare in cultivation.

C. acrostichoides, syn. *C. crispa* var. *acrostichoides* (rock brake)
Alaska, Canada, northern USA, H5–20cm (2–8in), W, Dry/Wet, Zone 2. Fronds tripinnate, lance-shaped. Ultimate segments of sterile fronds leafy. Fertile frond segments narrower because the margins are folded under to protect the sporangia, giving the fern a dimorphic appearance. A tuft-forming species. Fertile fronds are taller than sterile fronds. Sterile fronds are virtually wintergreen, fertile fronds die down in autumn. In cultivation this species rarely attains the sizes seen in nature but by planting among slates in an acid compost it can be grown as a beautiful semi-dwarf rock plant.

C. crispa (parsley fern)
Mountains of Europe, Asia, H7–30cm (3–12in), D, Dry/Wet, Zone 2. Fronds tri- to quadripinnate but otherwise similar to *C. acrostichoides* from which it differs by being completely deciduous. A very beautiful fern. Difficult to cultivate although possibly easier to grow than *C. acrostichoides* if given the same acidic conditions; only very rarely available commercially.

C. stelleri
Alaska, north-east USA, Canada, H12–38cm (5–15in), D, Dry/Wet, Zone 3. A smaller form of *C. acrostichoides* and completely deciduous. Quite similar to the other two species except it has creeping rhizomes and does not form a tuft of fronds. Of greatest significance is that, unlike the other two, it prefers calcareous composts.

CYATHEA

A large genus of about 600 species of tree ferns, widely distributed through the montane forests of the tropics, with a few species occurring in cool temperate regions. All cyatheas can be distinguished from the rather similar genera *Dicksonia* and *Cibotium* by the presence of scales on the stipe. Fronds are generally lanceolate-triangular, with a long stipe. All species like a humid site with a lime-free compost with plenty of humus. To establish newly imported trunks, water the trunk copiously during the growing season. To reduce the risk of rots setting in do not water into the crown over winter. Plant out of the wind. Younger plants are more susceptible to cold, therefore do not plant out very young plants in colder regions until they are well established, preferably with around 60cm (24in) of trunk. All species listed will do well in a frost-free greenhouse. Each species should survive unprotected in the zone given; if wrapped up over winter it should also survive in the next coldest zone.

Cyathea australis, from Australia and now being grown in Europe, is one of the hardiest tree fern species.

The species included here are only a selection: many more are available and many others have not been grown in temperate regions and may be worth trying whenever available. Sizes given are what might be attained in horticulture, specimens in the wild will often be bigger.

C. australis (rough tree fern)
Australia (Victoria, New South Wales, Tasmania), H Trunk to 5.5m × 30cm (18 × 1ft), Fronds 1.2–3m (4–10ft), D (even in Australia), Wet/Dry, Zone 9, or perhaps 8. Leaf

bases and stipe covered with short, blunt spines, hence the common name. Exterior of top of trunk covered with the spiny frond bases, base of trunk covered with a mat of roots. Fronds bipinnate-pinnatifid, broad lance-shaped, glossy light green on upper surface but matt and slightly glaucous beneath. Long yellow-brown stipe is densely covered by dark brown scales when young, but these are shed as the frond matures revealing a line of dark brown dashes along either side. An exciting prospect for gardens in colder areas as in the wild it grows in the same areas as *Dicksonia antarctica* except at slightly higher altitudes and in more open sites. On balance it should, therefore, be at least as hardy as the dicksonia. It has not been long in cultivation in Europe and its hardiness still needs to be proven over a few more winters. Cultivate in a sheltered site with adequate water and good light; some direct sun acceptable in early morning or evening. Plants offered in trade as *C. australis* are often *C. cooperi*.

C. brownii (Norfolk Island tree fern)
Norfolk Island, H Trunk to 3m × 15cm (10ft × 6in), Fronds 1.2–2.5m (4–8ft), E, Wet/Dry, Zone 10, possibly 9. Leaf bases covered with pale brown scales. Fronds bipinnate-pinnatifid, broad lance-shaped with orange-brown and white-brown scales. Spineless stipe has a line of white dashes running up either side. Superficially very similar to *C. cooperi*, cinnamon form, but differs in its more leathery laminae and by being very quick growing.

C. colensoi (creeping tree fern)
New Zealand, H Fronds 1–1.5m (3–5ft), E, Wet/Dry, Zone 7. Fronds bipinnate-pinnatifid, broad lance-shaped, hairy on upper surface. It looks like a young tree fern. A trunk may be formed but it is prostrate, perhaps creeping along the ground for a metre or so. *C. colensoi* grows in drier, colder forests than other tree ferns in New Zealand. Not widely grown in Europe but should be relatively hardy.

C. cooperi (lacy tree fern)
Eastern Australia, H Trunk to 2.5m × 12cm (8ft × 5in), Fronds 1.2–2.5m (4–8ft) E, Wet/Dry, Zone 9, possibly 8. Fronds bipinnate-pinnatifid, broad lance-shaped. Stipe long, with pimples near base, generously covered in pale chaff-like scales and with a line of grey-brown dashes along either side. Trunk covered with scales near top, and 'coin-spotting', where there are leaf abscission scars, is sometimes visible lower down. Plants in circulation as *C. australis* or the South American *C. delgadii* may be this species. *C. cooperi* survived, but did not thrive, in a straw shelter outdoors for four winters in central England

(zone 8). It would be better in a cool conservatory or outdoors in Zone 8 or warmer. In nature it is absent from Victoria and Tasmania, yet is frost tolerant.

'Brentwood' A robust selection made in the United States.

Cinnamon form Like the type plant but the rachis and stipe are covered with mats of cinnamon-coloured scales.

'Cristatum' A very heavily crested form, almost a grandiceps, was recently introduced into cultivation in Australia. It is hard to imagine what a mature plant will look like!

'Marleyi' Introduced in Australia. Differs from the type by being more graceful with all tips more finely pointed.

'Revolvens' Like the type plant except the lamina is curved down strongly. Not universally admired.

'Robusta' Similar to cinnamon form - perhaps the same?

C. cunninghamii (gully tree fern, slender tree fern)
New Zealand, south-east Australia, Tasmania, H Trunk 6m × 7cm (20ft × 3in), Fronds 1–2m (3–6ft), E, Wet/Dry, Zone 9. Fronds bipinnate-pinnatifid, lance-shaped with no stipe. Bunches of small pinnae are produced at the

Cyathea cooperi, the 'lacy tree fern', is a fast-growing species from eastern Australia.

base of each frond where it emerges from the crown, forming a 'wig'. Rachis is purple-brown, but black and spiny at the base and yellow brown towards the tip. It has mid-brown scales. Spines persist on old leaf bases encircling black trunk. In nature this fern is uncommon, usually growing in humid, dark gulleys. Coming from as far south as Tasmania it should be fairly hardy but its normally sheltered habitat would give it some frost protection. As a rule tree ferns with slender trunks are less hardy than fat-trunked species; however, experimentation with this in hardiness zone 8 with a very humid microclimate may prove rewarding, if it is not allowed to dry out. In my cold greenhouse this species is very quick growing, putting on about 15cm (6in) of trunk annually. In the wild in Australia it hybridizes with *C. australis* to make *C.* × *marcesens* (below). Spores produced only on mature specimens when the trunk may be 6m (20ft) tall. They are, therefore, very difficult to collect, making this fern scarce in cultivation. This is the only species of tree fern common to both Australia and New Zealand. It appears very similar in both regions but the New Zealand plant appears to have a narrower trunk, particularly near ground level.

The beautiful silver tree fern *Cyathea dealbata* is from New Zealand.

Cyathea medullaris has black scaly croziers which are awesome in spring.

C. dealbata (ponga, silver tree fern)

New Zealand, H Trunk 6m × 15cm (20ft × 6in), Fronds 1.2–2.5m (4–8ft), E, Wet/Dry, Zone 9. Fronds bipinnate-pinnatifid, broad lance-shaped, dull light green on top, silver below, stipe silver. The silver powdery covering does not develop on very young plants. Stipe with brown scales and brown dashes along either side. One of the world's most beautiful ferns and the national emblem of New Zealand. Grows very happily in south-west Eire (zone 9) without protection. It regenerates but young plants are lost in severe winters much as happens with *Dicksonia antarctica*. In the wild this is a tree fern with a preference for slightly drier climates than most other species: therefore, plant in well-drained soil.

C. dregei

South Africa, H Trunk to 3.5m × 45cm (12ft × 18in), Fronds 1.2–2.5m (4–8ft), E, Wet/Dry, Zone 9, possibly 8. Fronds bipinnate-pinnatifid, broad lance-shaped, deep green. Glossy brown scales on rachis. Grows at altitudes of up to 2100m (7000ft) in the Drakensburg Mountains, often in open sites by the sides of streams where it must endure severe weather. Large plants can survive grass fires as witnessed by their frequently grey trunks. Little is known about their cultivation in the northern hemisphere but this species is potentially one of the world's hardiest tree ferns. They should be given plenty of water, good drainage and plenty of light, ideally full sun in cold areas. Even in warm areas fronds die off annually.

C. × marcesens (skirted tree fern)
Australia (Victoria, Tasmania), H Trunk 6m × 30cm (6ft × 12in), Fronds to 1.8m (6ft), E, Wet/Dry, Zone 9, possibly 8. Fronds bipinnate-pinnatifid, broad lance-shaped. Rachis spiny and black with dark brown scales. Stipe short or absent producing some pinnae just above the crown. The common name refers to the persistent old fronds forming a 'skirt' around the trunk. Hybrid between *C. australis* and *C. cunninghamii* with characteristics intermediate between the parents. Although rare in the wild, this fern is surprisingly common in the forests of southern Victoria, where it sometimes outnumbers one parent, *C. cunninghamii*. Probably in horticulture only in Australia but attempts are being made to propagate it by tissue culture, which may lead to export of some stocks. In Australia it has the reputation of being one of the hardiest species, ie. it can withstand exposure and drought better than most; perhaps it can also withstand cold.

C. medullaris (black tree fern, Mamaku)
New Zealand, H Trunk to 4.5m × 10–22cm (15ft × 4–8in), E, Wet/Dry, Zone 10, possibly 9. Fronds bipinnate pinnatifid to tripinnate, broad lance-shaped, very long – up to 3m (10ft), even in cold areas. Rachis and stipe black except on very young plants; lines of white dashes along either side of stipe. Base of stipe may be yellow if the dark brown scales are removed prematurely. Trunks are surprisingly heavy; plants imported as trunks from New Zealand are often rather slim, around 7–10cm (3–4in) in diameter, to minimize weight and the costs of air freight. This fern has survived outdoors for a few winters at Portmeirion in North Wales, Tresco in the Isles of Scilly and in south-west Eire (all zone 9), but the odd severe winter has usually been critical. Fine in a greenhouse kept frost free. With care it makes a very quick-growing tree fern: in a cold greenhouse it may grow 7cm (3in) of trunk a year but a plant I was shown in an Australian garden had grown almost 30cm (12in) a year. Avoid damp in crown in winter.

C. milnei
Kermadec Islands, H Trunk to 1.5m × 12cm (5ft × 5in), Fronds 1–1.5m (3–5ft), E, Wet/Dry, Zone 10. Fronds bipinnate-pinnatifid, broad lance-shaped, slightly shiny on upper surface. Scales dark brown on croziers but pale with maturity. Rachis green with a line of brown dashes along either side. The trunk is stocky at the base. Superficially similar to *C. dealbata* but lacking any silver colouring.

C. princeps
Central America, H Trunk to 2m × 10–15cm (6ft × 4–6in), Fronds 1.2m (4ft), E, Wet/Dry, Zone 9. Fronds bipinnate-pinnatifid, broad lance shaped. Stipe, trunk and croziers abundantly covered with light golden-brown scales. Scaly unfurling croziers are a particular feature. I grew this for two years, one winter, in my garden in central England, in a shelter along with *Dicksonia antarctica*. The second winter was not as cold as the first but the crown rotted, perhaps due to the cold but more likely it got too wet in my shelter. It is a high-altitude tropical tree fern, like so many of the world's species. The partial success in my garden raises the hope that other more suitable species exist to be tested in cool-temperate gardens.

In nature *Cyathea smithii* grows further from the equator than any other species of tree fern.

Cyathea australis, detail

Cyathea cooperi, detail

Cyathea dealbata, detail

Cyathea medullaris, detail

Cyathea smithii, detail

Dicksonia fibrosa, detail

Dicksonia sellowiana, detail

Dicksonia squarrosa, detail

C. robertsiana
Australia (Queensland), H Trunk 3m × 2.5cm (10ft × 1in), Fronds 1m (3ft), E, Wet/Dry, Zone 10, possibly 9. Fronds bipinnate-pinnatifid, lance-shaped, pale green. Broad, blunt brown scales on green stipe and rachis. Broken line of white dashes, ageing black, along either side of stipe. Top of trunk green and fleshy. Despite being native to Queensland, where it is a primary colonizer of roadside banks, this fern is quite cold-tolerant. In my fernery it has survived short exposure to freezing temperartures with no serious damage. In Melbourne it thrives in the lath-house fernery at Rippon Lea where it may also experience occasional frost. A fascinating fern, ideal for a shady conservatory as its fronds are not huge but with the charm and elegance to equal any other tree fern. It must have adequate light. Unfortunately rarely available.

C. robusta
Lord Howe Island, H Trunk to 3m × 9in (10ft × 22cm), Fronds 1.8–2.5m (6–8ft) E, Wet/Dry, Zone 9, possibly 10. Fronds bipinnate-pinnatifid, broad lance-shaped. Rachis stout covered with pale scales. Stipe bases near glaucous. As its name suggests, a very robust tree fern, although young plants can be difficult to establish if overwatered. Brought into cultivation by Chris Goudey of Austral Ferns in Victoria from spores collected on Lord Howe Island. Unfortunately after the first flush of young plants there was a gap of several years before any plants in cultivation became old enough to produce new spores to restock the trade.

C. smithii (soft tree fern, Katote)
New Zealand, H Trunk to 3m × 30cm (10ft × 12in), Fronds 1.2–1.8m (4–6ft), E, Wet/Dry, Zone 10, possibly 9. Fronds bipinnate-pinnatifid, shiny above, narrowly lance-shaped with a short stipe. Mid-brown scales abundant on stipe, absent from laminae. Lines of small dark dashes along either side of stipe. This tree fern has the distinction of growing in the wild on the Auckland Islands, further from the equator than any other species of tree fern. It is also unusual in that its fronds are lance-shaped – very similar in shape and general appearance to *Dicksonia antarctica*, although the abundant scales will soon distinguish this from the dicksonia. Not common in cultivation, occasionally plants of *C. cooperi* are offered under this name. It may prove quite hardy but despite its provenance it is doubtful it will be as hardy as *Dicksonia antarctica*. Experimentation in zone 9 gardens will be interesting.

C. spinulosa
Himalaya, east Asia, H Trunk to 2.5m × 10cm (8ft × 4in), Fronds 1.8–2m (6–8ft), Zone 10, possibly 9. Fronds bipinnate-pinnatifid, broad lance-shaped, scales dark brown at base, orange-brown on stipe, which also has two lines of black dashes along either side. Leaf bases with short spines, more prominent as bases mature and become assimilated into trunk. Although from the Himalaya it is restricted to the warm valleys, for example around Kathmandu in Nepal. It will certainly stand slight frost and may do well in zone 9 sites. A very elegant fern which produces few fronds annually, although they are very long even on young plants.

C. tomentosissima
Papua New Guinea, H Trunk to 1m × 7cm (3ft × 3in), Fronds 1–1.5m (3–5ft), Zone 10, possibly 9. Fronds bipinnate-pinnatifid, dark green, lance-shaped. A mixture of orange-brown and pale brown scales abundant on stipe, rachis and even on pinnule midribs, making this a very beautiful fern. Trunk predominantly covered with pale brown scales. Ultimate pinnule segments are narrow and quite widely spaced giving the fronds an airy appearance. Only recently introduced into horticulture. Although it grows more or less on the equator in the wild, this plant grows at very high altitudes in alpine grassland where it experiences occasional short-lived frosts. Experimentation outdoors with larger specimens in zone 9 could therefore be successful. There is a form in circulation called 'Highland Lace'; I believe this to be no different from the type plant, but it is perhaps an attempt to introduce a pronounceable name. Tomentose means hairy (scaly) -issima means very, therefore the name is quite sensible.

CYRTOMIUM

A small genus of evergreen ferns from eastern Asia, especially Japan. Differences between species are rather subtle but in a garden situation all offer a dramatic contrast to other ferns and flowering plants. Fronds pinnate with a short stipe, pinnae broad and pointed.

C. caryotideum
Japan, east Asia, Hawaii, H45cm (18in), E, Dry/Wet, Zone 7. Fronds spreading, pinnate, pale green. Most pinnae have a prominent basal lobe (auricle).

C. falcatum (Japanese holly fern)
Japan, east Asia, H60cm (24in), E, Dry/Wet, Zone 8, possibly 7. Fronds pinnate, very dark green and glossy, some pinnae may have auricles. Reputed not to be reliably hardy but has thrived for many winters in central England. It may be advisable to protect the crown with a

stone or straw over winter. Both the species and the cultivars are widely grown as houseplants. It has escaped and become established in the wild in Europe and North America.

'Cristatum', syn. 'Mayi' A form with crested frond tips.
'Rochfordianum' A very pretty form with the pinnae margins deeply lacerated.

C. fortunei

Japan, east Asia, H60cm (24in), E, Dry/Wet, Zone 6, undoubtedly hardy in zone 7. Like *C. falcatum* except pinnae are pale, non-glossy green. Pinnae are also narrower.
var. *clivicola* Japan, H38cm (15in), E, Dry/Wet, Zone 6. Pinnae margins lobed and fronds more spreading.

C. lonchitoides

Japan, east Asia, H45cm (18in), E, Dry/Wet, Zone 7. Fronds slightly glossy, pinnate with smaller, rounder pinnae than the other species. The pinnae are set much closer together along the rachis than in *C. fortunei*.

C. macrophyllum

Japan, east Asia, H30cm (12in), E, Dry/Wet, Zone 7. Like

Cyrtomium fortunei is a striking evergreen species from Japan. Its narrow pinnae are a distinctive feature.

other species in this genus but fronds are more spreading, similar to *C. caryotideum* except it lacks basal lobe on pinnae. Very attractive.

CYSTOPTERIS (bladder ferns)

A genus of around 20 species scattered through cool-temperate regions. The common name refers to the bladder-shaped indusium enclosing the sorus. Only one or two species are common in cultivation. They are rather under used in the garden as they are beautiful in early spring, but unfortunately they die back rather early.

C. alpina, syn. C. regia (alpine bladder fern)

Central Europe, H10–22cm (4–9in), D, Dry/Wet, Zone 3. Fronds lance-shaped, tripinnate with ultimate divisions narrow, pinnules open giving fronds an elegant, airy appearance, mid-green. Pinnae narrowly triangular. In a rock garden will, in time, form a good-sized clump. Likes rocky, limy soil.

C. bulbifera (bulblet bladder fern)

USA, H38cm (15in), D, Dry/Wet, Zone 3. Fronds bipinnate-pinnatifid, narrow triangular, pale green. Plentifully furnished with bulbils along the rachis with a few on the pinnae midribs. These drop off and develop into new plants, eventually forming a colony. A form in cultivation with incised pinnae was tentatively named 'Incisa' by Jimmy Dyce; a form with wavy pinnae has been discovered in the USA. Other North American species, such as *C. tennesseensis* (below) and *C. laurentiana*, also produce bulbils but they are rare in cultivation.

C. diaphana

Mexico, south-west Europe, H15cm (6in), D, Dry/Wet, happy in high humidity but likes good drainage, Zone 8. Fronds bi- to tripinnate, ultimate segments broad and leafy, lance-shaped. Pinnae overlap along much of rachis. Clump spreads slowly to form a small patch. Requires a sheltered site, but has proved hardy in central England for many years.

C. dickieana (Dickie's bladder fern) (Plate IX)

Scotland, H10–15cm (4–6in), D, Dry/Wet with good drainage, Zone 4. As *C. fragilis* but smaller with pinnae set closer together on leaf axis, often overlapping. Pinnules also overlapping. This fern is only known from sea caves near Aberdeen in Scotland. On the basis of similar spore structure, a form that is widespread across Europe but is otherwise indistinguishable from *C. fragilis* has been grouped under this name. This may prove to be correct botanically but horticulturally the true *C. dickieana* is very distinct, constant in cultivation and comes

true from spores. Ideal in rock gardens. Occasionally crested forms occur in sowings.

C. fragilis (brittle bladder fern)
North America, Europe, including British Isles, H15–20cm (6–8in), D, Dry/Wet with good drainage, Zone 2. Fronds usually bipinnate; pinnae and pinnules usually distant from each other. Pinnules compact, lance-shaped, pale green; pinnae triangular. A very welcome little fern in my garden as it is one of the first to put up new fronds in spring. Easy to grow in any soil but prefers some lime. Apart from 'Cristata' there are no cultivars as such, but the appearance of the species varies throughout its range. The Victorian fern enthusiasts recognised several different species that have now all been sunk into *C. fragilis*. However, recently the Victorians have been proved right in other matters ferny, so I would not be surprised if modern biochemical research did not prove them right again here.

'Cristata' Frond apex and pinnae irregularly crested. Not a great beauty, but curious.

C. montana (alpine bladder fern)
Europe, including Scotland, Asia, North America, H15–30cm (6–12in), D, Wet/Dry, Zone 4. Fronds triangular, tripinnate, pale green on a long stipe. Basal pinnule against the rachis is the longest, ie. the pinnae are triangular, giving the frond a pentagonal outline. Laminae sparingly glandular. In nature it grows among dripping rocks where the water is lime-rich but in the garden it is quite easy in a limestone rockery.

C. moupinense
Central and east Asia, H15–30cm (6–12in), D, Wet/Dry, Zone 5. As *C. sudetica* except that it lacks glands on the laminae.

C. sudetica *(Plate IX)*
Central and north-east Europe, Asia, H15–30cm (6–12in), D, Wet/Dry, Zone 3. As *C. montana* except the basal pinnule against the rachis is not the longest, ie. the pinnae are oblong, therefore the frond is more typically triangular. Very rare in cultivation.

C. tennesseensis (Tennessee bladder fern) *(Plate IX)*
USA, H30cm (12in), D, Dry/Wet, Zone 5. Fronds bipinnate, triangular, pale green. Produces bulbils which drop to the ground and usually establish as new plants. This is a fertile species which has evolved from the hybrid between *C. bulbifera* (above) and *C. protusa*. It differs from

Davallia mariesii is an attractive fern, hardy in a sheltered niche in a rock garden. Note the relatively slender creeping rhizome.

C. bulbifera in that it is more finely dissected, more broadly triangular and generally more foliose.

DAVALLIA

A genus of very beautiful ferns with triangular, finely divided fronds produced on thick, scaly rhizomes that run along the surface of the growing medium. Unfortunately most species are frost tender.

D. mariesii, syn. *Araiostegia pseudocystopteris* (hardy hare's foot fern) *(Plate IX)*
Japan, H22cm (9in), D, Dry/Wet, Zone 8. Fronds finely divided, tripinnate, broad triangular with a long stipe. Creeping rhizomes covered with gingery scales. Hardy in a rock garden, if sheltered. Will eventually spread to become a small colony. Excellent for hanging baskets. Rhizome narrower than virtually all other davallias.

D. stenolepis
Japan, H30cm (12in), D, Dry/Wet, Zone 9, possibly 8. Fronds tripinnate, less finely divided than *D. mariesii*, lanceolate-triangular. Rhizomes covered with grey-brown scales. *D. stenolepis* lacks the delicacy of *D. mariesii* but it is more robust and quickly forms a large colony in my unheated polytunnel.

DENNSTAEDTIA

A small genus of creeping ferns scattered around the temperate regions of the world, but absent from Europe.

D. appendiculata
Asia, H60–75cm (24–30in), D, Dry/Wet, Zone 8. Fronds lance-shaped, bipinnate-pinnatifid, pale green erect on short creeping rhizomes. Rachis covered with white hairs. A very beautiful fern that has proved hardy for me over around ten winters. Unlike *D. punctiloba* it is not invasive, producing a dense clump of beautifully dissected pale green fronds.

D. davallioides (lacy ground fern)
Australia, H60cm (24in), D, Dry/Wet, Zone 9. An attractive fern with tripinnate, triangular fronds on creeping rhizomes. Common in shady forests in Victoria, South Australia where it will take occasional light frost.

D. punctiloba (hay-scented fern)
North America, H60–90cm (24–36in), D, Wet/Dry, Zone 5. Must have acid soil. Fronds bipinnate-pinnatifid, lance-shaped, hairy, yellow-green, erect carried on long creeping underground rhizomes. This fern can be invasive in moist, acid soil, perhaps a useful quality in large gardens. Can stand exposure to sun. In less than ideal conditions it normally stays where planted. Not the most

beautiful garden fern as the fronds lack any real character and can collapse like a pack of cards in dry conditions or severe winds. Glands on the fronds release the smell of new-mown hay when rubbed. The sori are similar to the dicksonia tree ferns, hence the synonym *Dicksonia punctiloba* in some old books.

D. wilfordii, syn. *Microlepia wilfordii*

East Asia, H15–30cm (6–12in), D, Dry/Wet, Zone 9, possibly 8. Delicate species with slender lance-shaped, bipinnate-pinnatifid, hairless fronds. Fertile fronds more delicately divided than sterile fronds. Rhizomes short creeping. Makes a most attractive tufted plant in a pot. I have grown this for around ten seasons in my unheated polytunnels with no problems. It should be hardy outdoors in zone 8; I have not tried.

DICKSONIA

A genus of around 20 species of tree fern distributed through the upland regions of the tropical and warmer temperate areas of the world. Dicksonias differ fundamentally from cyatheas through the presence of hairs, as opposed to scales, on the frond stipe. Although all species are stated to be evergreen, in colder weather all may lose their fronds.

Dicksonia fibrosa from New Zealand, a close relative of D. antarctica.

D. antarctica (soft tree fern)

Australia, including Tasmania, H Trunk to 6m × 75cm (20ft × 30in), Fronds 1.2–2.5m × 75cm (4–9ft × 30in), Wet/Dry, E to –8°C (17.5°F), Zone 9 or possibly 8. This is seemingly the hardiest of all tree ferns currently in cultivation. It has been hardy in my gardens in central England (zone 8), with protection, for the last 14 winters (min. recorded –15°C/5°F). Fronds bipinnate-pinnatifid, lance-shaped. Frond base covered with abundant purplish brown hairs. Stipe short or even absent. The trunk is made up of a central core of very hard woody vascular tissue. This is surrounded by old leaf bases through which root fibres grow. As the roots grow out they gradually increase the diameter of the trunk. In plants in cultivation the trunk is usually much shorter than the maximum figure given, and only up to 22cm (9in) in diameter. Inspection of the trunk of a plant growing in humid conditions in winter will often reveal actively growing pale-tipped roots; in summer active root growth is rarer. If possible grow out of winds and in fairly humid environment (see also pp.33–38). It is a common misconception that *D. antarctica* comes from New Zealand.

D. berteriana

Juan Fernandez Islands, Chile, H Trunk to 3m × 30cm (10 × 1ft), Fronds 1–1.5m × 45cm (3–5ft × 18in), E, Wet/Dry, Zone 9. Fronds tripinnate, some triangular, others broad lance-shaped, dark green, hairy on lamina above and below along veins. Stipe long, shiny, dark brown with abundant pale brown hairs. Despite usually lacking a trunk, at least in horticulture, this very attractive species is well worth growing.

D. fibrosa (wheki ponga)

New Zealand, H Trunk to 5.5m × 60cm (18ft × 24in), Fronds 1.2–2.5m × 75cm (4–8ft × 30in), E, Wet/Dry, Zone 9, possibly zone 8. This tree fern seems almost as hardy as *D. antarctica* here in central England – two well-protected plants have thrived with me over six winters outdoors and put on about 30cm (1ft) of trunk. Plants in cultivation are usually much smaller than the stated figure with trunks 22–30cm (9–12in) in diameter. Fronds bipinnate-pinnatifid, lance-shaped. They are darker green than *D. antarctica*, from which it differs most clearly in having up-turned margins to the pinnule segments, which make the upper surface of the frond feel rough when stroked gently (in *D. antarctica* the down-turned margins make the upper surface feel smooth). *D. fibrosa* also has a darker brown stipe and rachis with darker hairs

Dicksonia antarctica in a garden in Herefordshire, with new fronds 2.5–2.7m (8–9ft) long.

Dicksonia lanata at Inverewe, Scotland. This species is a creeping, non-arborescent tree fern.

than *D. antarctica*. The fronds of *D. fibrosa* tend to be shorter, too, not a diagnostic character but a very useful indication of the greater suitability of this species for smaller conservatories. Much is often made of the way the old fronds hang down the side of the trunk to form a 'skirt', a characteristic shared with *D. antarctica*. The specific name, *fibrosa*, refers to the matted roots making up the very fibrous trunk. This species seems to make more roots on the trunk than *D. antarctica*.

D. hispida

Northern New Zealand, H Trunk to 2.5m × 10–12cm (8ft × 4–5in), Fronds to 2m × 60cm (6 × 2ft), E, Wet/Dry, Zone 10. Fronds tripinnate, broad lance-shaped. Stipe long with dark red-brown hairs. Unlike most other tree ferns, the spores ripen over winter and are shed in spring. For many years this and *D. lanata* were considered the same species – under the name *D. lanata*, although in the middle of the nineteenth century Colenso proposed naming this forma *hispida*. Only very recently have the two forms been formally recognized at specific level and Colenso's name revived – nothing is new in pteridology! As a gardener I fully agree with the split. *D. hispida* is a handsome tree fern, well worth growing when available, although for most of us I fear it will have to be in a con-

servatory. I have been shown this in the Waipoua Forest north of Auckland but I have never grown it.

D. lanata

New Zealand, H Trunk prostrate, Fronds 1–1.5m × 45cm (3–5ft × 18in), E, Wet/Dry, Zone 9, possibly 9. Fronds tripinnate, broad lance-shaped to triangular on a long, red-brown-hairy stipe. Upper surface pale green and slightly glossy, undersurface slightly glaucous. Rhizomes branch eventually creating a tangled mass of trunkless crowns. Very similar to young plants of *D. squarrosa* but the frond shape should distinguish it. I have seen wonderful clumps of this fern at Inverewe in the north of Scotland (zone 8); it has also survived in Kenneth Adlam's garden near Ottery St Mary, Devon (zone 8). It is more or less confined to upland areas of New Zealand and could be one of the hardiest species, but it is rarely grown, perhaps because it lacks a trunk.

D. sellowiana

Brazil, H Trunk to 3m × to 30cm (10ft × to 12in), Fronds 1.8–2.5m × 60cm (6–8 × 2ft), E, Wet/Dry, Zone 9, possibly 8. I have not grown this species outdoors but a plant with a 1.2m (4ft) trunk in a garden near here in Hereford (zone 8) has so far thrived for two winters without sustaining any checks to growth; in the view of the

Dicksonia sellowiana differs from *D. antarctica* in having yellow hairs at the leaf base.

owner it is possibly doing better than *D. antarctica* and increasing its trunk height more noticeably. *D. sellowiana* is clearly very closely related to *D. antarctica* and *D. fibrosa*. In South America it does not grow any further south than southern Brazil (about latitude 40), but it matches the other two species for hardiness, compelling evidence to support the theory that hardiness is not always the dominant character in determining natural distribution of a species. Although superficially very similar to *D. antarctica*, *D. sellowiana* has yellower hairs in the crown and a different jizz that is hard to define. As in *D. antarctica*, the margins of the pinnule segments are downturned. Hooker (1840) observed that the stipes of

D. sellowiana are smooth, whereas in *D. antarctica* (and *D. fibrosa*) they are very slightly rough if rubbed; this certainly applies to my plants. A fern in circulation in Australia as *D. sellowiana* lacks these distinguishing features; while clearly not typical *D. sellowiana*, its true identity remains a mystery but it is distinct in its own right from the other species.

D. squarrosa (wheki, rough tree fern)
New Zealand, H Trunk to 3m × 7–10cm (10ft × 3–4in), Fronds 1–1.5m × 45cm (3–5ft × 18in), E, Wet/Dry, Zone 10, possibly 9. Less hardy than *D. fibrosa* or *D. antarctica*, this has struggled to do well in one of the warmest Cornish gardens (zone 9), but it may have been allowed to get too dry: its trunk needs copious applications of water, therefore it is difficult to establish outdoors. Fronds lance-shaped, bipinnate-pinnatifid with abundant dark

Dicksonia squarrosa is possibly the most elegant of the tree ferns but is less hardy than some.

brown hairs on the dark brown stipe and rachis. Rachis beneath contrasting beautifully with the slightly glaucous green on the undersides of the pinnae. Stipes are set vertically out of the crown but the fronds arch out elegantly to form a spreading crown, reminiscent of vaulting in a church roof. The slender trunk is covered with a sheath of vertical dark brown or black leaf bases, which do not stick out from the trunk as they do in the other species. Some aerial roots are produced along the trunk but far fewer than in *D. antarctica*, *D. fibrosa* or *D. sellowiana*, hence the stipes remain conspicuous a metre or so below the crown. Unusually among the tree-like *Dicksonia* in horticulture, this species produces side crowns up the trunk, as well as runners under ground to produce side shoots. If the main crown dies, do not throw away the stump: unlike in the other three species a new crown may appear. I have never grown this outdoors but it is ideal for a shady greenhouse where the trunk can be kept moist, or in a small conservatory where the shortish fronds reduce the pressure on space.

D. youngiae
Australia (Queensland), H Trunk to 2m × 10–15cm (6ft × 4–6in), Fronds 1.2–2m × 45cm (4–6ft × 18in), E, Wet/Dry, Zone 10. Fronds bipinnate-pinnatifid, lance-shaped. Stipe covered with purplish hairs. The develop-

ing purplish croziers are very attractive. Trunk is reported not to be very strong. Coming from Queensland it is likely that *D. youngiae* is not hardy, but it can withstand occasional frosts in Australia and may survive in sheltered Cornish gardens (zone 9); in colder areas it is best grown in a conservatory over winter.

DIPLAZIUM
A very large group of ferns closely related to *Athyrium*. A few are known to be hardy (zone 8) and future trial work will probably add many more to the list. All hardy species are deciduous.

D. hachijoense
Japan, H60–90cm (24–36in), D, Wet/Dry, Zone 7. Fronds bipinnate-pinnatifid, triangular, dark green on a long stipe. Rhizomes creeping. I was given spores under this name many years ago, but as there are many somewhat similar species the name is slightly tentative. Nevertheless, it has grown very well in the garden here at Kyre Park (zone 8) for several years such that it has colonized a few square metres of land. It is not dangerously invasive, and its exotic textured foliage makes it well worth growing.

D. pycnocarpon, see *Athyrium pycnocarpon*.

D. sibiricum, syn. *Athyrium crenatum*
Northern Europe, Asia, H15cm (18in), D, Wet/Dry, Zone 4. Fronds bipinnate-pinnatifid, triangular, rather similar to *D. hachijoense*. Rhizomes creeping. Unfortunately, I have never had material of this plant but, given its native distribution through Siberia, it can certainly withstand cold; however, it may not like the stop-start winters typical of the British Isles.

D. subsinuatum
Far eastern Asia, H30–45 × 2.5cm (12–18 × 1in), E, Dry/Wet, Zone 8 or 9. Typically for this species the fronds are entire, dull mid-green, narrowly lance-shaped, with a long stipe. The specimen I grow in my unheated polytunnel is crenately lobed, almost like *Asplenium ceterach*. It may not be correctly named; my plant may be *Deparia zeylanica*. It is a vigorous grower and could do well in a sheltered garden in zone 8.

DOODIA (rasp ferns)
A small genus of ferns mainly from the temperate zone of the southern hemisphere. New fronds are usually red tinted. Closely related to *Blechnum* but differ in having sori in one to two rows along either side of the midrib. In *Blechnum* there is a single, elongated sorus along each

side of the midrib. The species are all rather similar and can be difficult to distinguish one from another.

D. aspera
New Zealand (introduced), Australia, H15cm (6in), W, Dry/Wet, Zone 9, possibly 8. Fronds lance-shaped, pinnatifid; pinnae gradually reduce in size towards base of frond. Harsh to the touch. Young fronds pink. Sporing and sterile fronds similar. Needs warm, dryish conditions.

D. caudata (small rasp fern)
Australia, New Zealand, H15cm (6in), W, Wet/Dry, Zone 8. Sterile fronds pinnate, lance-shaped, spreading. Sporing fronds pinnate, lance-shaped and more erect, with narrower segments. The tip of the frond is somewhat caudate (drawn out into a point). Like all doodias (and blechnums) this little fern prefers acid soil. Ideal for rockwork. 'Perhaps hardy', Richard Rush, 1984. There is a crested form in cultivation which I have not seen.

D. media (Plate V)
Australasia, H25cm (10in), D, Wet/Dry, Zone 8. Fronds pinnate at least near base, lance-shaped, with sterile and fertile fronds similar. New fronds deep red, gradually turning pink then green. Outdoors needs sheltered spot. 'Hardy', Richard Rush 1984.

D. squarrosa
New Zealand, H15cm (6in), W, Wet/Dry, Zone 9. Fronds pinnate, lance-shaped, with sterile fronds more prostrate and the fertile fronds more upright. A rare fern from the Auckland district of New Zealand. Similar to *D. caudata* except the tip of the frond is less caudate. Excellent in a sheltered rockery.

DRYOPSIS

Easily confused with *Dryopteris* in name and appearance, but there are good botanical reasons why these ferns are kept separate. A small genus which contains one or two useful hardy ferns, the best being *Dryopsis nidus*.

D. nidus, syn. *Nephrodium nidus*
Himalaya, H45–60cm (18–24in), W, Dry/Wet, Zone 8. Fronds lance-shaped, pinnate-pinnatifid. Stipe, rachis and pinnae midribs covered with dark brown scales. Superficially similar to *Dryopteris wallichiana* but fronds more papery, stipes more slender, and the sori are produced only towards the tips of the pinnae segments. In the wild it is a high-altitude species and may prove hardy in zones colder than 8.

The richly coloured croziers of *Dryopteris affinis* subsp. *borreri* unfurling in spring.

DRYOPTERIS

This is the genus that contains by far the largest number of good garden ferns. Most are hardy in zone 7 and should form a pivotal part of any fern border. Many species have scaly stipes which can be dramatically beautiful in spring as the croziers are unfurling. Some species are evergreen, some wintergreen, and some are completely deciduous. Many are extremely easy to cultivate and will even do well in poorly lit and poorly watered areas. Many species have been brought into cultivation over the last 25 years due to the worldwide collections of Christopher Fraser-Jenkins. Unfamiliar names given here are almost certainly his introductions.

Many more of the 220 or so species, and even more numerous hybrids, could be included in this list, but I have restricted myself to those that I consider the most garden worthy. Other species are not in cultivation but may in time become more widely grown.

The descriptions here will not always enable a fern to be identified with certainty, but, hopefully, they will be adequate, in most cases, to determine what the plant is not. To really appreciate their distinctiveness, it is necessary to grow them.

D. aemula (hay-scented buckler fern) (Plate IX)
North-west Europe, including British Isles, with an outlying population in Turkey, H30–60cm (12-24in), W, almost E, Wet/Dry, Zone 5. Fronds fresh green, triangular, tripinnate, with margins of pinnule sections slightly turned up, giving a crisped appearance. Tips of pinnae curve down very gracefully. Minute glands on the fronds smell of hay when crushed. Stipe quite long, typically purple-brown on underside with a few red-brown slender scales. Does well in the garden if given plenty of shade and moisture. Prefers acid conditions with organic soil mix. Native of humid woods often near waterfalls, abundant in much of south-west Scotland in wooded margins of raised beaches. The Isle of Arran was dubbed 'Aemula Isle' by Jimmy Dyce. A beautiful fern that can be grown with great success, as at Greencombe garden at Porlock in Somerset.

D. affinis, syn. *D. borreri*, *D. pseudomas* (golden male fern) (Plate VII)
Europe, including British Isles, Asia, H1–1.2m (3–4ft), W, Dry/Wet, Zone 4. Fronds pinnate-pinnatifid, lance-shaped, dark green with golden-brown scaly stems. In winter they are likely to break and become untidy after gales or snow. Rhizomes erect with fronds forming a symmetrical crown. A magnificent garden fern that

deserves to be grown more often, it is tolerant of several hours of sun daily, and is also more wind resistant than most ferns. The unfurling ginger-brown croziers in spring are stunning. *D. affinis* is very similar to *D. filix-mas*, but it can always be distinguished by the presence of a black zone at the base of the pinna where it is attached to the rachis. Even hybrids with some *D. affinis* in their blood show this mark. It can also be recognised by the almost squared-off tips to the pinna segments. There are several subspecies which could arguably be considered separate species, but because it is difficult for even botanists to distinguish between them it is generally agreed to leave them as subspecies. All subspecies are apogamous: this means that all cultivars come true from spores. Very rarely new sports arise; for example 'Cristata Angustata' is a sport of 'Cristata'. Subsp. *affinis* is very robust and very scaly. Subsp. *cambrensis* has fewer scales but they are an attractive purplish-brown and the lamina is crisped. Subsp. *borreri* has relatively few brown scales and looks most like *D. filix-mas*. But it is not always that easy – there are intermediates and hybrids. There are hybrids between each subspecies and *D. filix-mas*: they too are difficult to distinguish and are collectively called *D.* × *complexa*.

Cultivars of subsp. *affinis*

'Congesta Cristata' H15cm (6in), E. Fronds congested with neat crests on pinnae and frond tip. Raised by Dr Lyell in 1886. Very rare.

'Crispa Cristata Angustata' *(Plate VII)* H15cm (6in), E. Fronds crested, congested and narrowed – a congested form of 'Cristata Angustata'. Very rare, first raised by Lang in the nineteenth century.

'Crispa Gracilis' *(Plate VII)* H22cm (9in), E. Fronds very congested and crisped, tips of pinnae upturned and seem pointed, dark green, not crested. Green and handsome throughout the winter in sheltered site. First grown by Dr Lyell, 1880s. Often grown as 'Crispa Congesta'.

'Cristata' (king of the male ferns) H90cm (36in), W. A robust fern often more than 90cm (36in). The tips of the pinnae and the tip of the frond are crested, fronds mainly erect. Like 'Cristata Angustata' but fronds normal width and more erect.

'Cristata Angustata' H60–90cm (24–36in), W. An elegant fern with narrow, long, arching fronds. Frond and pinnae tips crested.

'Grandiceps Askew' H60cm (24in), W. Heavily crested. I do not grow this cultivar. It is a neat form but rare.

'Pinderi' H60–90cm (24–36in), W. Uncrested with frond narrowed terminating in a slender point. Found in 1855 in the Lake District by the Rev. Pinder. A more compacted form of *D.* × *complexa* 'Stableri'. Formerly considered a cultivar of *D. oreades*.

'Polydactyla Mapplebeck' *(Plate VII)* H1–1.2m (36–48in), W. In some ways similar to 'Cristata' but the crests much larger and not so neat. Strictly a grandiceps form as the crest is broader than the frond. Found in Westmorland in 1862 by Mapplebeck.

Cultivar of subsp. *cambrensis*

'Crispa Barnes' *(Plate VII)* H60cm (24in), D, Dry/Wet. Fronds as in the type plant but the lamina crisped. First recognized by J.M. Barnes in the Lake District in 1865 but since found in many places. It is, in fact, simply a well developed form of subsp. *cambrensis*.

Cultivars of subsp. *borreri*

'Polydactyla Dadds' *(Plate VII)* H90cm (36in), D, Dry/Wet. Similar to 'Polydactyla Mapplebeck' but not so robust and the crests often little more than forks on the pinnae. This cultivar and Mapplebeck's form were recently differentiated by the notable botanist Christopher Fraser-Jenkins. Working in the herbarium at Kew he came across original named specimens of both forms and could instantly see that they were polydactylous (crests were many-fingered) forms of different subspecies. It was then easy to name both forms in cultivation with confidence. This and other cultivars of *D. affinis* can reappear in the wild. I found this form on Keswick Railway Station in the Lake District around 1970 – clearly an escape from a nearby garden – nearly 100 years after it was first raised by Dadds in 1872.

'Revolvens' H60cm (24in), D, Dry/Wet. A rare form with the pinnae rolling back from the rachis forming an open tube-like shape. Tubular form of fronds becomes more striking with older plants. An old Victorian cultivar first found in the Lake District.

Cultivars of × *complexa*

'Decomposita' H60cm–1.1m (24–46in), D, Dry/Wet. Fronds uncrested but pinnae lobes themselves lobed, the frond is thus almost pinnate-bipinnatifid.

'Ramosissima Wright' H60–90cm (24–36in), D, Dry/Wet. A very rare cultivar which is sterile and can, therefore, only be propagated by division. The fronds branch several times from the base. The pinnae and all the frond divisions are crested. Discovered in North Wales by Wright in 1864.

'Stableri' H1–1.2m (36–48in), D, Dry/Wet. Despite hybrid origins this cultivar is easily raised from spores. The fronds are uncrested but narrowed and very large. Raised by Stabler in the Lake District. One of the largest hardy ferns for a cold garden.

'Stableri' (crisped), syn. 'Crispa Angustata' *(Plate VII)* H60–75cm (24–30in), D, Dry/Wet. A dwarf form of 'Stableri' with slightly crisped pinnae. This cultivar does not appear to be in any of the early fern books and is, therefore, probably a newish break, perhaps from the European continent. The synonym seems a more suitable name but is, unfortunately, apparently unacceptable. 'Stableri Heerlen' may prove to be correct.

D. aitoniana

Atlantic Islands, Madiera, H60cm (24in), W, Dry/Wet, Zone 8. Delicately divided fern, the frond bipinnate, triangular or broadly lance-shaped with a long stipe. Laminae covered with stalked glands that can be seen with a hand lens.

D. amurensis

North-east Asia, H45–60cm (18–24in), D, Wet/Dry, Zone 4. Rhizomes creeping, fronds broadly triangular, tripinnate on a long stipe. Frond in outline reminiscent of *Gymnocarpium robertianum*. I have never seen this species.

D. arguta (Californian wood fern)

South-west USA, H20–60cm (12–24in), W, Dry/Wet, Zone 8. Fronds narrowly triangular, bipinnate. Similar to *D. submontana* but paler green. This fern is not terribly easy to grow in central Britain; it is hardy but it seems to need the Mediterranean-type climate, ie. warm wet winters and hot dry summers.

D. × australis (D. celsa × D. ludoviciana)

North-east USA, H1–1.2m (36–48in), D, Dry/Wet or Wet/Dry, Zone 5. Fronds narrowly lance-shaped, erect, pinnate-pinnatifid. Pinnae bearing sporangia shorter than non-soriferous pinnae. As this is a hybrid the spores are rarely fertile but the rhizomes creep slowly, and frequently branch producing a mass of growing tips. Each of these can be removed to produce a new plant. Always rare, but so striking it is worth taking some trouble to find it. Much admired at the Chelsea Flower Show. Seems very unfussy regarding growing conditions but spreads well beside a pool here in Worcestershire.

D. azorica

Azores, H60–90cm (24–36in), W, Wet/Dry, Zone 8. Like *D. dilatata* (see below) except stipe scales are lance-shaped. This is one for the specialist. There is one excellent cultivar, 'Cristata'. Introduced in the nineteenth century, it is a good cristatum with neat crests on pinnae and frond tips. Unfortunately now very rare.

D. bissetiana

Japan and east Asia, H30–60cm (12–24in), W, Wet/Dry, Zone 7. Fronds triangular, bipinnate-pinnatifid, dark green with all segments fairly narrow and pointed. Rachis and stipe covered with pale scales unlike the otherwise similar *D. erythrosora* var. *prolifica*. Prefers a sheltered spot, perhaps in a rock garden.

D. blandfordii

Himalaya, H60cm (24in), D, Wet/Dry, Zone 7. Fronds bipinnate-pinnatifid, lance-shaped, can be almost tripinnate at the base. A rather variable species but often superficially very similar to *D. filix-mas*. *D. blandfordii* is typically densely dark-scaly; however, plants in circulation seem to lack dark scales and I suspect that a mistake has been made. The plant in horticulture is not distinct from *D. filix-mas* to the untrained eye and is not, therefore, worth growing unless *D. filix-mas* is not available.

D. campyloptera

North America, H60–90cm (24–36in), Dry/Wet, Zone 4. Fronds triangular, tripinnate. Very similar to the European *D. dilatata* (see below) from which it is distinguished with difficulty. One for the specialist.

D. carthusiana (narrow buckler fern)

British Isles, Europe, H60cm (24in), D, Wet/Dry, Zone 3. Fronds bipinnate-pinnatifid, lance-shaped. Like *D. dilatata* (see below) but fronds narrower and lance-shaped, with scales at frond base uniformly pale. Excellent for damp areas, quite at home in bogs.

'Cristata' is a very good crested form from Europe. It is not mentioned in any fern book I have seen and is presumably, therefore, new to cultivation, making the name I give here unacceptable!

D. caucasica

Turkey and CIS, H60–90cm (24–30in), D, Dry/Wet, Zone 4. Similar to *D. filix-mas* except fronds bipinnate, at least at base, and pinnule margins more deeply serrate. *D. filix-mas* is derived from the hybrid between *D. caucasica* and *D. oreades*.

D. celsa

North America, H60–90cm (24–36in), Dry/Wet, Zone 5. Fronds lance-shaped, pinnate-pinnatifid. In appearance not unlike a small *D. goldiana* – one of its ancestral parents.

PLATE VII
Dryopteris affinis and relations

*All fronds shown
approximately half size*

Dryopteris affinis subsp.
cambrensis 'Crispa Barnes'

Dryopteris affinis
subsp. *affinis* 'Polydactyla
Mapplebeck'

Dryopteris × *complexa*
'Stableri' (crisped)

Dryopteris affinis subsp.
affinis 'Crispa Gracilis'

Dryopteris affinis
subsp. *affinis* 'Crispa
Cristata Angustata'

Dryopteris affinis
subsp. *affinis*
'Cristata'

Dryopteris affinis
subsp. *borreri*
'Polydactyla Dadds'

*Dryopteris
affinis* subsp.
affinis 'Cristata
Angustata

D. championii

East Asia, H60cm (24in), E, Dry/Wet, Zone 7. Fronds triangular, bipinnate. Similar to *D. erythrosora* but pinnules are stalked, more glossy and round tipped.

D. chrysocoma

Nepal, south-east Asia, H60cm (24in), D, Dry/Wet, Zone 8. Fronds bipinnate, lance-shaped, dull green. Pinnae somewhat leathery. Stipe covered with pale brown scales at base. Fronds arching. Easy in a shaded border.

D. clintoniana

North America, H60–90cm (24–36in), D, Dry/Wet, Zone 4. Fronds pinnate-pinnatifid, narrowly lance-shaped on a long stipe. A broader form than *D. cristata* (below). A very elegant fern, easy to grow. If kept out of strong winds, it is ideal for most gardens.

D. cochleata

Nepal, south-east Asia, H60cm (24in), D, Wet/Dry, Zone 8. Fronds triangular-lanceolate, bipinnate-pinnatifid. Stipe long with many pale scales at base. Fertile fronds much less leafy and more erect than sterile fronds.

D. conjugata

Himalaya, H90cm (36in), D, Dry/Wet, Zone 7. Fronds glossy dark green, pinnate-pinnatifid, lance-shaped. Recently introduced from the Himalaya by Christopher Fraser-Jenkins. Very handsome.

D. coreano-montana, syn. *D. sichotensis*

Japan, H60cm (24in), W, Dry/Wet, Zone 6. Fronds pinnate-pinnatifid, triangular, undulating, an outstanding species for the flush of pale green fronds in spring. Easy to grow, deserves to be more widely cultivated.

D. corleyi

Northern Spain, H60cm (24in), W, Dry/Wet, Zone 8. A European species fairly recently discovered by Christopher Fraser-Jenkins. It is of hybrid origin with *D. aemula* as one parent. Fronds bipinnate, narrowly triangular, lamina undulating.

D. crassirhizoma, syn. *D. buschiana*

Japan, H75cm (30in), D, Dry/Wet, Zone 6. Fronds pinnate-pinnatifid, pale green and glossy, otherwise similar to *D. wallichiana*. Responds to a sheltered site. As with so many Japanese and east Asian species, the plants have 'colour'! The green is a yellow-green and quite eye-catching.

D. crispifolia

Azores, H60–90cm (24–36in), W, Dry/Wet, Zone 8. Fronds triangular, tripinnate with margins of pinnule segments crisped up and down. Very similar to *D. dilatata* 'Crispa Whiteside', which at one time was thought to be the same fern. Also has much in common with *D. aemula* but is less elegant.

D. cristata (crested buckler fern)

Europe, including British Isles, North America, H60cm (24in), D, Wet/Dry, Zone 3. Fronds pinnate-pinnatifid, erect and narrow. Very distinct among European species but closely related to several North American species including *D. clintoniana*. One of the rarest British ferns, only ever common in the Broads area of Norfolk, but easy to cultivate in a damp spot.

D. cycadina

Japan, H60cm (24in), W, Dry/Wet, Zone 5. Fronds pinnate; pinnae narrow, lance-shaped, dark green with serrated margins. Shape rather like *D. affinis* with all the pinna segments confluent (joined together). Fronds fairly erect and arching. Black scales on stipe. A very robust fern for colder gardens. It is one of the few ferns to regenerate naturally in my garden. This fern is often distributed in error as *D. atrata*, which is a tender species. *D. hirtipes* is another similar species which may be hardy.

D. darjeelingensis, see *D. gamblei*.

D. dickinsii

Japan, H60cm (24in), D, Dry/Wet, Zone 6. Fronds pinnate; pinnae linear with lobed margins. Beautiful yellow-green laminae contrast with dark scales on rachis. Similar to *D. cycadina* but more leafy and a paler green.

D. dilatata (broad buckler fern)

Europe, including British Isles, H1–1.2m (3–4ft), W, Dry/Wet, Zone 4. Fronds tripinnate, triangular or broadly lance-shaped with pinnule margins often recurved. Distinguished from *D. carthusiana* by stipe scales having a dark central zone. One of the commonest British ferns. There are a few good cultivars still in cultivation but several are possibly forms of closely related species.

'Crispa Whiteside' H60cm (24in). Like parent except leafy part of the frond is crispy. First grown by Robert Whiteside and returned to general cultivation by Reginald Kaye about 20 years ago. Whiteside, a keen fern collector for over 50 years, considered this his best wild find.

'Cristata' H60cm (24in), D. Small crests at tip of fronds and pinnae. A form with bunched crests can appear in sowings of 'Grandiceps', and a distinct form with more elegant, small, fingered crests recently occurred wild in the National Trust for Scotland garden at Inverewe in northern Scotland. Hopefully it still thrives there. This plant may be a cultivar of *D. expansa*. Another crested form, rare in cultivation, may in fact be a crested form of *D. azorica*.

'Cristata Roberts', syn. 'Cristatogracilis' H45cm (18in), D. Fronds bipinnate-pinnatifid, lance-shaped with a short stipe. Frond tips and pinnules have neat, flattish crests. Pinnules short, also showing hints of crests. An extraordinary cultivar I thought long extinct until a plant turned up in Jimmy Dyce's garden some twenty years ago. I find it hard to believe it is a cultivar of *D. dilatata*: the frond shape is anything but typical for the species, but it was found in 1870 by Roberts at Llanberis, North Wales. It must therefore be a British native and I can think of no other species it could be. An attractive fern still rare in cultivation. Unfortunately slightly depauperate, as are all its offspring.

'Grandiceps' H60cm (24in), D. Large crest at head of fronds; pinnae also crested. Terminal head is rarely broader than the frond so strictly speaking plants rarely qualify as true grandiceps! Raised by Barnes.

'Jimmy Dyce' H45cm (18in), D. Like the type plant except the fronds are stiff, erect and crowded. A very neat fern. I was nearby when this fern was found by the combined talents of Jimmy Dyce and Fred Jackson on the Isle of Arran in 1969. *D. expansa* was common locally and this may be the parent species.

'Lepidota' H45cm (18in). Leafy parts of the laminae reduced in width, and frond very scaly on rachis and pinna midribs. Not crested. Rarely seen. Sometimes called 'Hymenophylloides', which was a dwarf congested form, and 'Stansfieldii', which had thick and crispy pinnae. I believe both these latter cultivars are extinct. I sometimes wonder if this and 'Lepidota Cristata' are cultivars of *D. expansa*.

'Lepidota Cristata' H60cm (24in). A crested form of 'Lepidota' with the leafy parts of the laminae similarly reduced in width. A very elegant, airy plant.

Recurved form Origin unknown, possibly North America. Edges of pinnules are all curved downwards. Surprisingly attractive. Young plants reminiscent of *Gymnocarpium dryopteris*.

D. erythrosora (autumn fern)

Japan, China, Taiwan, H60cm (24in), E, Dry/Wet, Zone 6. Glossy, bipinnate, triangular fronds emerge pink in spring, turning bronze then green as the season progresses. Stipe quite long. Sori on underside of fronds bright red, hence the species name: *erythro* (red) *sora* (sorus). One of the best garden ferns. The common name refers to the apparent autumn colours that the fronds produce in spring. There is possibly a complex of species in cultivation under this name (for example,

D. championii, D. cystolepidota, D. fuscipes, D. gymnosora, D. purpurella). Not all have the red sori (eg. f. *viridisora*), but in every other respect seem to be the same fern. This fern, and the next, are surprisingly evergreen; during snowdrop flowering (mid-February in Britain) the fronds are usually erect and unbroken and still have good yellow colour. It is possible some botanical research has been published sorting out this group: if so I have overlooked it. Research published in Japanese is difficult to understand for a westerner!

var. *prolifica*, syn. *D. koidzumiana*, Japan. All leafy parts of the fronds are narrowed, giving a very airy appearance to the plant. Bulbils are sometimes produced.

D. expansa, syn. *D. assimilis*, *D. dilatata* var. *alpina* (alpine buckler fern)

Europe, including British Isles, Asia, North America, D, Dry/Wet, Zone 4. In Europe this is a northern species, only occurring on mountains in the south. Fronds pale green, finely divided. Prefers acidic soils. Very similar to *D. dilatata*, from which it is often difficult to separate. Mentioned here as some cultivars of *D. dilatata* should perhaps be included here (see above). A very nice congested form has recently been brought into cultivation.

D. filix-mas (male fern)

Europe, including British Isles, Asia, North America, H1–1.2m (3–4ft), D, Dry/Wet, Zone 4. Fronds erect, pinnate-pinnatifid, mid-green, lance-shaped. Rhizomes usually erect but plants can develop a large number of crowns over the years. Along with bracken (*Pteridium aquilinum*) the commonest British fern, found almost everywhere in woods, on roadside banks, walls, waste ground, stream sides and so on. At higher altitudes it is replaced by *D. affinis* and *D. oreades*. The common name refers to the robust (masculine) nature of the fern – like almost all ferns it is hermaphrodite, producing both sex organs on the prothallus. The lady fern, *Athyrium filix-femina* is likewise hermaphrodite, being called lady fern because it is delicate (feminine). In the garden *D. filix-mas* is just about the most adaptable fern. All gardens have a dark, difficult corner, perhaps near the compost heap or site of the dustbin; *D. filix-mas* will thrive in such places with a little help during establishment. Furthermore, although easy to grow, it will not spread and take over a border, although sporelings may eventually grow where you do not want them. While common in Europe, it is very rare in North America being confined to calcareous woodland. It is possible the North American plant may turn out to be a different species – I have never grown it.

PLATE VIII
Dryopteris filix-mas

All fronds shown approximately half size

'Crispa Cristata'

'Barnesii'

'Linearis
Polydactyla'

'Cristata
Martindale'

'Grandiceps Wills'

'Bollandiae'

Cristata Group

Despite its name, the fronds of *Dryopteris filix-mas* 'Depauperata Padley' are not really depauperate.

Quite a few cultivars are still in cultivation:

'Barnesii' *(Plate VIII)* H1–1.2m (36–48in). Very tall fern, potentially one of the tallest for dryish borders. Fronds narrow, pinnate-bipinnatifid. Perhaps a parent of *D. × complexa* 'Stableri'.

'Bollandiae' *(Plate VIII)* H90cm (36in). Plumose form. Fronds bipinnate-pinnatifid, the pinnules attractively lobed. Unfortunately, there are always some pinnae or pinnules missing, or short pinnae (depauperations) on the fronds. The plant is sterile: although sori are produced there are no good spores. Found once in the wild in Kent in 1857 by Mrs Bolland (see p.15). All plants in cultivation are, therefore, parts of the original clump, and all are well over 100 years old – living antiques. Eventually this will make a fine clump, I have seen a plant in Shropshire with hundreds of fronds 1–1.2m (3–4ft) long.

'Crispa Cristata' *(Plate VIII)* H60cm (24in). Fronds crispy with lightly crested pinnae and frond tips. Pale green.

'Crispata' H60cm (24in). Fronds more leafy than usual with crispy pinnules. First found by Hodgson in 1864 in the Lake District.

Cristata Group *(Plate VIII)* H60cm (24in). Pinnae tips lightly crested, frond tips more heavily crested, fronds not crispy. Pale green. There are quite a lot of different forms of cresting in *D. filix-mas*: it is, therefore, often wise to use the group name.

'Cristata Jackson' H60–90cm (24–36in). Crest on pinnae broad and mainly in one plane. Prominent frond tip crest.

'Cristata Lux Lunae' H60cm (24in). An old cultivar that has small streaks of yellowish-white scattered through the frond. My plant came from Reginald Kaye, where I believe it was a chance sporeling.

'Cristata Martindale', syn. 'Martindalei' *(Plate VIII)* H60–90cm (24–36in). Found in 1872. Crests small on all terminals but the characteristic feature is the way the pinnae in the upper part of the fronds are sickle-shaped (falcate), sweeping towards the tip of the frond.

'Decomposita' H60cm (24in). Like the type plant except fronds bipinnate-pinnatifid. Pinnae a little narrowed but similar texture to normal. A rather foliose cultivar. First discovered in Devon by Allchin.

'Depauperata Padley' H45–60cm (18–24in). Fronds bipinnate with confluent pinnules. Misleadingly named – the fronds are not really depauperate. It is a pretty fern, well worth growing when available. Found by Padley in 1868 on Exmoor.

'Grandiceps Wills' *(Plate VIII)* H60–90cm (24–36in). Found by John Wills in Dorset in 1870. Frond tip has a broad multi-branched crest. Small pinnae crests. A very robust fern once well established. There are fine stands at Harlow Carr Gardens in Harrogate. Plants in cultivation are no doubt all sporelings but seem identical to the original. Jimmy Dyce found an identical form wild on Whitbarrow in the Lake District in the 1980s.

'Jervisii' H60–90cm (24–30in). A crested form that always has parts of the fronds missing or deformed (depauperate). Once a plant is well established it is, however, quite attractive.

'Linearis' H60cm (24in). An old cultivar, named by Wollaston in the nineteenth century but with an unknown origin. Fronds darker green, bipinnate with very narrow, leathery pinnules. Tends to be slightly depauperate, sometimes leading to misidentification as 'Depauperatum'. The plant looks very delicate and almost wispy, but in reality it is very tough, being able to tolerate windy spots in the garden.

'Linearis Congesta' H15–30cm (6–12in). A congested, dwarf form of 'Linearis'.

'Linearis Polydactyla', syn. 'Linearis Cristata' *(Plate VIII)* H75cm (30in). A crested form of 'Linearis'. Fronds bipinnate; pinnules narrowed and leathery; fronds and pinnae crested. Crests often long and fingered, hence 'Polydactlya' is often a more appropriate name. Darker green than most *D. filix-mas* cultivars. The crested forms are much commoner than straight 'Linearis'. In the 1980s Philip Coke raised one with a very wide pendulous head.

'Polydactyla' This name occasionally appears in lists. I cannot remember ever seeing the plant. 'Linearis Polydactyla' or 'Polydactyla Dadds' in *D. affinis* may be the fern intended.

'Succisa' H45–60cm (18–24in). Fronds erect, uncrested. Pinnae flat as in the type plant but tips of pinnae and frond abort producing a depauperate but distinctive frond. *Succisa* means 'bitten' and the fronds certainly look bitten. The history of this cultivar is obscure: I do not know who found it or when; for some years it was thought to be a cultivar of *D. dilatata*.

D. formosana

Taiwan, Japan, H60cm (24in), W, Dry/Wet, Zone 7. Fronds triangular with distant pinnae. Tripinnate especially at the base of the basal pinnae, where the basiscopic pinnules are very long. Undersides of midribs covered with black and brown scales. New fronds are yellowish-green and have a similar texture to *D. erythrosora*, but are more open. In my garden the new fronds are produced

Although the fronds are 'bitten' *Dryopteris filix-mas* 'Succisa' is a structurally useful fern with erect fronds.

very late in the season but they persist well, sometimes all winter.

D. fragrans (Plate IX)

Arctic Europe, North America, 7–15cm (3–6in), D but almost E, Dry/Wet, Zone 3. A remarkable dwarf species with a very attractive tufted growth form. Fronds lance-shaped, bipinnate-pinnatifid. Pinnae 1–2.5cm (½–1in) long; pinnule margins crenately lobed. Stipe very short, covered with pale brown scales. Greens-up early in season. Prolifically fertile with indusia present on every lobe of established plants. Leaf surface covered with sessile glands that are fragrant when rubbed. Hardy outdoors but also excellent as a display alpine.

D. fuscipes

East Asia, H60cm (24in), E, Dry/Wet, Zone 7. Fronds triangular, pinnate-pinnatifid. Pinnae distant but pinnules crowded and round-tipped. Texture leathery. See also *D. erythrosora*.

D. gamblei, syn. D. darjeelingensis

Himalaya, H50–75cm (20–30in), D, Dry/Wet, Zone 8. Fronds pinnate, lance-shaped. Pinnae deeply and rectangularly lobed. Very similar to *D. cycadina*.

D. goeringiana, syn. D. laeta

China, Japan, Korea, H45cm (18in), D, Dry/Wet, Zone 8. Fronds triangular, bipinnate, pale green. Stipe medium length with pale scales. This is quite a delicate-looking fern, rather similar to the green form of *Athyrium niponicum*. Possibly this name was misapplied to the athyrium hence it is sometimes called *Athyrium goeringianum*.

D. goldiana (Goldie's fern)

North America, H1–1.2m (36–48in), D, Wet/Dry, Zone 4. Fronds pinnate-pinnatifid, broad lance-shaped, but not triangular, with a long stipe. Very leafy, slightly arching, golden green; not, however, named for its colour but for its discoverer. Rhizomes short creeping, gradually forming a clump. One of the tallest ferns for a sheltered shady garden. *D. monticola* is similar and native to eastern Asia.

D. guanchica

South-west Europe, H30–60cm (12–24in), W, Wet/Dry, Zone 8. Fronds tripinnate-pinnatifid, broadly lance-shaped, almost triangular. Laminae slightly undulating, glossy. Stipe purplish-brown, scaly at base. Similar in general appearance to *D. aemula* but less crispy with not so strongly triangular fronds. A pretty little fern worth trying in a humid, sheltered spot.

D. hawaiiensis

Hawaii, H60cm (24in), D, Dry/Wet, Zone 8. Newly described species. Fronds triangular, tripinnate, dark green. Stipe and rachis covered with dark brown scales. Despite coming from Hawaii, this fern has thrived in my garden for years.

D. intermedia
Eastern North America, H60cm (24in), W, Dry/Wet, Zone 4. Very lacy, tripinnate species. Fronds lance-shaped, almost oval, pale green, covered with minute glands, particularly on the underside. Overall rather similar to European D. carthusiana, but distinct.

D. juxtaposita
Himalaya, H60–90cm (24–36in), D, Dry/Wet, Zone 7. Fronds triangular, bipinnate, pale green; margins of pinnae conspicuously serrated. Stipe abundantly covered with scales at base. There is a small black mark at the point where the pinna midrib joins the rachis. (See also D. affinis.)

D. kuratae
Japan, H60cm (24in), D, Dry/Wet, Zone 8. Often confused with D. pycnopteroides, which is a very similar but larger species from China and has more densely scaly rachis. D. kuratae has lance-shaped, pinnate, spreading fronds. Pinnae narrowly triangular; margins regularly scalloped. Rachis moderately scaly. I plan to try this shortly; it may be hardy in zone 7.

D. lacera
Eastern Asia, H45–60cm (18–24in), D, Dry/Wet, Zone 7. Fronds pinnate-pinnatifid, narrowly triangular. Spores are produced at the tip of the frond on just a few pinnae which are smaller than would be expected. In addition these pinnae shrivel up once the spores are shed, the remainder of the frond staying green into autumn. Prefers acid soil, but not essential.

D. lepidopoda
Himalaya, H60cm (24in), D, Dry/Wet, Zone 7. Fronds lance-shaped or narrowly triangular, pinnate-pinnatifid. This fern was originally collected as D. wallichiana: it was only when it produced pink fronds that it was realised it was a new species. It is superficially similar to D. wallichiana except for the pink new fronds, which go bronze then green within a few weeks of unfurling. Also the lamina is a little glossy on the upper surface.

D. ludoviciana
North America, H60–90cm (24–36in), D, Wet/Dry, Zone 6. Fronds pinnate-pinnatifid, narrowly lance-shaped. At home in wet woodland but apparently not particularly fussy in gardens. Likes lime. One of very few ferns listed here that I have not grown or seen growing. It is one of the parents of D. × australis.

D. marginalis
North America, H60–75cm (24–30in), W, Wet/Dry, Zone 4. Fronds triangular, bipinnate, bluish-green. Rhizomes erect and slow to branch, hence plants can produce a magnificent single crown. Name refers to the presence of the sori along the margins of the pinnulets. Very common in North America where it seems to fill the role that D. filix-mas plays in Europe. Good robust garden fern.

D. marginata
Himalaya, Far East, H60–90cm (24–36in), W, Dry/Wet, Zone 8. Fronds triangular, tripinnate, broad and leafy. Pinnules broad, margins serrated. Sori not marginal on pinnulets. Not to be confused with D. marginalis of North America.

D. munchii
Chiapas in Mexico, H60cm (24in), D, Dry/Wet, Zone 8. Fronds triangular, bipinnate-pinnatifid. Pinnae tend to overlap on the frond but pinnules are distant from each other. A pretty little fern for the enthusiast. Despite coming from Mexico in the tropics, this has proved hardy in several gardens in Britain.

D. neorosthornii
Himalaya, H60–90cm (24–36in), W, Dry/Wet, Zone 7. Fronds lance-shaped, bipinnate. Pinnules slightly squared at tip and crenately lobed along the sides. Scales on rachis are larger, more numerous and blacker than D. wallichiana. Stipe short, very scaly. This must be the most striking of this group of dryopteris. In spring the uncurling croziers are black and wonderfully mysterious. A plant in my garden, shown on the Gardener's World programme on TV, drew the biggest response to any fern I have ever known.

D. oreades, syn. D. abbreviata (dwarf male fern)
Europe, including British Isles, Asia, H45–90cm (18–36in), D, Dry/Wet, Zone 4. Fronds lance-shaped, pinnate-pinnatifid. Pinnules frequently crisped up. Unless this species is in typical form it is easily confused with D. × complexa and D. filix-mas: both ferns contain genetic material of D. oreades. It is distinguished from D. filix-mas by the rounded, crenate teeth on its pinnae segments, and from D. affinis subsp. cambrensis by its lack of a dark spot at the point where the pinna midrib joins the rachis. The Asian form, which comes from Turkey, is slightly different. The common name is confusing as, in low-level woods in mountainous districts, this fern can easily have fronds 90cm (36in) long. One of the first ferns to die down in winter, but its crispy fronds make it a pretty

garden plant. There are a number of cultivars still in cultivation:

'Crispa Glen Shee' H45cm (18in). A particularly crispy form selected by Jimmy Dyce from a roadside bank in Glen Shee, Scotland.

'Cristata Barnes' Found by Barnes in Westmorland in 1870. A genuine cristatum with the frond tip terminating rather abruptly and the terminal crest pleasantly rounded.

'Decomposita', syn. 'Incisa Crispa'. An uncrested form with narrow pinnules, with wavy margins.

D. panda

South-east Asia, H60cm (24in), larger in warmer climates, D, Dry/Wet, Zone 8. Fronds lance-shaped, pinnate-pinnatifid; pinnae lobes cut about halfway to pinnae midrib. Pinnae quite distant from each other. Rhizomes creep. Very pretty.

D. polylepis

North-east Asia, H60cm (24in), D, Dry/Wet, Zone 7. Lamina lance-shaped, pinnate-pinnatifid. Pinnae lobes squared at tip as in *D. affinis* but segments slightly narrower and longer.

D. pseudofilix-mas

Mexico, H60–90cm (24–36in), D, Dry/Wet, Zone 6. Fronds lance-shaped, pinnate-pinnatifid. Very similar to *D. filix-mas* but mentioned here as further evidence of hardy ferns occurring at high altitudes in the tropics.

D. pulcherrima

Nepal, most of Himalayan region, H30–60cm (12–24in), D, Dry/Wet, Zone 7. Fronds lance-shaped, pinnate-pinnatifid. Stipe very short; stipe and rachis densely covered with dark brown or black scales. Differs from *D. wallichiana* by its much neater habit. Pinnae segments very neatly squared off. Occurs in the Himalaya at up to 4000m (13,000ft) altitude. Very pretty fern that deserves to be more widely grown.

D. pulvinulifera

South-east Asia, H45–75cm (18–30in), D, Dry/Wet, Zone 9, possibly 8. Fronds triangular, tripinnate-pinnatifid. Pinnae also triangular. Rhizomes creep. Not generally in cultivation but included here because I have recently heard from Christopher Fraser-Jenkins that he has found an exciting heavily crested form in Assam. Hopefully, it will be brought into cultivation.

D. × remota

Central Europe, H65cm (26in), D, Dry/Wet, Zone 5. Tough fertile hybrid between *D. affinis* and *D. expansa*. Finely divided, bipinnate lamina, narrowly lance-shaped.

Dryopteris sieboldii is quite unlike the typical members of the genus.

D. scottii

South-east Asia, H60cm (24in), W, Dry/Wet, Zone 8. Fronds lance-shaped, pinnate. Pinnae lance-shaped and entire apart from crenate lobing along margins. Similar to *D. cycadina* but differs by not carrying an indusium on the sorus and by its broader pinnae. *D. hirtipes* is similar but appears less hardy.

D. sieboldii

Japan, H45–60cm (18–24in), D, Dry/Wet, Zone 6. Fronds leathery, triangular or broadly lance-shaped, pinnate, occasionally bipinnate at base, pale green. Pinnae margins finely serrate but at a glance appear smooth, quite unlike any other dryopteris.

D. stenolepis

Himalaya, H60cm (24in), D, Dry/Wet, Zone 8. Fronds lance-shaped, pinnate. Superficially similar to *D. cycadina* but pinnae are narrower and more widely spaced. Rachis scales dark. The plant in cultivation may turn out to be *D. meghalaica*.

D. stewartii
Western Himalaya, H60cm (24in), D, Dry/Wet, Zone 7. Fronds broadly triangular, bipinnate-pinnatifid to tripinnate, pale green.

D. sublacera
India, Nepal, H60cm (24in), W, Dry/Wet, Zone 5. Fronds broadly lance-shaped, bipinnate, but pinnules lobed at base; dark dull green above, pale silvery green below. Pinnae taper to tip. Rachis and stipe covered with dark brown scales. A robust plant worth growing when available.

D. submontana (rigid buckler fern)
Europe, including British Isles, North Africa, H30–45cm (12–18in), D, Dry/Wet, Zone 5. Fronds dark blue-green, erect, narrowly triangular, bipinnate, surface covered with glands. In the wild this is a plant of limestone pavements, which are common in parts of northern England. In the garden it likes an alkaline soil, but it is not essential if a suitable well-drained site exists. Soon forms a clump. For well over a century this fern was known as *D. villarii* to British botanists, but in the early twentieth century it was realised that it differed from the original *D. villarii* and had to be given a new name. No sooner than we are used to this, up pops yet another name which pre-dates *D. submontana* – *D. mindshelkensis*. In view of the unstable naming of this fern I will stick with *D. submontana* for the time being.

D. tokyoensis
Japan, H60–90cm (24–36in), D, Dry/Wet, Zone 7. Fronds erect, narrowly lance-shaped, pinnate, pale green. Pinnae are wide at their base gradually tapering to a point. A very distinctive fern, deserving to be grown more widely. I have seen it in an Italian garden approaching 1.2m (4ft) tall.

D. × uliginosa
Europe, including British Isles, H60cm (24in), D, Wet/Dry, Zone 4. Fronds tall, lance-shaped, pinnate-pinnatifid. Creeping rhizomes allow it to spread slowly. Individual crowns can then be cut away to increase numbers. A sterile hybrid between *D. cristata* and *D. carthusiana*.

D. uniformis
Eastern Asia, H30–60cm (12–24in), W, Dry/Wet, Zone 6. Fronds broadly lance-shaped, bipinnate, leathery. Black scales a feature on croziers. *D. uniformis* 'Cristata' is a crested form in some collections. It is perhaps correctly, but rather mysteriously, known as 'Crispata'.

D. villarii
Southern Europe, H60cm (24in), D, Dry/Wet, Zone 7. Fronds lance-shaped, bipinnate, pale green. Like *D. submontana* this often grows in limestone pavements. Although for a long time the two species were treated as one, they are easily separable. Worth growing in a rock garden.

D. wallichiana, syn. *D. parallelogramma*
Hawaii, Mexico, Jamaica, Himalaya, H60–120cm (24–48in), W, Dry/Wet, Zone 6. Fronds lance-shaped, pinnate-pinnatifid. Pinnae segments neatly squared off at the tips. Stipe short. Stipe and rachis liberally covered with (usually) brown scales; the form most common in cultivation, however, has black scales. It has been refound in the wild near Darjeeling by Fraser-Jenkins and he has segregated it as subsp. *himalaica*. Another subspecies described by Fraser-Jenkins is subsp. *nepalensis* which is a robust form with an attractive glossy upper surface. In the past I have distributed this as 'intermediate between *D. wallichiana* and *D. lepidopoda*'. Plants from all parts of the natural range appear to be hardy in Britain.

D. yigongensis
China, H60–90cm (24–36in), D, Dry/Wet, Zone 7. Fronds numerous, pale green, bipinnate-pinnatifid, lance-shaped. Stipe short with dark brown scales. This is a very attractive fern producing an open shuttlecock. It is rather like a feathery form of *D. filix-mas*. Unfortunately, this is probably not the corrct name for the fern in cultivation; it is more likely to be *D. khullarii*.

EQUISETUM (horsetails)

Equisetums, or horsetails, are not true ferns. They are, however, closely related plants of garden merit worthy of a mention here. They are not normally propagated by spores; all species have creeping rhizomes allowing division of clumps periodically. Some species can be rather aggressive colonizers: for this reason I always recommend confining horsetails to containers. A container plunged into the ground so that the rim is at soil level is not noticed in the garden. Horsetails look particularly good in a gravelled area.

The aerial part of the plant consists solely of stems: there are no leaves as such. The stems are green and perform the function of leaves. Most horsetails seem to prefer some lime in the soil, but they appear to do well in all but very peaty soils. There are several species native to colder regions but, in my opinion, those listed below are the best for cultivation.

E. gigantea
South America, H to 2.5m (8ft), E, Dry/Wet, Zone 9.

Stems green, fat, up to 1cm (½in), unbranched with a large central air space and easily squashed. This is an extraordinary plant. Stems are upright but often sag under their own weight, therefore it is best given support from other vegetation. Can thrive in moist or dryish conditions. I first saw it escaping from a coldframe at the Fraser-Jenkins garden in South Wales. Hardy with me.

E. hyemale (Dutch rush, scouring rush)
Europe, including Britain, Asia and North America, H60–90cm (2–3ft), E, Wet/Dry, Zone 3. Stems slim 3–5mm (⅛–¼in) in diameter, dark green, erect, usually unbranched, fairly firm if squeezed. Stem sections 5–7cm (2–3in) long, each separated by a white sheath with a black band at its base – very attractive and a good contrast with almost any other plant. Stem surface densely covered with silica grains creating a very finely abrasive surface: handfuls of stems can be used for scouring pots, hence the common name scouring rush. Individual stem sections can be used for refining reeds in woodwind musical instruments.

E. scirpoides
Northern Europe, Asia, North America, H15cm (6in), E, Dry/Wet, Zone 1. Stems very slim, 1–2mm (¹⁄₁₆in), wiry and characteristically slightly wavy, often semi-prostrate. Usually unbranched. An established plant makes a curious tangled mat that can provide interest in many garden situations. Due to its small size, it is less invasive than other species but can get out of control and I still recommend planting in a container.

E. sylvaticum (wood horsetail)
Europe including British Isles, North America, H30–60cm (12–24in), D, Wet/Dry, Zone 2. Stems pale green, erect, with numerous whorls of branches along all but the basal few centimetres of the stem. Sheath associated with each whorl is brown and divided characteristically into four distinct teeth. This is an extremely pretty plant, but once established it can take over if not in the recommended container. Of all the species this one seems to tolerate less alkaline conditions; in Essex, north-east of London, it is quite common in acid woodland.

E. telmateia (giant horsetail)
Europe, including British Isles, Asia, North America, H60–180cm (2–6ft), Wet/Dry, Zone 6. Stems virtually white with numerous whorls of green branches along all but the basal few centimetres. I was not sure whether to include this species – early in the season the white stems are very eye-catching, but they usually collapse quite early and brown off at points of damage; it is also very invasive. Sporing stems are produced early in spring before the vegetative stems.

GLEICHENIA

A genus of ferns that forms thickets in the wild. The fronds tend to be of indeterminate length and repeatedly branch, getting tangled together. Rarely seen in horticulture in Britain but widely grown in Australia and other warmer countries. One or two species should be hardy to zone 8. Plants can only be transplanted if very small. Although the rhizomes are creeping, it is very difficult to establish separate sections. At the Royal Botanic Gardens at Kew, it has been discovered that a tip of rhizome will root in a new pot alongside an established plant, and once there is a good rootball, the connection with the mother colony can be severed (for further information see Holttum and Woodhams, *Bulletin of the British Pteridological Society*, 154–158, 1976).

Do not allow plants to dry out but give reasonable drainage and keep in high levels of light. Too much shade will eventually kill the plant. Use a compost low in nitrogen and phosphorus – the peaty soil found under stands of bracken is ideal. Some of the plants listed here are rare in cultivation but, if available, all are well worth trying. I think species from the far south of Chile (for example, *G. quadripartita*) are not in cultivation but they could be well adapted to cool temperate areas.

G. alpina, syn. *G. dicarpa* var. *alpina* (alpine coral fern)
Tasmania, New Zealand, H25–50cm (10–20in), W, Wet/Dry, Zone 7. Fronds forked several times but laminae short compared with length of stipe. Croziers a stunning pinky-orange in spring. Perhaps not in cultivation but well worth trying when spores are available.

G. dicarpa (pouched coral fern)
Australasia, H30–60cm (12–24in), E, Wet/Dry, Zone 7. Fronds fork repeatedly, eventually producing pinnate pinnae with scaly midribs to the pinnules. The margins of the pinnulets strongly recurved forming a pouch. Laminae pale green, but dark green in shade. Some authorities consider *G. alpina* to be an environmental form of *G. dicarpa*.

G. microphylla (scrambling coral fern)
Australia, H30–60cm (12–24in), E, Wet/Dry, Zone 9, possibly 8. Fronds fork repeatedly eventually producing pinnate pinnae with a dark midrib and pale green lamina. Midrib to the pinnule lacking scales and pinnulets flat – not strongly recurved as in *G. dicarpa*. In the wild

fronds can be 1.8m (6ft) long but in cultivation they are usually much shorter. Rhizomes creeping.

GYMNOCARPIUM

A small genus of charming little ferns. The thin, papery lamina is almost always held at close to 90 degrees to the stipe. All species can be propagated by division or from spores. Albeit rarely, many of the species cross in nature. The resulting hybrids can usually be detected by abortive spores; no hybrids have been found in the British Isles. The whole genus is ideal for cultivation in a shady herbaceous border or among rocks.

G. dryopteris (oak fern)
Europe, including British Isles, Asia, North America, H22–30cm (9–12in), D, Wet/Dry, Zone 3. Fronds pale green (blue-green in deep shade), tripinnate, triangular. Stipe erect, delicate, long, with few colourless scales but no hairs. Rhizomes far creeping. A delightful little fern but can become invasive in neutral to acid, well-watered soils.

'Plumosum' (plumose oak fern) Broader, more luxuriant and foliose, laminae broader; pinnules and pinnae overlapping. Another beautiful fern, first discovered in the early 1900s by Mr Christopherson on a limestone hill in the Lake District. The lime may have been leached out of the site as this is usually an acid loving fern. Possibly more correctly called 'Foliosum' as it is fertile, coming true from spores.

G. fedtschenkoanum
East Asia, H15–30cm (6–12in), D, Dry/Wet, Zone 7. Similar to G. dryopteris except slightly more finely cut and a slightly fresher green. Records of G. dryopteris in Asia may be this species.

G. jessoense
East Asia, H15–30cm (6–12in), D, Dry/Wet, Zone 7. Fronds bipinnate-pinnatifid, triangular with glandular laminae and stipe. Similar to G. robertianum except fronds are a fresher green. The segregate subsp. *parvulum* is confined to North America.

G. oyamense
East Asia, H15–30cm (6–12in), W, Wet/Dry, Zone 7. Fronds a beautiful blue-green, pinnate-pinnatifid. Lamina triangular, but less markedly so than other species in the genus. A beautiful fern. It is surprisingly hardy: I have grown it outdoors for years with little effort, and it also

Gymnocarpium fedtschenkoanum has fronds that are slightly more delicately divided than the commoner G. dryopteris.

The beautiful *Gymnocarpium oyamense (left)* is often evergreen and is quite unlike other ferns in the genus.

seems quite hardy in my unheated polytunnels. It is often evergreen, unlike other ferns in the genus, and it would not surprise me greatly if eventually a new genus is created to accommodate it.

G. robertianum (limestone polypody) *(Plate IX)*
Europe, including British Isles, Asia, North America, H15–30cm (6–12in), D, Dry/Wet, Zone 3. Fronds pale yellowish-green, bipinnate-pinnatifid, triangular with a long stipe covered with minute stalked glands. Not so leafy as G. dryopteris with the margins of the lamina often down-turned. The lamina is not so strongly angled from the stipe as in other species. Limestone polypody likes to grow on limestone screes and rockwork. In Britain it is uncommon in native habitats but occurs from time to time on old walls.

GYMNOPTERIS

This is one of those generic names that does not rest comfortably with taxonomists. My good friend Christopher Fraser-Jenkins places these ferns in *Notholaena*, but since the one species in cultivation is quite well known as *Gymnopteris* I have decided to leave it here.

G. vestita, syn. *Notholaena himalaica* (mouse-ear fern)
Central Asia to Taiwan, H15–30cm (6–12in), E, Dry, Zone 8. Fronds pinnate. Pinnae almost oval but with a slight bulge on the acroscopic side. Stipe and underside of pinnae densely covered in pale brown hairs, giving the frond a woolly appearance. Sori obscured by massed hairs

PLATE IX
Miscellaneous species

*Dryopteris
fragrans*

*Polystichum
nepalense*

Dryopteris aemula

*Pseudophegopteris
levingei*

Cystopteris sudetica

Davallia mariesii

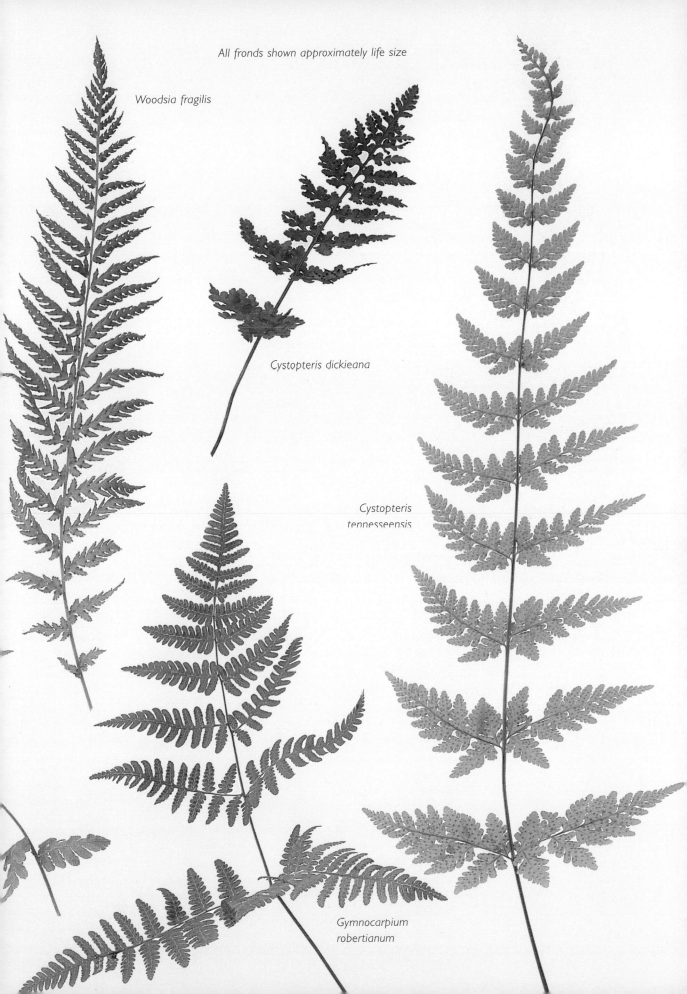

All fronds shown approximately life size

Woodsia fragilis

Cystopteris dickieana

Cystopteris
tennesseensis

Gymnocarpium
robertianum

The 'mousy ears' of *Gymnopteris vestita*. This specimen is in the West Midlands garden of Clive and Doreen Brotherton.

but spores produced along veins on underside of pinnae. A very attractive species that I have overwintered in my unheated polytunnels without problem. It has also thrived for several years just outside the filmy fern house at the Royal Botanic Gardens at Kew. In colder gardens some protection is wise: plant in a well-drained spot, perhaps with overhead protection. Treat as *Cheilanthes*. *Paraceterach reynoldsii* is another very similar species from Australia.

HISTIOPTERIS

A very small genus closely related to *Pteridium*.

H. incisa (water fern, bat wing fern)

Tropics and temperate southern hemisphere, H60–120cm (24–48in), D, Wet/Dry, Zone 7. Frond tripinnate, triangular, pale glaucous green. Basal pinnules adjacent to, and tending to clasp, the main rachis (hence bat wing fern). Rhizomes far creeping. Invasive when established, not unattractive but can become weedy. Occasionally imported on trunks of *Dicksonia antarctica* from Australia. Needs acid soil and good protection over winter.

HYMENOPHYLLUM

A large genus of filmy ferns that are superficially similar to *Trichomanes* (see p.164), but with the receptacle (which carries the sporangia) not protuding beyond the indusium. Botanical taxonomists have split *Hymenophyllum* into several different genera – for the fern grower I suspect the one name will suffice. The fronds of filmy ferns are usually one cell thick, and transparent when held up to the light. They are confined to humid, poorly lit situations and reflect light in such a way as to look as though they are perpetually wet. Most species are mat-forming on rocks or tree trunks in the wild. In cultivation they are usually grown in a terrarium or Wardian case. However, in the nineteenth century it was fashionable to excavate an underground fernery where the humidity was always high. Such a fernery was constructed at James Backhouse's fern nursery in York, and some enthusiasts within the British Pteridological Society are building similar structures today.

This is a large genus of mainly tropical ferns, but there are some interesting temperate species, especially from Australasia. In cultivation, plants often fail to develop sporangia, which makes specific identification difficult.

Hymenophyllum species are difficult to grow from spores so plants are invariably sourced from the wild. However, mats prized off rocks are unlikely to thrive and should not be disturbed. Species that grow on rocks include the native British and European species *H. tunbrigense* and *H. wilsonii* – although *H. tunbrigense* is abundant on the *Dicksonia antarctica* at Dereen, near Kenmare, Co. Kerry, south-west Eire. Plants in cultivation usually become available as epiphytes on tree ferns imported from Australia and New Zealand. Even dead tree fern trunks sometimes produce hymenophyllums if in a humid environment. The following species are most likely to occur.

H. armstrongii
New Zealand, H10mm (½in), E, High humidity but good drainage, Zone 8. Fronds translucent, simple strap-shaped, perhaps forking at base, sori produced at tip. Margin of lamina spiny. Rhizomes slender, creeping. A minute fern of interest to collectors; close inspection of mossy tree fern trunks may well reveal it.

H. australe
Australia, H5–12cm (2–5in), E, High humidity but good drainage, Zone 8. Fronds triangular, tripinnatifid, translucent, without hairs. Sori formed mainly in central part of frond lamina, not on extremities. Rhizomes slender, creeping.

H. demissum
New Zealand, H5–25cm (2–10in), E, High humidity and good drainage, Zone 8. Fronds triangular, tripinnatifid, translucent, without hairs. Often not sporing but sori occur in the central part of the lamina. Rhizomes slender, creeping. Superficially similar to *H. australe* but I have seen this species growing outdoors on the ground at Rosdohan, a very humid garden in Kerry, south-west Eire, ten years after it was first introduced. Of all the hymenophyllums in cultivation this is the easiest to grow. In a terrarium it forms a good colony quickly and seems able to withstand exposure to drier conditions better than most other species.

H. dilatatum
New Zealand, H15–45cm (6–18in), E, High humidity and good drainage, Zone 8. Fronds translucent, triangular, bipinnate-pinnatifid. Lamina very foliose. A beautiful fern, the largest filmy fern in New Zealand. Well worth growing when available.

H. flabellatum
Australia, New Zealand, H5–25cm (2–10in), E, High humidity but good drainage, Zone 8. Fronds narrowly triangular, pinnate-bipinnatifid, translucent, ultimate segments gracefully elongated. Sori formed on tips all over frond. Rhizomes slender, creeping. Established on Australian tree ferns at Garinish Island, Kerry, Eire.

H. rarum
Australia, New Zealand, H5–12cm (2–5in), E, High humidity but good drainage, Zone 8. Fronds linear, pinnate-pinnatifid, translucent. Sori borne on tips of segments. Rhizomes slender, creeping.

HYPOLEPIS

A genus of ferns related to bracken. Like bracken, they spread, but not normally so rapidly. Various species of hypolepis are occasionally introduced on trunks of *Dicksonia antarctica* from Australia. Unless protected from all but the slightest frost, they do not persist.

H. millefolium (thousand-leaved fern)
New Zealand, H30–38cm (12–15in), D, Dry/Wet, Zone 7. Fronds broadly ovate, tripinnate-pinnatifid. Stipe covered with brown hairs. Creeping rhizomes. Not usually invasive, this fern can spread to form a very attractive, good-sized clump. The finely divided leaves and the clumping growth habit instantly separate it from almost every other garden fern. Unfortunately this has not done well with me in my alkaline gardens; however, a friend only 20 miles away grows it beautifully on her slightly sandy, acidic soil.

LASTREOPSIS (shield ferns)

A very beautiful genus of ferns, many from Australasia. I grow certain species as pot plants but in zone 9 most should do very well. Closely related to *Polystichum*, hence the common name. The two species listed here both occur in Tasmania and are probably the best candidates for cultivation. If you are successful with these two species, there are many more awaiting trial. (See C. Goudey, *A Handbook of Ferns for Australia and New Zealand*, 1988.)

L. acuminata (shiny shield fern)
Australia, H45–60cm (18–24in), E, Wet/Dry, Zone 9. Fronds shiny, narrowly triangular, bi- or tripinnate at base. Rachis with inconspicuous hairs in a shallow groove. Stipe has a pink tinge. Compared with *L. hispida* not a particularly delicate-looking fern. Rhizomes are erect, therefore fronds are tufted. Should do well in shady, sheltered gardens. Can grow well in relatively open sites.

L. hispida (bristly shield fern)
Australia, New Zealand, H45–60cm (18–24in), E,

Wet/Dry, Zone 9. Fronds triangular, tri- or quadripinnate. Rachis conspicuously covered in hairs, hence 'bristly' shield fern. Lamina dark green, delicately divided. Rhizomes creeping, therefore fronds arise singly and not in large tufts. Should do well in shady, sheltered gardens where there is adequate atmospheric humidity.

LEPTOPTERIS

A small genus from south-east Asia, north Australia and New Zealand. All ferns in this genus have delicate fronds and they need to be grown in a terrarium or in a very humid environment. They cannot stand high light levels. Spores are green and need to be sown when fresh. Well grown, mature plants will produce short trunks.

L. hymenophylloides (single crepe fern)
New Zealand, H75–90cm (30–36in), E, Wet, Zone 9, possibly 8. Fronds broad lance-shaped or triangular, bipinnate-pinnatifid, translucent, lamina slightly crisped but more or less in one plane. Stipe long. Can hybridize with L. superba so look out for intermediate plants. Cultivate as L. superba.

L. superba (Prince of Wales feathers, double crepe fern)
New Zealand, H60–75cm (24–30in), E, Wet, Zone 9, possibly 8. Frond elliptic (tapering to base and tip), bipinnate-pinnatifid, translucent, lamina crisped (three-dimensional). Stipe short. I have grown this in a terrarium (fish tank) for nine years. Despite almost total neglect it has thrived, although it has remained small, which is just as well given the size of the tank. I water it perhaps once or twice a year with rainwater; the glass on the top is loose fitting. The terrarium is housed in the darkest corner of my tree fern house, minimum temperature 0°C (32°F). I am sure this would thrive outdoors in some of the dark, dank tree fern gardens of south-west Eire.

LOPHOSORIA

A genus of a single species closely related to *Cyathea*, resembling a small tree fern.

L. quadripinnata
Central and South America, H Trunk to 1m (3ft), Fronds to 2m (6ft), E, Wet/Dry, Zone 9, possibly 8. Frond triangular, tripinnate-pinnatifid, fairly leathery. Usually glaucous beneath. Plants from southern Chile, in the far south of its natural range, are probably more hardy but

Hypolepis millefolium creeping through the acidic, well-drained soil at Lydiate Ash garden near Birmingham.

rarely seem able to produce a trunk. Trunk or rhizomes covered with golden hairs. It is very variable; in time the southern type may be recognized as a separate species. I have grown the Mexican plant outdoors in my tree fern shelter for four or five years. It has survived but does not thrive and has still not started to produce a trunk. I have heard of L. quadripinnata of more southerly origin doing well in south-west Britain, producing large fronds but, again, no trunk. This is a beautiful, potentially dramatic fern that deserves to be more widely grown.

LYCOPODIUM

A large genus of fern allies that are difficult to cultivate. I do not grow any and have decided to omit them from the A–Z.

LYGODIUM

Lygodiums are climbing ferns. Their roots are in the ground but their fronds are of virtually indeterminate length as they climb up through vegetation. The pinnae midribs and the rachis have the ability to wind round any support, just like a pea tendril. Sporing pinnules smaller and neater than others. Spores are green and must be sown soon after harvest.

L. japonicum
South-east Asia, Japan, H1–1.5m (3–5ft), but much taller in the wild, D, Dry/Wet, Zone 9. Frond tripinnate and narrowly triangular but, because of its climbing habit, the shape is rarely obvious. Pinnae triangular, spreading horizontally. A beautiful and fascinating fern well worth taking the trouble to grow. I know of one garden in England where it has survived, so far, at the base of a warmish wall. The soil is a well-drained loam with some organic fibre added, and the fern gets some shade in summer. I have not tried it outdoors yet. It is wise to mulch the crown to protect against cold winters. Very easy to grow from spores: it was the first fern I ever grew back in 1965 and I had thousands of plants that I did not know what to do with.

L. palmatum (Hartford fern)
South-eastern North America, H1–1.5m (3–5ft), but more in the wild, E, Wet/Dry, Zone 4. Fronds with palmate pinnae, usually with six lobes. Towards the tip of the frond, the pinnae are usually all fertile and are irregularly shaped, divided into many tiny, hand-like pinnules. Rachis wind and twine as it climbs through vegetation. This fern is included here because it is undoubtedly hardy and very pretty, but I know no one who grows it.

If available it is difficult to establish: it needs moist slightly acid, humus-rich soil. *L. palmatum* is superficially very similar to *L. articulatum* of New Zealand.

MARSILEA

This is a genus of water ferns found in very wet places at margins of pools. Reproduction is by pea-like spore-bearing structures (sporocarps) produced at the base of the fronds.

M. quadrifolia (water clover)
Southern Europe, H15–25cm (6–10in), D, Wet, Zone 6. Fronds resemble a four-leafed clover. Rhizomes creeping. No other fern is quite like this, indeed it does not look like a fern until you see the fronds characteristically unrolling. I have never kept it going for very long, although it should be hardy here in central England. It is probably most easily grown in a pan stood permanently in water, but it is worth trying to introduce it into the mud of shallow garden pools. Propagate by division.

MATTEUCCIA

Although a small genus, this is a very important one in temperate gardens where some moisture is available.

M. intermedia
Nepal to China, H Vegetative and fertile fronds H60–90cm (24–36in) (fertile fronds shorter in most

The beautifully symmetrical shuttlecock fern, *Matteuccia struthiopteris*, is ideal for wet ground and water sides.

Chinese populations), D, Wet/Dry, Zone 7. Fronds lance-shaped, pinnate with pinnae shallowly crenately lobed. Intermediate between *M. struthiopteris* and *M. orientalis* and probably derived from the hybrid betwen the two. Usually recognized by the relatively long fertile frond.

M. orientalis
Asia, H Vegetative fronds 60–90cm (24–36in), Fertile fronds 15–22cm (6–9in), D, Wet/Dry, Zone 7. Fronds lance-shaped, pinnate-pinnatifid, spreading. Stipe quite long with pinnae not markedly reduced in length at base of frond. Fertile fronds spreading, or even drooping, initially green but soon turning brown, lacking any lamina. Produced on a creeping caudex (rhizome). A pretty fern for a sheltered spot, its spreading foliage makes it distinctive in the garden. Deserves to be grown more widely.

M. pensylvanica (ostrich fern, shuttlecock fern)
North America, H Vegetative fronds H90–120cm (36–48in), Fertile fronds 30cm (12in), D, Wet, Zone 3. I will be criticized by botanists for recognizing this fern as being different from *M. struthiopteris* at specific level. It is, however, fairly distinct, with both species deserving to be grown. It differs from *M. struthiopteris* in that the base of the stipe is glaucous and the fronds are less erect, giving a more open shuttlecock. Rare in cultivation in Europe.

M. struthiopteris, syn. *M. germanica* (ostrich fern, shuttlecock fern)
Central Europe, H Vegetative fronds H1–1.5m (36–60in), Fertile fronds H30–45cm (12–18in), D, Wet, Zone 3. Fronds lance-shaped with pinnae, markedly reduced in length, right to the base, pale yellow green, pinnate-pinnatifid, mainly produced in a single flush in spring as a beautiful, almost erect, shuttlecock. Stipe almost absent. Fertile fronds are produced in autumn and are completely given over to spore production. They lack any laminae and are very dark green when first produced but soon turn brown. Do not mistake these stunted fronds for evidence of disease. The spores are green and ripen in mid-winter. They are not viable for long and need to be sown immediately after collection. I collect my spores by cutting a sporing frond around Christmas. I leave it to dry on a piece of white paper for about half an hour, then, as if by a miracle, thousands of spores are released onto the paper. The main caudex (rhizome) is erect and, eventually, in suitable damp conditions a small trunk up to 15cm (6in) tall can develop. Creeping stolons 4–15mm ($\frac{1}{8}$–$\frac{1}{2}$in) in diameter are also produced. These do not produce occasional fronds along their length but rather, when ready, suddenly produce a new crown. In

time quite a colony can be formed. If the new crowns appear in the wrong place they are easily removed and replanted elsewhere. The stolon is near the surface so, despite its creeping nature, can be kept in check with little difficulty. Plant in shade otherwise sun may burn fronds by midsummer.

MICROSORIUM

A group of ferns closely related to *Polypodium*.

M. diversifolium (kangaroo fern)
Australia, New Zealand, H30cm (12in), E, Dry, Zone 9. Frond pinnatifid, occasionally simple, glossy, leathery produced on creeping rhizomes. Occasionally introduced on the trunks of *Dicksonia antarctica* where it can persist with little attention. Can be grown on a free-draining bank, as at Par in Cornwall, or more usually as an epiphyte on trees, as at Dereen and other gardens in south-west Eire. I have seen it festooning trees from ground level to 5–6m (15–20ft) above the ground in several Irish gardens. Although I have not attempted to grow it outdoors in central England it has done well in an unheated polytunnel. A closely related Australasian species, *M. scandens*, is slightly more delicately cut, but also slightly less hardy.

NEPHROLEPIS

Normally considered a houseplant in Britain but I have seen this species thriving outdoors in a garden in north Lancashire, not far from the sea.

N. cordifolia
Tropics, extending to New Zealand and Japan, H30–60cm (12–24in), D, Dry/Wet, Zone 9. Frond pinnate, narrowly oblong. Rhizomes short, creeping. Stolons produced above ground sometimes bear tubers. The plants I have seen were on a sunny limestone rockery. In the wild this is a fern of sunny clearings growing at quite high altitudes (up to 3000m/10,000ft on Java).

Notholaena himalaica, see *Gymnopteris vestita*.

OLEANDRA

A small genus of epiphytic ferns related to *Polypodium*.

O. wallichii
Himalaya, H12–25cm (5–10in), D, Dry, Zone 9, possibly 8. Fronds entire, lance-shaped produced on creeping rhizomes. Sori arranged in a single row along either side of the midrib. An epiphytic fern that flourishes in my unheated polytunnel; in a sheltered moist area it may do well on old tree stumps or rockwork. The rhizomes benefit from protection with moss.

ONOCLEA

A genus containing a single species, but one of the best and most distinctive ferns for general cultivation.

O. sensibilis (sensitive fern)
North America, H60cm (24in), D, Wet, Zone 2. Fronds triangular pinnate, blue-green with crenately lobed pinnae. Stipe long. Creeping rhizomes, therefore spreads rapidly in wet ground. Fertile fronds, produced late summer, have laminae replaced by spore-carrying beads. As with *Matteuccia* the spores are green, ripen in midwinter and can be induced to shed in a heated room in around half an hour. Spores need to be sown as soon as possible after shedding.

O. sensibilis is ideal for planting in a damp site where there is plenty of room; in small gardens it may become a little invasive, but its distinct foliage usually makes it a welcome invader. The rhizomes are near the soil surface and can usually be peeled back from areas where the fern is not welcome. A form in cultivation has red fronds in spring. It is rare but worth hunting down – the red colour persists in the stipes almost all season but the laminae eventually turn green. It is called sensitive fern because it dies down with the first autumn frost; conversely, late spring frosts do not seem to be damaging. I have recently been given a dwarf form which may prove constant.

ONYCHIUM

A small genus of several closely related species. The following have proved tolerably hardy with me in north Herefordshire in sheltered niches in the garden.

O. contiguum
East Asia, H30–45cm (12–18in), D, Dry/Wet, Zone 8, possibly 7. Fronds are triangular, tripinnate. Stipe long, black at base. Very similar to *O. japonicum* but the pinnules are somewhat further apart, giving the frond a more open appearance.

O. japonicum (carrot fern)
East Asia, H30–45cm (12–18in), D, Dry/Wet, Zone 8, possibly 7. Fronds triangular tri- or quadripinnate at base. Stipe long, dark yellow at base. A very pretty fern looking like a carrot leaf.

OPHIOGLOSSUM (adder's tongues)

A large group of rather primitive ferns. Their common name is very appropriate, referring to the shape of the

single vegetative frond enclosing the single spike-like sporing frond. There are a few very closely related species scattered around the temperate regions of the world, but I think *O. vulgatum* is the only cold-hardy species in cultivation. Epiphytic species from the tropics are sadly not hardy but they are fascinating plants, worth growing in a heated greenhouse when material is available.

O. vulgatum (adder's tongue)
Europe, including British Isles, North America, Asia, H7 15cm (3–6in), D, Wet/Dry, Zone 6. Vegetative frond simple, ovate, smooth and leathery, lacking midrib, pale green on a short green stipe. Fertile frond appears from where the lamina and stipe join. It is simple, erect, longer than the vegetative frond and usually less than 7mm (¼in) wide. The sporangia are borne towards its tip. This is usually a curiosity confined to the gardens of enthusiasts, but it does have a distinct charm. Propagation by division, rarely from spores – Jack Bouckley, then President of the British Pteridological Society, raised it from spores a few years back and it took about seven years.

OREOPTERIS

A very small genus formerly included within the very large genus *Thelypteris*.

O. limbosperma, syn. *Thelypteris limbosperma* (mountain fern, lemon-scented fern)
Europe, including British Isles, H60–90cm (24–36in), D, Wet/Dry, Zone 4. Frond elliptic with the pinnae tapering in size to base and tip, pinnate-pinnatifid, pale green, smell of lemons when crushed. Stipes absent (pinnae produced from ground level). Rhizomes erect, creating a tufted plant. Rarely in cultivation despite being very common in nature on banks in hilly, acid soil districts. It likes high rainfall, good drainage, good light and no lime in the water or soil, therefore usually grown best in gardens in acid, mountainous districts. The scent is very attractive but crushing fronds to generate it is a bit destructive! In the nineteenth century many cultivars were described, none of which seem to be in cultivation today. The fern still sports, it is just a case of looking! I have found the following cultivars but know of no others currently in cultivation.

'Angustifrons' H60cm (24in). Fronds 5–7cm (2–3in) wide, apex long drawn out into a point. Very attractive. I found this in Radnorshire, Wales in 1985 in a coniferous

Onoclea sensibilis makes an eye-catching specimen beside a stream at Burford House gardens, Tenbury Wells, Shropshire.

Oreopteris limbosperma 'Angustifrons' is one of very few cultivars currently known for this species.

plantation, one of my best finds ever. It was originally found by George Whitwell in Patterdale in the Lake District in about 1900.

Cristata Gracilis Group H60cm (24in). Fronds delicately crested at their tips and at tips of pinnae. I found this in a coniferous plantation near Dartmoor in Devon in 1978 and wonder if it is similar to a crested form C. T. Druery found in the same area almost 100 years earlier.

Revolvens Group H45–60cm (18–24in). Fronds elliptic, pinnae more widely spaced than usual with pinnules reflexed along midrib. Found by me in the eastern Lake District in 1984. Curious, not a great beauty, but nevertheless quite strikingly different among a colony of normals.

OSMUNDA

A genus of about 10 species, well suited to water gardens or damp places. They are majestic plants, being the largest garden ferns hardy in areas too cold for tree ferns. Sporangia are produced on pinnae of reduced size that usually lack any lamina. Early in the season, when the spores are unripe, the sporangia are green; they soon turn black or brown as the spores ripen. The spores are shed by midsummer leaving the sporangia brown and shaggy for most of the growing season. The spores are green and need to be sown within a month of collection. Osmundas generally prefer acidic soil conditions, but do well in alkaline gardens, if given a good fibrous compost. If provided with adequate moisture, osmundas will grow satisfactorily in full sun.

O. asiatica, see *O. cinnamomea* var. *fokiensis*.

O. cinnamomea (cinnamon fern)
North America, H60–120cm (24–48in), D, Wet, Zone 2. Fronds of two types. Vegetative fronds green, lance-shaped, pinnate-pinnatifid, produced in a shuttlecock. Fertile fronds are slightly taller than vegetative fronds and lack any green lamina. The pinnae are covered with cinnamon-coloured sporangia and confined to the top half of the frond. These pinnae are held almost upright close to the rachis, giving the frond the shape of a slender pampas grass flower stem. Several sporing fronds are produced in the centre of the ring of vegetative fronds, creating a stunning effect. There are brown hairs mixed within the sporangial clusters. The sporing fronds wither in about three weeks, once the green spores are shed, but the vegetative fronds persist until autumn. This is one of my favourite ferns.

var. fokiensis replaces the type in eastern Asia. It differs in having black as well as brown hairs mixed among the sporangia and is quite distinct. Another taxon, *O. asiatica* may be the same as *O. cinnamomea* var. *fokiensis*.

O. claytoniana (interrupted fern)
North America, H60–90cm (24–36in), D, Wet, Zone 2. Fronds lance-shaped, pinnate-pinnatifid. Sterile fronds green throughout, forming a slightly open shuttlecock. Fertile fronds differ in being erect and having two or three sets of sporing pinnae mid-frond. In these pinnae the green lamina is completely replaced by massed sporangia. The sporangia blacken as they ripen and shrivel soon after shedding the green spores. The frond is thus interrupted, hence the common name. A fascinating garden fern that is easy to establish in a damp spot.

O. gracilis, syn. *O. regalis* var. *gracilis*
Origin unknown, H60–120cm (24–48in), D, Wet, Zone 7. Very similar to *O. regalis* 'Purpurascens' except smaller, much more delicate and fronds are red in spring. The red fronds with green sporangia on the terminal pinna are a beautiful sight. The differences between this fern, *O. regalis* 'Purpurascens' and *O. regalis* var. *spectabilis* need further investigation.

O. japonica
Japan, H60–90cm (24–36in), D, Wet, Zone 7. As *O. regalis* except the fertile fronds have a very long stipe bearing fertile pinnae at the tip only, totally lacking green pinnae lower down the frond. Vegetative fronds resemble those of *O. regalis* except they are a little more leafy. Plants with vegetative fronds only are rather difficult to distinguish from *O. regalis*.

O. lancea
Eastern Asia, H60–90cm (24–36in), D, Wet, Zone 8. As *O. regalis* except characteristically pinnules are lance-shaped, running to a point at tip and base. It is also much smaller and red tinted in spring. A beautiful, elegant fern, unfortunately rather rare.

O. regalis (royal fern, flowering fern)
Europe, including British Isles, Asia, H1.2–2m (4–6ft), D, Wet, Zone 3. Fronds broadly lance-shaped, bipinnate; pinnules oblong-ovate with smooth margins. Stipe long

Osmunda regalis 'Cristata' is a more compact form of the royal fern and well suited to smaller gardens.

The stunning purple croziers of *Osmunda regalis* 'Purpurascens' with *Onoclea sensibilis* behind at Kyre Park.

and smooth. Rhizomes branched, erect, massive, over many decades eventually becoming 30–60cm (1–2ft) tall and the same, or more, across. Fertile fronds produced among the first flush of fronds in spring are erect. Later, vegetative fronds are often more spreading and usually longer. Sporangia are borne at the tip of the fertile frond on reduced pinnae which are given over totally to spore production. These sporing tips are brown for the later part of the season and stand conspicuously against the green of the other foliage. With the onset of the first frosts the foliage turns a buttery golden colour; although only short-lived, perhaps a week, it is an attractive plus point helping to brighten up autumn. This fern was called the flowering fern because the sporing fronds resembled flowering spikes of astilbe or docks. I prefer the other common name because it truly is a regal plant. Unfortunately *O. regalis* does like wet conditions, being happiest at the sides of lakes, as at Savill Gardens *(photo p.20)* where it is luxuriant and self perpetuating, or in bogs. However, those of us without these conditions can still grow good specimens (see pp.22–23). If allowed to get too dry the fertile fronds readily shrivel and do not recover, but there is usually no damage to the vegetative

fronds. There are a few cultivars, all worth growing when available.

'Cristata' H1–1.2m (3–4ft). As the type, except the pinnae and pinnule tips are flat crested. This form is usually more compact, with a bushier outline and the sporing spikes are shorter and less conspicuous. *O. regalis* is often considered lime hating, but this form, and many others, thrives beside the stream in the limestone rockery garden managed by the National Trust at Sizergh Castle in the Lake District. This cultivar was discovered among a large batch of plants collected from the wild in 1857 while dormant. A nurseryman bought the entire batch from the fern dealer, but it was only in the following spring that one plant produced crested fronds and was noticed by a great fern man, Dr G.B. Wollaston. He offered £25 (a fortune then) for the plant but his offer was declined. This was a mistake as the cultivar comes true from spores and in no time at all it was widely distributed. £25 would buy ten plants today. Occasionally sporelings produce a branched stipe and have been called 'Ramocristata', or large bunched crests at the top of the fronds and have been called 'Corymbifera'.

'Decomposita' H1.2–2m (4–6ft). As the type, except that the pinnules are divided into pinnulets, hence the frond is tripinnate. Pinnules near the extremities of the frond are less deeply divided. First discovered by Cowan in 1901 in County Kerry, Eire. Lost to cultivation until I chanced upon a plant in a ditch 90 years later, also in Kerry, but not near the original find.

'Philip Coke' H1.2–2m (4–6ft). As the type, except that the fronds come up deep purple in spring. It differs from 'Purpurascens' by the frond shape being identical to the type. Found in Eire in the 1970s by Philip Coke. A grand, robust fern, not widely in cultivation, but potentially a stronger grower than 'Purpurascens'. The buttery-yellow autumn colour is particularly well marked on this form. Philip could not remember where he found the plant, but it is worth noting that osmundas from warmer climates do have a greater tendency to produce red fronds in spring. I have found red-fronded plants in the far south of France.

'Purpurascens' Possibly from the Atlantic Isles. H1–1.2m (36–48in). As the type except the stipe is deep purple and the laminae purple when young, turning green. It is also more delicately divided than normal *O. regalis* with smaller pinnules relatively more widely spaced on the pinna midrib, making me wonder if this is a different species or subspecies. This form comes almost true from spores, but some plants are less strongly purple. It may be less hardy than the other cultivars, perhaps needing some protection in zones 3 and 4.

var. spectabilis North America, H1.2–2m (4–6ft), Zone 3. Similar to *O. regalis* except it is a more upright plant, potentially taller. It is transiently red-tinted in spring. This is the North American form of the species.

'Undulatifolia', syn. 'Crispa', 'Undulata'. Europe, not British Isles, H1–1.2m (36–48in). As the type, except that the lamina, not the rachis, is wavy.

O. schraderi 'Contorta'
Eastern Asia, H90cm (36in), D, Wet, Zone 8. Similar to *O. gracilis* except all the pinnules are distorted, usually into small fan shapes. Pinnules few along side of pinna, terminal pinnule more prominent. Very slow in cultivation, needs protection over winter.

OSMUNDIASTRUM

A genus limited to a single species from eastern Asia. Closely related to *Osmunda*. Spores green.

O. banksifolium, syn. *Osmunda banksifolia*
China, Japan, other east Asian offshore islands, H60–90cm (24–36in), W, Wet, Zone 8. Fronds lance-shaped, spreading, pinnate with a long rachis. Pinnae margins serrated. Normal pinnae in middle of fertile fronds replaced by bunches of sporangia (see also *Osmunda claytoniana*). I have grown this fern outdoors for several winters with just a little straw to protect the dormant crown. It has survived −10°C (14°F) or colder.

PAESIA

A genus with a single species.

P. scaberula (ring fern)
New Zealand, H30–60cm (12–24in), D, Wet/Dry, Zone 7. Fronds lance-shaped, tripinnate pinnule segments small and delicate looking. Stipe straight but rachis characteristically zig-zagging. Rhizomes creeping. In New Zealand it is a colonizer of waste ground and can be weedy, looking unattractive in dry spells if the fronds become matted. Conversely, in cultivation in colder regions it is not aggressive and forms a very attractive small clump. In my cold Herefordshire garden, the ring fern held its own well in an acid bed I had created for rhododendrons.

PARACETERACH

A genus of one or two species confined to Australia. Very easily confused with *Gymnopteris*.

P. reynoldsii
Australia, H15–25 × 3.5cm (6–10 × 1½in), E, Dry, Zone 8. Fronds erect, narrowly lance-shaped, pinnate. Pinnae round to elliptical, with fawn hair-like scales on upper and lower surfaces. Croziers silvery and woolly. Spores produced in a band around the periphery of each pinna. Hardy through recent winters in central England. Cultivate as *Cheilanthes*. See also *Gymnopteris vestita*, a very similar species.

PELLAEA

A large genus of nearly 100 species with several species hardy in an alpine house in Britain. Some species are fully hardy. See section on *Cheilanthes* for cultural requirements.

P. andromedifolia (coffee fern) *(Plate VI)*
USA, Mexico, H30–45cm (12–18in), E, Dry, Zone 8. Frond triangular, tripinnate. Pinnae narrowly triangular, distant, lacking scales and hairs. Pinnules orbicular. Stipe light brown. May survive outdoors in a protected spot in colder areas. Prefers acid conditions.

P. atropurpurea (purple cliff brake)
North-east USA, H15–45cm (6–18in), E, Dry, Zone 3. A naturally occurring fertile hybrid between *P. glabella* and *P. ternifolia*. Fronds blue-green, narrowly triangular to oblong, bipinnate. Pinnules narrowly triangular, no scales or hairs. Rachis and stipe black, sparingly hairy. Prefers calcareous conditions, preferably limestone rock. Despite the fact that it comes from very cold areas of North America I find this difficult in cultivation. I think it would be best suited to a sheltered cleft between two rocks or with the crown protected by an overhanging rock.

P. cordifolia
Mexico, H30–60cm (12–24in), E, Dry, Zone 8. Fronds leathery, light green, tripinnate; pinnulets triangular. Stipe straight, unlike *P. ovata* which characteristically has a zig-zagging rachis and secondary rachis. Hardy in central England given the shelter of a wall.

P. glabella
Central North America, H10–25cm (4–10in), E, Dry, Zone 3. Fronds bipinnate, oblong; pinnules large, narrowly triangular. Stipe usually brown and hairless (compare with *P. atropurpurea*). Difficult to cultivate in the open in Britain as it needs a well-drained calcareous mix – winter damp is the problem, not the cold, and it is good in an alpine house.

P. ovata
North and Central America, H60–90cm (24–36in), E,

Dry, Zone 8. 'Semi-hardy', Richard Rush, 1984. Fronds tripinnate, scandent. Rachis pale brown and zig-zagging. Rhizome creeping. Segments heart-shaped and dark green. Neutral or alkaline soil.

P. rotundifolia *(Plate VI)*
New Zealand, H15–30cm (6–12in), E, Dry/Wet, Zone 7. Fronds pinnate borne in a flat rosette; pinnae rounded, dark green. Acid soil. This survived over winter in central England for a few years and eventually died from summer drought. I had it under conifers where the worst winter extremes were diluted, but where summer neglect was a problem. 'Semi-hardy', Richard Rush, 1984.

P. ternifolia *(Plate VI)*
Mexico, USA, Hawaii, H15–25 × 1cm (6–10 × ½in), E, Dry, Zone 8. Fronds narrow, lacking conspicuous scales or hairs. Pinnae 3-lobed. Stipe black. Survived outdoors in central England in a sheltered, well-drained site, but probably best in an alpine house in colder areas.

PENTAGRAMMA

A genus recently split from *Pityrogramma*, the following species is occasionally grown.

P. triangularis, syn. *Pityrogramma triangularis* (goldback fern)
Western USA, Mexico, H22–38cm (9–15in), D, Dry/Wet, Zone 8. Fronds triangular, almost pedate, because of the elongated pinnules at the base of the lowest pinnae, pinnate-pinnatifid. Dark green on top but covered with pale yellow wax glands beneath. Stipe black and long. A beautiful fern but unfortunately difficult to overwinter in central Britain because it needs to be kept dry with excellent drainage so is often best in an alpine house. Can be tried in dry regions in full sun in acid soil. The leaves may roll up temporarily in very dry weather.

PERANEMA

A curious genus closely related to *Dryopteris*. The sori hang from the undersurface of the frond on short stalks.

P. cyatheoides
Himalaya to east Asia, H60–90cm (24–36in), D, Dry/Wet, Zone 7. Fronds pale green, broadly ovate, tripinnate. Stipe long, covered with brown scales. An attractive fern that looks like a young cyathea (tree fern) before it has begun to produce a trunk, hence the specific name. *Peranema*, however, will not produce trunk. I have grown this on a wooded bank for years. It produces plenty of sori with me but I always fail to collect good spores: perhaps our summers are not long enough for them to ripen?

PHANEROPHLEBIA

A genus very closely related to *Cyrtomium* and not always recognized as distinct.

P. macrosora
Central America, H38–50cm (15–20in), E, Dry/Wet, Zone 8. Fronds dark green, ovate to narrowly trianular, pinnate. Laminae very leathery. Stipe long, covered with scales when young. Sori arranged in up to 5 rows along the underside of the frond. Another surprisingly hardy species from high altitudes in Mexico. This has survived outdoors with me for over 10 years on a well-drained slope, with a stone over the crown for some protection. I originally thought my plant to be *P. pumila* – a very dwarf species – but it has now grown so large it can only be *P. macrosora*!

PHEGOPTERIS

A small group of deciduous ferns often lumped into the large, mainly tropical, genus *Thelypteris*.

P. connectilis, syn. *Thelypteris phegopteris* (beech fern)
Europe, including British Isles, North America, Asia, H15–38cm (6–15in), D, Wet/Dry, Zone 2. Fronds produced singly on creeping rhizomes, pale green, ovate, pinnate-pinnatifid with a long stipe. Lamina typically longer than broad. The basal pair of pinnae are not connected to adjacent pinnae and are slightly shorter than those immediately above, characteristically pointing forward. A strong colony of this fern looks charming on a bank, the fronds facing forward and the very conspicuous basal pinnae. It has been used to very good effect at Branklyn garden in Perth in Scotland where it thrives in a peaty soil. In the wild, beech fern often grows under bracken or among wet, shady, acidic rocks.

P. decursive-pinnata, syn. *Thelypteris decursive-pinnata* (Japanese beech fern)
Kashmir to Taiwan, Japan, H38cm (15in), D, Wet/Dry, Zone 5. Fronds pale green, pinnatifid, lance-shaped. Pinnae shorten towards frond base, stipe quite long. Pinnae deeply serrate. Rhizomes grow slowly horizontally, gradually forming a clump.

P. hexagonoptera, syn. *Thelypteris hexagonoptera* (broad beech fern)
North America, H30–45cm (12–18in), D, Wet/Dry, Zone 5. Fronds triangular, bipinnatifid with a long stipe. Fronds usually broader than long. Basal pair of pinnae are connected to adjacent pinnae by a wing of lamina and do not point forward so conspicuously as in *P. connectilis*. Fronds produced singly on creeping rhizomes.

PILULARIA (pillwort)

A small genus of grass-like ferns that are members of the same family as *Marsilea*. Like *Marsilea* the spores are produced in a pill-like structure borne at the base of the leaves. One species is popular with enthusiasts.

P. globulifera (pillwort)
Europe, including British Isles, H7–15cm (3–6in), D, Wet, Zone 5. Fronds erect, simple threads like a dwarf rush, produced on creeping rhizomes, eventually forming a mat. In mature colonies, round pills up to 6mm (¼in) in diameter are produced at intervals along the rhizomes. Easily overlooked, recognized as a fern by the unrolling new fronds. Best cultivated in low-nutrient acid soil in a pan stood permanently in lime-free water. In suitable acidic gardens it could be introduced into shallow water. Propagation by division. A rare plant only occasionally in cultivation.

PLECOSORUS

A monotypic genus from Central America, very closely related to *Polystichum* but the pinnule segments are not spiny.

P. speciosissimus
Central America, H30–60cm (12–30in), E, Dry/Wet, Zone 8, possibly 7. Fronds lance-shaped, leathery, bipinnate, with pinnules crenately lobed. Stipe relatively short very abundantly covered with mid-brown scales, up to 10cm (4in) long. Rhizomes stout, erect. Hardy with me for a few years, apparently also hardy in the Seattle region of north-west America. A very handsome plant, worth special attention when available.

PNEUMATOPTERIS

Closely related to *Thelypteris*. There is one species in cultivation.

P. pennigera
Australia, New Zealand, H60–90cm (24–36in), D, Wet/Dry, Zone 9. Fronds lance-shaped, pinnate with linear pinnae lobed almost halfway to midrib. An attractive yellow-green. Hardy in my unheated polytunnels. Included here because it sometimes appears spontaneously on trunks of newly imported tree ferns. Surely hardy in sheltered gardens in south-west England and Eire.

POLYPODIUM

A large genus, many species being hardy in cool temperate areas. Although the species are rather similar to one another at a glance, certain species have given us a wonderful range of cultivars far exceeding the beauty of typical wild plants. *Polypodium* was at one time a much larger group of species: however, in the narrow sense used here it is a relatively small genus with many of the ferns split off into newer genera, such as *Microsorium* and *Pyrrosia*, on botanical technicalities that are mostly irrelevant for this book. Those included here all have sori lacking an indusium. All polypodiums have creeping rhizomes.

All hardy polypodiums need good drainage plus free air movement around the fronds. In particularly humid sites the fronds can get too big and heavy and hang down on the soil. Also in too-humid or wet conditions, the fronds may develop black blotching, which can be physiological or a fungal disease.

P. amoenum, syn. *Polypodiodes amoena*
Himalaya to Taiwan, H30cm (12in), D, Dry, Zone 8. Fronds pinnatifid, light green, underside of rachis scaly. Rhizomes creeping, densely covered in scales. Hardy with me for many years with the rhizome under a stone in an otherwise exposed site, but new fronds are always late appearing – I interpret this as an indication that it is only just surviving. With better shelter, I am sure it could do much better in zone 8.

P. amorphum, syn. *P. montense*
North-west America, H7–15cm (3–6in), E, Dry, Zone 6. Fronds pinnatifid, narrowly lance-shaped, erect; pinnae close together, often overlapping, often crenately lobed. A very pretty little fern, well suited for rockwork or an alpine house.

P. australe, syn. *P. cambricum* (southern polypody) *(Plate X)*
Europe, including British Isles, Asia, North Africa, H7–60cm (3–24in), W, Dry/Wet, Zone 6. Fronds thin-textured, pinnate, broadly ovate, almost triangular, with the second pair of pinnae from the bottom usually the longest. Stipe long, rhizomes creeping and covered in pale brown scales. Fronds produced in late summer-early autumn and persist through winter to disappear late spring-early summer. This is probably the best fern (perhaps even the best herbaceous plant) for fresh green foliage throughout winter; even if severely frosted it bounces back as if nothing had happened. The species is believed to have evolved in the Mediterranean region of Europe where the summers are hot and dry and the winters wet and warm. Any self-respecting fern prefers warm and wet weather so, not surprisingly, the annual cycle of *P. australe* has adjusted to grow during the warm wet

winters. Over the millennia, as the species migrated up the western seaboard of Europe, it retained the characteristic of autumn-winter growth, even in the British climate. It needs a well-drained site and, although not essential, it actually likes limey soil. That difficult corner in the garden where the builders left all their rubble is often perfect, as this mimics its natural habitat on walls and limestone rocks. In Britain it is uncommon but has a particular affinity with castle walls.

'Cambricum' This is a group of at least 7 named, and one or two unnamed, clones. All are top-quality gems. In general, fronds are pinnate-pinnatifid with deeply lacerated pinnae and pointed segment tips. The fronds are always sterile (ie. sori are lacking on the underside), so all forms have to be propagated by division of the rhizome. The various forms differ slightly in detail and need to be well established and well grown before they produce fronds in good character: only then can a realistic attempt be made to name the different clones. Curiously all the forms described here were before 1894, no new cultivars having been discovered in the wild since. I do not know why. I have devised a system that I hope will facilitate identification of the clones – splitting them into two sections: Cambricum base section and Barrowii section.

Barrowii section has thick-textured, almost leathery fronds. Pinnae segments not finely serrated. Fronds almost triangular to narrowly ovate. **Cambricum base section** has thin-textured, almost transparent fronds. Pinnae segments finely serrated. Fronds triangular.

Barrowii section clones

'Cambricum Barrowii' H38–45cm (15–18in). Found at Witherslack in the south of the Lake District, in 1874 by T Barrow. It differs from 'Cambricum Henwood' in having pinnae lamina more twisted, making the frond more three dimensional and spiky. The texture of the frond is more solid and slightly more glossy. Very rare in cultivation, with 'Cambricum Wilharris' (see below) often grown as 'Cambricum Barrowii'.

'Cambricum Hadwinii' Found at Silverdale, north Lancashire by Hadwin in 1875. Unfortunately I have never knowingly seen this cultivar. It may be extinct. It was a narrow, robust form very similar to 'Cambricum Wilharris'. No collection in the past ever seemed to grow both cultivars so I wonder if they are actually the same plant. Further reason for suspicion is the old records for 'Hadwinii Reversion'. This was a pulcherrimum type (ie. completely fertile), which certain parts of

Polypodium australe 'Cambricum Barrowii', one of the rarest forms of 'Cambricum'.

'Cambricum Hadwinii' apparently reverted to. I have seen this happen only once – to a pan of 'Cambricum Wilharris'! If my suspicions are correct, by the laws of precedence, 'Cambricum Hadwinii' will be the correct name for 'Cambricum Wilharris'.

'Cambricum Prestonii' (Plate X) H20–30cm (8–12in). Found at Yelland, north Lancashire in 1871 by Preston. It was growing in a block of limestone pavement and Preston could not extricate it, so he took the whole block home and gradually grew the fern out of its crevice. Similar to 'Cambricum Barrowii' except the frond is narrowly ovate. The lacerations of adjacent pinnae overlap more strongly, hence this cultivar has been called 'Congestum Preston'. This is in every sense a smaller, more delicate plant than all the other cambricums.

'Cambricum Wilharris' H38–45cm (15–18in). Found by 'Wilharris' at Pennard in Somerset in about 1893. I wonder if Wilharris was in fact the Mr Harris who was then Head Gardener at Bristol Zoological Gardens, where a large fern collection was housed – perhaps his Christian name was Wil? I also wonder if this was

PLATE X
Polypodium australe and cultivars

'Semilacerum
Falcatum O'Kelly'

'Cristatum Forsteri'

'Cristatum'

'Omnilacerum
Superbum'

'Semilacerum'

'Hornet'

'Pulcherimum
Addison'

Polypodium
australe

'Cambricum
Prestonii'

'Pulcherimum
Trippitt'

'Richard Kayse'

All fronds shown
approximately half size

Polypodium australe 'Cambricum Wilharris' is the commonest 'Cambricum' in cultivation, but often labelled 'Barrowii' in error.

'found' in a garden as there is no obvious outcropping of limestone at Pennard. Similar to 'Cambricum Barrowii', with which it is often confused, but differs in being much narrower fronded – the frond is lance-shaped. This is the commonest clone of 'Cambricum' in cultivation. See also under 'Cambricum Hadwinii'.

Cambricum base section

'Cambricum'   H38–45cm   (15–18in).   Origin unknown, it may have originated in Eire in the nineteenth century. Fronds quite papery, lamina along each pinna slightly twisted, making the frond moderately three dimensional and spiky. One of the most beautiful ferns and fortunately not too rare.

'Cambricum Henwood' seems identical to the base form; it was found by Henwood near Cromer in Norfolk in about 1910 and was growing with 'Cristatum Henwood', a long way from the nearest known colony of *P. australe*. I, therefore, think it was a garden escape.

'Cambricum   Oakleyae'   H20–30cm   (8–12in). Found at Raglan, South Wales by Mrs Oakley in 1868. Similar to the base form except the pinnae lacerations are shorter, and it is smaller, largely due to the stipe being shorter. This cultivar may be extinct. Plants in cultivation under this name are invariably fertile and, therefore, correctly forms of *P. australe* 'Pulcherrimum'.

'Richard Kayse' *(Plate X)* H38–45cm (15–18in). Very similar to the base form but always more spiky and the pinnae are not twisted. Probably the most beautiful form of cambricum. Found at Dinas Powys in South Wales by Richard Kayse of Bristol in 1668, and was still in its original locality in 1980, albeit in small quantity. It is on a sheer limestone cliff – out of reach of all but rock climbers – where I hope it will remain for many more centuries. Plants in gardens under this name are parts of the original plant, since it is sterile, and can surely, therefore, lay claim to being one of the oldest herbaceous plants in existence. We are not talking about sporelings here, but the original plant. This is the form seen by Linnaeus and named *P. cambricum* by him, but which recent research has shown to be a cultivar of *P. australe*. As it was named by Linnaeus, some have argued it should be used as the type plant and the species name changed to *P. cambricum*. I reject this because if *P. australe* is changed to *P. cambricum* it makes it very difficult to know just which form is being referred to.

'Crenatum' H25cm (10in). Margins of pinnae roundly lobed, ie. crenate.

'Cristatum',   syn.   'Cristatum'   (old   form),   'Cristatum Perry' *(Plate X)* H25cm (10in). Found in 1854 by H.S. Perry in County Cork, Eire. The pinnae and the frond tip all carry smallish, curled crests. Frequently the crest at the frond tip is slightly depauperate lacking small pieces of lamina and having an extended spike of midrib at some tips. The terminal crest is usually narrower than the frond lamina.

'Cristatum Forsteri', syn. 'Cristatum Clewarth', 'Grandiceps Forster' *(Plate X)* H25cm (10in). Found in 1876 by 'Jas.' Clewarth in County Clare, Eire. A neat cultivar with large crests at tips of pinnae and frond. The terminal crest is usually broader than the frond lamina. Easily distinguished from 'Cristatum' by the larger crests and the lack of depauperation within the crests. Very rare.

'Diadem' (Cristatum Group) H30cm (12in), W, Dry. Fronds broadly ovate. Crests of pinnae and frond tip small. Distinct. This is a new cultivar raised by our nursery. E. J. Lowe used the name 'Diadema' in the nineteenth century; this may or may not be a similar form, but the name 'Diadem' seemed appropriate.

'Trippitt's Crested' (Cristatum Group) H7–20cm (3–8in). Raised by Bob Trippitt c1975 as a sporeling of 'Pulchritudine'. Fronds bipinnatifid with all terminals fan crested. Very distinct and apparently a completely new break. It is amazing that no evidence can be found for the existence of this cultivar when ferns were being more widely raised from spores in the past. I have subsequently raised identical plants from the same parent, as well as some smaller forms.

'Grandiceps Fox' H30cm (12in) Found at Grange-over-Sands in the Lake District by Mrs Fox in 1868. Similar to 'Cristatum Forsteri' except this is a more robust cultivar with larger crests on all terminals. Despite being named 'Grandiceps' the crest is often narrower than the frond lamina; however, this is a large cultivar and the crest is always big.

'Grandiceps Parker', syn. 'Multifido-cristatum Parker' Found on a wall near Weston-super-Mare in Somerset in 1854 by Henry Parker. The individual crests are longer than in other forms and branch repeatedly making the terminal head very broad, hence the alternative name multifido-cristatum. All fronds clearly in true grandiceps character. The frond sometimes reduced to a huge crest without any pinnae; where present the pinnae also crested. The 'fingers' of the crest slim. This cultivar may be extinct but a very fine form recently introduced into Britain from British Columbia by Judith Jones strongly resembles the surviving specimens in the Kew herbarium. The British Columbia form is considered to be a cultivar of *Polypodium glycyrrhiza*, certainly the rhizome tastes of licorice, but the resemblance is uncanny. Curious as it may seem it is just possible that the two ferns are one and the same! I cannot believe that *P. glycyrrhiza*

Polypodium australe 'Grandiceps Fox' is a large cultivar with large crests although they are narrower than the frond.

Polypodium australe 'Hornet' is a dwarf curiosity with a short bristle at the tip of each pinna.

could have established itself near Weston-super-Mare, but it is possible that Joseph Wiper (a founder member of the British Pteridological Society and inventor of Kendal Mint Cake) took material of 'Grandiceps Parker' with him when he emigrated to Canada at the beginning of the twentieth century, only for it to return here by a happy coincidence.

'Hornet' *(Plate X)* H7–20cm (3–8in) Found by me near Llandudno in North Wales in 1983. It was growing on a limestone cliff among many normal plants of *P. australe* in a private garden. I have no doubt that it was a cultivar naturally occurring in that locality. All pinnae and frond tips are truncate with the midrib protruding like a small horn.

'Macrostachyon' Found in the Burren district of western Eire by P.B. O'Kelly early in the twentieth century. The frond is normal except the lamina narrows abruptly and ends with a single long, terminal pinna. Sometimes this cultivar is called 'Caudatum' or 'Longicaudatum' in error. An established plant of 'Macrostachyon' is very attractive with the massed, erect terminal pinnae creating quite an effect.

'Omnilacerum Aldrenii' H45–60cm (18–24in). Found by J.A. Aldren at Milnthorpe, Lancashire in 1873. Similar to 'Omnilacerum Superbum', but tends to be truncate at tip. Probably extinct.

'**Omnilacerum Bennett**' H60cm (24in). Found by Bennett on Goodrich Castle in Herefordshire in 1848. This cultivar is probably extinct but deserves mention here for two reasons. It is historically significant as a very early named cultivar of *P. australe*, and it was very distinct. It may turn up in a collection or garden somewhere: indeed, an apparently identical cultivar was found on Cleeve Abbey in Somerset in 1864. When in good character all the pinnae were deeply lacerated very much like a more open form of 'Cambricum' base form, but they were copiously covered with sori.

'**Omnilacerum Superbum**', syn. 'Omnilacerum Oxford', 'Omnilacerum Superbum Williams' *(Plate X)* H to 75cm (30in). Found at Tregony in Cornwall sometime before 1897 possibly by J.S. Tyerman, or a Mr Williams. Pinnae lacerated along their length and along the length of the frond although the lacerations are shallower towards the tip of the pinnae and the tip of the frond. A well-grown frond in silhouette can approach 'Cambricum' but it differs by being fully fertile. Probably the tallest cultivar of *P. australe*. Unless well cultivated it can look like a form of *P. australe* with slightly lacerated pinnae at the base of the frond only. There is a form in cultivation called 'Oxford Gold' which apparently has golden blotches when grown in full sun; I have not seen it.

'**Pulcherrimum**' Pulcherrimum means 'most beautiful' – an appropriate name for this group of rather similar cultivars. Fronds regularly bipinnatifid, the ends of the pinna segments not sharply pointed. Segments are close together giving the frond a pleasant yet solid appearance. All moderately well-established plants produce some sori, albeit sometimes sparingly. Sori confirm that the plant is not a Cambricum form. The texture of the frond is relatively thick, also quite unlike Cambricum forms. When well grown, the fronds can become tripinnatifid but may get rather heavy and lie on the ground.

There are a few named clones that differ a little from each other.

'**Pulcherrimum Addison**', syn. 'Pulcherrimum Barnes' *(Plate X)* The original find from Whitbarrow in the south of the Lake District by Addison in 1861. For some time it was considered a form of 'Semilacerum' but under cultivation enthusiasts realised it was something special. Fronds large, usually pale green.

'**Pulcherrimum May**' Selected by H.B. May's nursery early in the twentieth century, very similar to 'Pulcherrimum Addison' but usually darker green.

'**Pulcherrimum Trippitt**' *(Plate X)* Not an official

The beautiful dark green fronds of *Polypodium australe* 'Semilacerum Robustum'.

name and as such unacceptable, but this is a very good form raised by Bob Trippitt about 25 years ago. It is distinguished by the relatively long-drawn-out and pointed tips of the pinna segments. Sparingly fertile.

'**Pulchritudine**' Raised by E.J. Lowe in late 1884. Along the general lines of 'Pulcherrimum' except the tips of frond, pinnae and segments are slightly crisped giving the frond a slightly concave appearance. The margins of the segments are crenately lobed. Sparingly fertile. This is a beautiful cultivar to which I have given Lowe's old name, based on his short description in *British Ferns* (1890): 'A handsome finely cut variety. Fronds concave 12 × 4½in …' This is not a lot to go on but no other description fits this beautiful fern which I feel sure must have been in cultivation for many years.

'**Semilacerum**', syn. 'Hibernicum' *(Plate X)* There have been many finds of this form, indeed many good wild populations of *P. australe* support occasional plants of this type. *Semilacerum* means half lacerated, and fronds in character are irregularly bipinnatifid along the lower half of the frond and normal along the top half. Wild finds can be poor when found but in cultivation they often settle down into interesting plants. First named 'Semilacerum' by Link in 1841. Some of the best named forms are:

'**Carew Lane**' (**Semilacerum Group**) H38cm (15in). I found this wild in South Wales. Pinnae segments rather broad, almost overlapping, with rounded tips. Dark green, robust.

'Chudleigh' (Semilacerum Group) H38cm (15in). I found this wild in Devon in about 1980. Similar to 'Carew Lane' but more space between pinnae segments, giving a more open frond, and paler green.

Crisped form (Semilacerum Group) H38cm (15in). I found this wild at Buckfast in Devon in 1980. Bottom half of frond irregularly bipinnate; lamina crisped. Quite distinct, having a different texture to other forms.

'Semilacerum Falcatum O'Kelly' *(Plate X)* H45–60cm (18–24in). Found in County Clare, Eire by O'Kelly around the beginning of the twentieth century. The fronds are lance-shaped (uncommon in *P. australe*), and the pinnae are sickle-shaped (falcate) and curved towards the tip of the frond. The bipinnatifid pinnae can extend more than halfway up the frond in well-grown specimens. This is a beautiful fern; the arching fronds somehow give a feeling of movement.

'Semilacerum Lowei', syn. 'Semilacerum Jubilee' H38–45cm (15–18in). Found in Eire by A. Lowe 1856. Segments crowded on pinnae and those from adjacent pinnae overlapping. Very late appearing in late summer-early autumn.

'Semilacerum Robustum' H45–60cm (18–24in). Found on Whitbarrow in the south of the Lake District by Barnes in 1863. A large robust form of 'Semilacerum'. Lacerations deep and quite regular. Tall, erect grower

Polypodium glycyrrhiza 'Malahatense'. This is the fertile form – a robust garden plant, but somewhat coarse.

'Semilacerum Undulatum' H45–60cm (18–24in). Found on Warton Crag, north Lancashire, probably by Bolton, around 1910. Fronds dark green, more leathery than normal *P. australe*. Lower half of frond bipinnatifid, the pinnae segments are often short, being little more than deep crenations. Pinnae slightly twisted.

P. azoricum
Azores, H12–38cm (5–15in), E, Dry, Zone 8. Frond pinnatifid, broadly lance-shaped, pinnae undulate and sometimes lobed, very similar to *P. australe* but differs by being slightly glossy. This description fits plants grown in relatively high humidity; in drier sites the frond is more leathery and shiny, approaching the appearance of *P. scouleri*.

P. californicum
West USA, H10–20cm (4–8in), E, Dry/Wet, Zone 8. Fronds pinnatifid, lance-shaped. Very similar to European *P. interjectum*. Occasionally cultivated but not excitingly distinct.

P. cambricum, see *P. australe*.

P. glycyrrhiza, syn. *P. vulgare* 'Acuminatum' (licorice fern)
Western North America, H45–60cm (18–24in), E, Dry, Zone 6. Frond bipinnatifid, darkish green, papery texture, erect. Sori quite small, dark orange-brown when ripe. Pinnae tips acuminate. The rhizome tastes of licorice if chewed. Believed to have been used by west coast Indians as a sweetener for food. There is a species in Japan, *P. fauriei* which is superficially similar.

Bifid form *(Plate XI)* H30cm (12in). Not yet officially named but raised by the late Ray Coughlin around 1985. I believe it is a hybrid between *P. glycyrrhiza* 'Longicaudatum' and *P. vulgare* 'Bifido-cristatum'. Scientific analysis of plant enzymes supports this theory. If correct it is a hybrid new to science that awaits a name. I propose *P.* × *coughlinii*.

Grandiceps Group *(Plate XI)* H20–30cm (8–12in). Fronds heavily crested; rhizomes taste weakly of licorice but I wonder if this *P. australe* 'Grandiceps Parker'.

'Longicaudatum' *(Plate XI)* H25–38cm (10–15in). Introduced into Britain around the time of the First World War. Fronds pinnatifid, each with a long-drawn-out tip. Does not taste as strongly of licorice as the type.

'Malahatense' H25–38cm (10–15in). Found at Malahat in British Columbia, Canada. Fronds bipinnatifid and sterile, along the lines of *P. australe* 'Cambricum'. Not a robust grower with me, new fronds come later in season than normal *P. glycyrrhiza*. There is a rather similar fertile form, which is bipinnatifid but more coarse. It can be

PLATE XI
Polypodium species and cultivars

Polypodium glycyrrhiza 'Longicaudatum'

Polypodium × mantoniae 'Bifido-grandiceps'

Polypodium glycyrrhiza Grandiceps Group

Polypodium interjectum

Polypodium scouleri

All fronds shown approximately half size

Polypodium vulgare
'Trichomanoides
Backhouse'
(both frond
types)

Polypodium vulgare
'Cornubiense Grandiceps'
(both frond types)

*Polypodium
× mantoniae*
'Cornubiense'
(bipinnatifid frond)

*Polypodium
× mantoniae*
'Cornubiense'
(normal frond)

*Polypodium
glycyrrhiza*
Bifid form

The curious *Polypodium interjectum* 'Glomeratum Mullins', no two fronds of which are the same.

identified by the occasional sorus. I am not aware of any name for it.

P. hesperium

North-west America, H10–20cm (4–8in), E, Dry, Zone 6. Frond narrow, oblong, similar to *P. amorphum* but the pinnae are more widely spaced. Beautiful neat fern for rockwork.

P. interjectum (intermediate polypody) *(Plate XI)*

Europe, including British Isles, H45cm (18in), E, Dry, Zone 5. Fronds pinnatifid, narrowly ovate, somewhat leathery. Marginally the longest pair of pinnae is about the sixth pair from the base. Usually a bluish-green. Stipe quite long, produced from creeping rhizomes covered with pale brown scales. Very common in Europe on neutral to lime-rich rocks, walls and banks. In an evolutionary sense this is a modern species which arose as a hybrid between *P. vulgare* and *P. australe*. Rarely on trees. Fronds produced in midsummer. There is one cultivar of garden merit.

'Glomeratum Mullins' H15–22cm (6–9in). Found by Job Mullins, gardener to Lady Oylander, at Beaminster,

Dorset in 1873. A curious form with no two fronds the same. Pinnae can be missing or crested, frond tips can be plain or crested. Despite its extraordinary variability it can make an attractive clump in the garden. Propagate by division as it does not come true from spores. Although some spores are viable I do wonder if this is properly a cultivar of *P.* × *mantoniae*.

P. macaronesicum

Canary Islands, H30cm (12in), W, Dry, Zone 8. Fronds pinnate; all pinnae more or less the same length, pale green, papery texture, very slightly shiny. Like *P. australe* this species loses its fronds in summer. It differs from *P. australe* by not having triangular fronds.

P. × mantoniae

Europe, including British Isles, H45cm (18in), E, Dry, Zone 5. Fronds pinnatifid, narrowly ovate, somewhat leathery, with the longest pair of pinnae usually the fifth or sixth pair from the base. Hybrid betweeen *P. vulgare* and *P. interjectum*. Very similar to *P. interjectum* except the sori never ripen to enclose uniform yellow sporangia; instead the sorus tends to be a mixture of blacks, browns and yellows. Most spores are, therefore, abortive. Included here because the following cultivars are excellent garden plants and the most widely grown polypodiums.

'Bifido-grandiceps' *(Plate XI)* H45–60cm (18–24in). History obscure, but it probably arose in cultivation as a hybrid between *P. vulgare* 'Bifido-cristatum' and normal *P. interjectum* early in the twentieth century. It is a very robust fern with abortive spores. Fronds pinnatifid with pinnae ending in flat crests. Crest at tip of frond very wide and flat, more or less in one plane, much wider than the rest of the frond lamina. Propagate by division. A handsome fern with very attractive arching fronds.

'Cornubiense' *(Plate XI)* Origin unknown, but quite recent. It was unknown in Victorian times unless it is the same as 'Cornubiense Foliosum' raised by Clapham in the nineteenth century. Fronds of two types, normal or bipinnatifid. I have never seen good spores on any of my plants, therefore almost certainly a hybrid. I believe it arose accidentally as a cross between *P. interjectum* and *P. vulgare* 'Elegantissimum', but this is speculation on my part as it has not yet been checked by any scientific technique. Propagation is by division, but because it is a strong grower this excellent cultivar is, fortunately, relatively common. *P. vulgare* 'Elegantissimum' used to be called 'Cornubiense', but this hybrid form has taken over the name. Rather than change the name for what is now a very well-known plant, I propose that this form continues to be called 'Cornubiense' while the original plant reverts to its alternative name of 'Elegantissimum' (see below).

'Cornubiense Bifidum' H38cm (15in). Like 'Cornubiense' above but with tips of pinnae very lightly crested, often merely forked.

P. polypodiodes (resurrection fern)
Southern USA, tropical America, H12–25cm (5–10in), E, Dry, Zone 7. Fronds pinnatifid, oblong, densely covered with scales on the upper surface. In dry weather the frond can curl up only to reopen when rain arrives. I have overwintered this in central England but I lost it eventually. It needs good drainage in winter and is perhaps best suited to an alpine house. Well worth the effort as it is a very distinctive species.

P. scouleri (leather polypody) *(Plate XI)*
North-west America, H20–38cm (8–15in), E, Dry, Zone 7. Fronds pinnate, not broad; pinnae all more or less same length, leathery, shiny on both surfaces, dark green above. Tips of pinnae blunt. Leathery texture in ferns, especially polypods, is common among species from a largely maritime environment. Surprisingly hardy inland in central England, eventually forms a good-sized clump.

P. scouleri × *P. glycyrrhiza*
North-west America, H30–45cm (12–18in), E, Dry, Zone 5. Fronds pinnate, broadly lance-shaped, pinnae longest in centre of frond, slightly leathery, shiny on both surfaces, dark green above. Tips of pinnae acuminate. A beautiful fern, sadly very rare. Propagate by division.

P. sibiricum
Northern Asia, northern North America, H10–20cm (4–8in), E, sometimes D, Dry, Zone 3. Frond pinnatifid, narrowly triangular; pinnae longest towards base of frond, papery texture, upper surface dark green, not shiny. Pinnae narrow and relatively distant from each other. A pretty little polypod but I have lost this in the garden. I suspect it needs snow cover in cold weather.

P. virginianum
Western North America, H30cm (12in), E, Dry, Zone 3. Fronds pinnatifid, narrowly lance-shaped, very similar to European *P. vulgare*. Apparently not in general cultivation in Europe. There is at least one excellent cultivar.

'Cambricoides', syn. 'Bipinnatifidum' H25cm (10in). Fronds regularly bipinnatifid, papery, probably sterile. A beauty but possibly not in cultivation.

P. vulgare (common polypody)
Europe, including British Isles, Asia, H38cm (15in), E, Dry, Zone 3. Frond pinnatifid, papery, with pinnae

The leathery-fronded *Polypodium scouleri* is from coastal regions of north-west America.

shorter than those of *P. interjectum* and more or less the same length for most of the frond. New fronds appear early summer. In nature this is a fern of acid banks and rocks, and also tree branches in high rainfall areas. It is rare for the other species of polypodium to colonize tree branches. In the garden it is not that fussy over soil pH but it does do very well on acid soils, better than *P. interjectum* or *P. australe*. It benefits from planting in a site with good drainage.

'Bifido-cristatum' H30–38cm (12–15in). Found in North Lancashire by Thomas Walmsley in 1867. Fronds pinnate, all pinnae with neat bifid branches forming fan-shaped crests. Terminal crest also a flat fan shape but much wider than the rest of the frond. Strictly speaking a true grandiceps. Comes true from spores.

'Cornubiense Grandiceps' *(Plate XI)* As 'Jean Taylor' but lacking any quadripinnatifid fronds. This was first raised by A. Clapham around 1875. It is a hybrid between *P. vulgare* 'Bifidocristatum' and *P. vulgare* 'Elegantissimum'. It comes more or less true from spores but is usually propagated by division.

'Elegantissimum', syn. 'Cornubiense', 'Whytei' H30–38cm (12–15in). Found in Cornwall in 1867 by the Rev J.R. Whyte. A remarkable cultivar that produces fronds of three types: perfectly normal fronds, very finely cut tripinnatifid (or even quadripinnatifid) fronds, together with bipinnatifid ones. By happy chance the very finely cut fronds usually predominate. One could be forgiven for thinking that different cultivars have become mixed except careful scutiny will usually reveal two or more characters mixed on the same frond. This is a beautiful fern, but unfortunately rather rare. As far as I am aware this cultivar is unique among polypods in occasionally producing bulbils on the upper surface of the frond. So far neither I, nor other more notable growers before me, have ever succeeded in raising and plants from these bulbils. One frond up to 1cm (½in) long is produced but never any roots.

'Jean Taylor' H7–20cm (3–8in). A crested form of 'Elegantissimum' from which it was raised by Jack Healey around 1950 and named after his wife. It has the three kinds of fronds but is a bit inclined to be coarse with fewer and fewer quadripinnatifid fronds being produced as the plant ages. Other similar forms have been raised by spores from the same parentage; one recently raised by Robert Sykes has mainly quadripinnatifid fronds and seems more stable.

'Ramosum Hillman' H30–38cm (12–15in). Found in Hampshire by C. Hillman in 1860. Fronds branch near their base, usually into three, and again near the tips. The overall effect is a fan-shaped frond. Was rare in cultivation but recently refound on a wall in Borrowdale in the Lake District. Comes true from spores, but usually propagated by division.

'Trichomanoides Backhouse' *(Plate XI)* H15–30cm (6–12in). Raised at Backhouse's nursery before 1873 as a sporeling of 'Elegantissimum'. Fronds of two kinds: quadripinnatifid or normal. It lacks the intermediate bipinnatifid fronds. Some selections are reputed to produce quadripinnatifid fronds only. This is a gem!

POLYSTICHUM

A large genus including many of the best hardy garden ferns, all of which like good drainage, often with some lime in the soil. Almost all species are evergreen with a fairly leathery texture to the frond. The margins of the pinnae are usually serrated with bristles, appearing spiny, at the tip of each serration, hence *poly – stichum*. The spring croziers of most species are a strong feature,

attracting many admiring comments: the curled up tip of the frond is rolled in towards the crown but the weight of the crozier acts to bend the tip of the frond away from the crown, creating a wonderful S-shape in the unfurling fronds, which open in a flush as a spreading shuttlecock. The attraction is further enhanced in a number of species by the presence of abundant scales on the croziers. Most species have short, erect rhizomes.

On the debit side polystichums can suffer from an unpleasant disease called *Taphrina wettsteiniana*. Fortunately, it is not common but it can get a hold where a lot of polystichums are grown in close proximity, it is quite commonly present on plants of *P. setiferum* in the wild in western Britain. Symptoms are patchy browning and shrivelling of fronds, especially young fronds. It is difficult to control but systemic fungicides sprayed into the crown in early spring, before the croziers start to move, will keep it at bay. Ideally also remove all affected fronds or parts of fronds: this can set the plant back but it should keep the disease in check. As the disease is spread by water, sickly plants can be grown in a greenhouse for a season or two to regain health. Care should be taken not to wet the crown.

P. acrostichoides (Christmas fern)
North-east America, H90cm (36in), E, Dry/Wet, Zone 3. Fronds lance-shaped, pinnate, mid-green. Sporing fronds differ from vegetative fronds by narrowing at the tip where spores are produced. The common name refers to its evergreen nature: it is an attractive plant at Christmas in the northern hemisphere. When the new croziers flush in spring they arch out very distinctively. Easy to grow in a reasonably well-drained site.

P. aculeatum (hard shield fern)
Europe, including British Isles, H75–90cm (30–36in), E, Dry/Wet, Zone 4. Fronds lance-shaped, bipinnate, deep green and glossy. Pinnae continue and narrow right to base of frond; stipe therefore very short. Distinguished from *P. setiferum* by the angle at the base of the pinnule where it is attached to the midrib being less than 90 degrees, ie. acute. Young plants and plants in mountainous areas may only develop pinnate-pinnatifid fronds. This form is sometimes called var. *cambricoides*. It can be mistaken for *P. lonchitis*, but in *P. lonchitis* the pinnae are unlobed. Both types are very handsome, forming neat shuttlecocks of spreading fronds. I like to see this fern on a shady bank where the fronds can arch out very elegantly. In the past several cultivars have been described; I believe that all are now extinct or have

been reassigned as cultivars of *P. setiferum*.

P. alticola

South Africa, H30–38cm (12–15in), E, Dry/Wet, Zone 8. Fronds narrowly lance-shaped to oblong, pale green, not glossy, bipinnate. Pinnules small, neat with margin only shallowly toothed, pale creamy-brown hairs along top of pinna midrib. Scales on rachis and stipe pale creamy-brown. I have overwintered this for many years in an unheated polytunnel, and have no reason to doubt it would be hardy here if tested. In the wild it only grows at high altitudes, mainly in the Drakensberg Mountains.

P. andersonii

North-west America, H60–75cm (24–30in), E, Dry/Wet, Zone 6. Fronds lance-shaped, pinnate-pinnatifid, pale green. Stipe short. Proliferous bud near the tip of most fronds. In my opinion a rather nondescript fern, usually only noticeable for the bud near the frond tips.

P. bonseyi

Hawaii, H45–60cm (18–24in), E, Zone 8. Fronds broadly triangular to ovate, bipinnate, drab green. Pinnules ovate, toothed with tips of teeth turned up. Despite coming from an unpromising source this has been hardy with me in central England despite 11 years of neglect!

P. braunii

Central Europe, North America, eastern Asia, H60–90cm (24–36in), E, Dry/Wet, Zone 4. Fronds fairly narrowly lance-shaped, bipinnate, leathery, bright or yellowish-green. Stipe short. Shininess of frond partially disguised by light covering of hairs. Stipe and rachis well covered with pale brown scales. The forms from each region differ in detail: the American form called var. or subsp. *purshii*, is diploid, the European and Asian forms are tetraploid. All forms have been hardy with me for years. Very similar to *P. setigerum*.

P. cystostegia

New Zealand, H15–30cm (6–12in), D, Dry/Wet, Zone 7. Fronds lance-shaped, erect, bipinnate pinnatifid, fresh green. Pinnae triangular, turned at right angles to the rachis, crowded at tip of frond, well-spaced at base. Stipe scales uniformly pale brown. I have never grown this fern but it is the most alpine of New Zealand ferns and, when available, should be well adapted to cool temperate gardens or alpine house conditions, given good light and drainage.

P. deltodon

Far eastern Asia, H38–45cm (15–18in), E, Dry/Wet, Zone 8, possibly 7. Fronds slightly shiny on upper surface, mid-green, oblong or very narrowly lance-shaped, up to 3.5cm (1½in) wide. Pinnate, the pinnae rectangular with obtuse tips and irregularly, shallowly crenate margins. Stipe long with few scales at base. Sporangia just in from the margin of the pinna. A very interesting fern unlike any other I grow, hardy with me now for many years totally unprotected. There are several closely related species in China and it is possible that the fern described here is one of these.

P. drepanum

Madeira, H45–60cm (18–24in), E, Dry/Wet, Zone 8. Fronds triangular, bipinnate, leathery. Pinnae narrowly triangular not overlapping; pinnules ovate. Despite being one of the world's rarest ferns, this is in cultivation as it comes quite well from spores. It has been hardy in zone 8 for the last two winters.

P. × dycei

H60–120cm (2–4ft), E, Dry/Wet, Zone 7. Synthesized hybrid (*P. proliferum* × *P. braunii*) created by Ann Sleep at Leeds University. Fronds lance-shaped, bipinnate, mid- to dark green. Stipe very scaly. One or a few bulbils are produced near the tip of the frond. These can form into small plants while still held aloft. Along with *P. munitum* probably the largest polystichum for general garden conditions. Sterile but can be propagated from the bulbils. Rare.

P. excellens

China, H30–45cm (12–18in), E, Dry/Wet, Zone 8. Fronds oblong, pinnate, pale green. Pinnae sickle-shaped, acutely pointed at tip with neatly serrated sides and quite a conspicuous 'thumb' at base of acroscopic side. Stipe long. The identification of this fern is provisional – it may be *P. hecatopterum*. It has done well for several seasons in my unheated polytunnel.

P. falcinellum

Madeira, H45–60cm (18–24in), E, Dry/Wet, Zone 8. Fronds pinnate, leathery, erect, lance-shaped, conspicuous auricle on the base of each pinna on the acroscopic side. Very similar to *P. munitum*, which has less leathery and slightly more spreading fronds, and only two sets of chromosomes – *P. falcinellum* has eight. Hardy with me for many years.

P. fallax

Australia, H30–60cm (12–24in), E, Dry/Wet, Zone 9, possibly 8. Fronds lance-shaped to triangular, bipinnate, glossy mid-green. Pinnae oblong with an acute tip. At one time considered a form of the European *P. aculeatum*. I grew this for a few years in my unheated polytunnel but lost it when I moved the nursery.

P. haleakalense

Hawaii, H60cm (24in), E, Dry/Wet, Zone 8. Fronds lance-shaped, bipinnate, glossy dark green. Pinnules spiny along outer margin. Stipe short. Very similar to *P. braunii*, but darker glossy green. Another Hawaiian fern hardy in central England for 11 winters now.

P. hancockii

Japan, China, Taiwan, H7–20cm (3–8in), E, Dry/Wet, Zone 8. Fronds linear, pinnate with the two basal pinnae enlarged and themselves pinnate, like small fronds. The whole frond shaped like a dagger. A charming little fern, a dwarf version of *P. tripteron*.

P. × illyricum

Europe, including British Isles, H30–60cm (12–24in), E, Dry/Wet, Zone 4. Hybrid *P. lonchitis* × *P. aculeatum*. Fronds narrow lance-shaped, pinnate-pinnatifid, dark green, glossy. Pinnae sickle-shaped. Stipe short. Rarely available but a good garden plant, much easier than *P. lonchitis*.

P. imbricans

North-west America, H30–60cm (12–20in), E, Dry/Wet, Zone 6. Very similar to *P. munitum* except pinnae are closer together and often overlap. Fronds stiffly erect, pinnae twisted to nearly right angles with the plane of the rachis.

'Grandiceps' H30cm (12in). Grown by Reginald Kaye. Tip of fronds heavily crested; pinnae uncrested. Might be cultivar of *P. munitum*.

P. kruckbergii

North-western America, H15–30cm (6–12in), E, Dry/Wet, Zone 6. Frond linear-lanceolate, pinnate-pinnatifid. Pinnae short, triangular, with usually six teeth either side (the very similar *P. scopulinum* has 8–25 teeth each side and the pinnae are more distinctly lobed). A fertile species created from the hybrid between *P. lemmonii* and *P. lonchitis*. A very high-altitude fern well suited to an alpine house, not as hardy in the open, probably due to excesive winter damp.

P. lemmonii

North-western America, H15–22cm (3–9in), E, Dry/Wet, Zone 6. Fronds linear-lanceolate, bipinnate to bipinnate-pinnatifid. Pinnae short triangular, deeply lobed to the midrib. Differs from the rather similar *P. kruckbergii* and *P. scopulinum* by being clearly bipinnate.

P. lentum

South-east Asia, H15–38cm (6–15in), E, Dry/Wet, Zone 8. Fronds lance-shaped, arching, pinnate-pinnatifid, dark green, slightly glossy. Pinnae acute pointed, short, sickle-shaped. Most fronds have a bulbil produced a few centimetres before the tip. I did not expect this to be hardy in central England but it has done well for years.

P. lepidocaulon

South-east Asia, H30–60cm (12–24in), E, Dry/Wet, Zone 8. Fronds pinnate, dark glossy green, oblong. The tips of mature fronds develop into long rhizomatous runners which root where they touch the ground. Pinnules sickle-shaped. Another species that has proved much hardier than I expected and is well worth growing when available.

P. lonchitis (holly fern)

Europe, including British Isles, North America, H15–38cm (6–15in), E, Dry/Wet, Zone 3. Fronds narrowly lance-shaped, pinnate. Pinnae conspicuously toothed with a noticeable 'thumb' on the acroscopic side at the base. Stipe very short, except when growing in deep crevices. Can be difficult to grow in lowland or warm gardens. I find it does well if given good drainage and planted so that the caudex (base, including roots) is protected by an overhanging stone – this reduces the penetration of winter wet into the crown. Lime in the mix is not essential, but it helps.

P. longipaleatum, syn. P. discretum

Himalaya, H60cm (24in), E, Dry/Wet, Zone 7. Fronds lance-shaped, bipinnate, dark green, arching. Laminae covered with long golden-brown hairs, which are partly deciduous. Stipe about a fifth the length of the frond, scaly. A very distinct fern which is unfortunately rare.

P. luctuosum

South Africa, H30–60cm (12–24in), E, Dry/Wet, Zone 8. Fronds ovate to narrowly triangular, bipinnate, dull, dark green above, leathery, scales on rachis and stipe black. A spiky-looking fern with sharp-pointed fronds, pinnae and pinnules. Very pretty; a good garden plant, separated from *P. tsus-simense* by being much more leafy and less finely divided.

P. makinoi

Eastern Asia, H45–60cm (18–24in), E, Dry/Wet, Zone 6. Fronds triangular to broadly lance-shaped, arching, quite leathery, bipinnate, drab green shiny on upper surface. Pinnae midribs purplish-brown contrasting strongly with lamina. Pinnules acutely pointed at tip, frequently lobed at base, sometimes with a thumb. Stipe long. Excellent garden plant. Rather similar and also in cultivation is *P. pseudomakinoi*; it differs in not being shiny.

P. manmeiense

Himalaya, H60–90cm (24–30in), E, Dry/Wet, Zone 8. Fronds lance-shaped, slightly glossy fresh green on upper surface, bipinnate. Pinnules ovate, crowded, overlapping especially towards tip on pinnae. Overall reminiscent of *P. setiferum,* but distinct.

P. mehrae

Himalaya, H15 × 2.5cm (6 × 1in), E, Dry/Wet, Zone 8. Often confused with *P. acanthophyllum.* Frond narrow oblong to narrow triangular, bipinnate, dark green, glossy. Rachis abundantly covered with mid-brown scales. Stipe short. New fronds red in spring. A beautiful small fern for rockwork or alpine house. In effect a dwarf version of *P. neolobatum,* except frond is not noticeably lance-shaped. Some plants in cultivation as *P. mehrae* are, I suspect, *P. neolobatum.*

P. mohroides

South America, H22–38 × 7cm (9–15 × 3in), E, Dry/Wet, Zone 6. Fronds lance-shaped, bipinnate. Pinnae narrowly triangular, acute-tipped. Rachis and stipe very scaly. There are two forms of this fern in cultivation. I grow the one described above; the North American plant is narrowly lance-shaped, pinnate to bipinnate. Pinnae short triangular, blunt-tipped, stipe short or absent. It is very reminiscent of, but distinct from, *P. lemmonii.*

P. monotis

East Asia, H30cm (12in), E, Dry/Wet, Zone 7. Fronds lance-shaped to narrowly triangular, dark glossy green, leathery, pinnate except for the base of the frond where

Polystichum lonchitis, here growing on a Scottish mountain, has pinnae that are conspicuously toothed.

a few pinnae have a detached 'thumb' at their base on their acroscopic side. Pinnae lobed. Similar to *P. xiphophyllum* except pinnae lobed and broader, making the frond altogether denser.

P. mucronifolium, syn. P. tacticopterum

Himalaya, H60–90cm (24–30in), E, Dry/Wet, Zone 7. Fronds lance-shaped, dark glossy green, bipinnate. Pinnules acute at base and tip; pinnules confluent towards tip of frond and tips of pinnae. Name is currently in doubt but Fraser Jenkins (1997) places it here until further research can be carried out.

P. munitum (western sword fern)

North-west America, H90cm (36in), E, Dry/Wet, Zone 6. Fronds pinnate, dark green, slightly lax and spreading, with a conspicuous auricle at the base of each pinna on the acroscopic side. One of the larger evergreen ferns and extremely useful in the garden. Forms a loose shuttlecock.

Crisp form Introduced into Europe by Judith Jones. Pinnae twisted. Fertile.

var. incisoserratum Possibly not in cultivation in Europe. Mid-frond pinnae deeply incised. Not constant, some years not in character.

P. neolobatum

Japan, H45cm (18in), E, Dry/Wet, Zone 7. Fronds lance-shaped, dark green, glossy, bipinnate – at least at base. Underside of frond pale green, but also shiny. Pinnules acute-angled at base and tip. Rachis and stipe covered with dark brown scales. Whole frond very tough and rough to the touch. A beautiful garden fern, ideal with its crown planted in the shelter of a rock or stump.

P. nepalense (Plate IX)

Himalaya, H30–45cm (12–18in), E, Dry/Wet, Zone 7. Fronds oblong, pinnate, pinnae not tapering to base of frond. Stipe is about a quarter the length of the lamina. Pinnae not conspicuously toothed and lacking an obvious 'thumb' on the acroscopic side at the base. Pinnae often crisped. Similar to European *P. lonchitis* but the above characters should separate the two species.

P. piceopaleaceum

Himalaya, H60cm (24in), E, Dry/Wet, Zone 7. Fronds lance-shaped, bipinnate, glossy yellow-green. Pinnules ovate, very few with a basal lobe or thumb, margins bristly.

P. polyblepharum

Japan, H45–60cm (18–24in), E, Dry/Wet, Zone 6. Fronds lance shaped, bipinnate, glossy, yellow-green and covered in golden bristles in spring, gradually turning deep

Polystichum prescottianum is a charming dwarf alpine fern.

green. Acroscopic pinnules enlarged into a 'thumb'. The golden-bristled croziers in spring are a beautiful feature; the tips are boat-shaped. Fronds spreading when mature. This species is becoming naturalized around at least one garden in Cornwall.

P. prescottianum
Himalaya, H10–25cm (4–10in), D, Dry/Wet, Zone 7. Fronds pinnatifid or nearly pinnate, narrowly lance-shaped, soft in texture. Pinnae deeply serrate with hair-like points. A charming little fern that did well for me in a well-drained rather rocky spot, but it did need some watering over summer. One of very few deciduous polystichums.

P. proliferum (mother shield fern)
Australia, H45–90cm (18–36in), E, Dry/Wet, Zone 8. Fronds lance-shaped, bipinnate (approaching tripinnate), dark green. One or a few proliferous buds produced near the tip of the frond. Pinnae narrowly triangular. A beautiful dark green fern, well suited to most gardens. Can produce massive rootstocks with age. Easily multiplied from the bulbils.

P. retrosopaleaceum
Japan, H60–75cm (24–30in), E, Dry/Wet, Zone 6. Fronds lance-shaped, bipinnate, glossy mid-green. Stipe long, covered with mid-brown scales. Superficially very

similar to *P. polyblepharum* but the pinnules are smaller and not conspicuously enlarged at the base of the pinna.

P. richardii
New Zealand, H30–60cm (12–24in), E, Dry/Wet, Zone 8. Fronds narrowly triangular to ovate, bipinnate, blue-green. Pinnae ovate, not deeply lobed, midrib purplish. Stipe scales entirely dark brown. Should do well in good light in a well-drained, sheltered site.

P. rigens
Japan, H38cm (15in), E, Dry/Wet, Zone 6. Fronds lance-shaped, bipinnate, tough, with pinnae tips sharply pointed. New foliage delightfully yellow tinted in spring. When mature, fronds are matt mid-green.

P. scopulinum
North-west North America, H12–30cm (5–12in), E, Dry/Wet, Zone 5. Fronds lance-shaped, pinnate-pinnatifid. Pinnae with 8–25 teeth either side (*P. kruckbergii*, an otherwise quite similar species, usually has 6). Good in a rocky area or in an alpine house.

P. semifertile
Himalaya, H30–45cm (12–18in), E, Dry/Wet, Zone 8. Fronds oblong-lanceolate, pale green, bipinnate. Pinnules with a prominent terminal spine. Rachis and stipe covered with pale brown hairs and scales. A lowish-altitude fern that has survived well in an unheated polytunnel for ten or so years. It would no doubt do well outside if tried.

P. setiferum, syn. *P. angulare* (soft shield fern)
Europe, including British Isles, H75–90cm (30–36in), E, Dry/Wet, Zone 5. Fronds lance-shaped, bipinnate, light green. Pinnae do not continue to the base of the frond, therefore there is a stipe. Distinguished from *P. aculeatum* by the angle at the base of the pinnule, where it is attached to the midrib, being more than 90 degrees. Fronds arching in the wild type but the cultivars differ widely in this respect.

Over 300 cultivars have been described; most are now lost to cultivation and many others not sufficiently distinct to warrant naming. Cultivars of *P. setiferum* were the special area of interest of the late Jimmy Dyce, the author of a specialist handbook on the subject (in press).
'Acrocladon' H38cm (15in). Found by Mrs Thompson in South Devon in 1858. Fronds oblong with a large forked, terminal crest, erect, dark green, bipinnate. Pinnae crested. Pinnules often acute at point of attachment to the midrib, hence often placed in *P. aculeatum*. Pinnules confluent towards tip of pinnae. Fertile. A selected form of 'Grandiceps'.

'Acutilobum' (Plate XII) H60–90cm (24–36in). Fronds sub-erect, lance-shaped, bipinnate, dark green, leathery. Pinnules mostly undivided although some towards the base of the frond have a single lobe or 'thumb'. All pinnules have an acute angle at point of attachment to the pinna midrib. Like 'Divisilobum' below, it is easy to place 'Acutilobum' as a cultivar of P. aculeatum by mistake. A very striking cultivar, not as widely grown as it deserves. I have never seen bulbils on true 'Acutilobum'.

'Broughton Mills' (Plate XII) H30cm (12in). Found by Reginald Kaye and Jimmy Dyce at Broughton Mills in the Lake District, about 1960. Fronds stiffly erect, ovate to triangular, congested. Ends of pinnae turn up and are slightly crisped. Pinnules ovate with bristles 1–2mm (1⁄16in) long at tips of teeth around distal margin. Contrary to some opinion this cultivar is not crested: it simply looks crested with the pinnae tips turned up. A very pretty cultivar, becoming rare. A type of 'Congestum'.

'Capitatum' Occasionally occurs in sowings. Large crest at tip of frond with pinnae uncrested.

'Carrugett' Found in Cornwall by G. Matthews and Bridget Graham in 1988. Fronds lance-shaped, bipinnate. Pinnules missing from basal part of lower pinnae, remaining pinnules narrowed and serrated. A type of 'Lineare'.

'Congestum' (Plate XIII) H15–25cm (6–10in). Fronds erect, triangular lance-shaped. Rachis short; pinnae overlapping. An excellent fern for the front of a border, or rockwork, or even in a trough. The form in cultivation is probably 'Congestum Padley' found by Padley in 1865 in South Devon. I grow another form that I found in Devon about 1980. It has narrowly lance-shaped fronds.

'Congestum Cristatum' H15–25cm (6–10in). Spore sowings of 'Congestum' frequently produce a small proportion of crested or ramose plants. The crests are not immediately obvious and do not add greatly to the beauty of basic 'Congestum'.

'Congestum Grandiceps' H15–25cm (6–10in). Tip of frond has a broad crest; pinnae crested. Pinnae and pinnules congested.

'Conspicuolobum' H60–75cm (24–30in). Lobe or 'thumb' at base of pinnule distinct as a separate lobe. Uncommon.

'Cristato-gracile Moly' H45cm (18in). Found by James Moly in South Devon in 1868. Fronds bipinnate, spreading, lance-shaped. Tips of frond and pinnae very lightly crested. Occasionally pinnae tips are slightly branched as well as slightly crested. Pinnules not crested but very bristly at tip giving the impression of gentle cresting. Pinnules and pinnae not overlapping. A very neat cultivar that could arguably be described as a crested 'Acutilobum'. Sporelings do not all come true; I have a range of plants that differ in detail – crests are bigger and fronds are branched.

'Cristato-pinnulum' (Plate XIII) H90cm (36in). Found by Dr Wills in Dorset in 1878. Fronds lance-shaped, bipinnate, pale green. Pinnules fan-shaped, not crested. Sparingly fertile. Occasionally produces bulbils, although my plants have not produced any for years. For a long time I called this cultivar 'Flabbeli-pinnulum' but it is clearly named 'Cristata-pinnula' (sic) in Jones Nature Prints (first published 1878, reprinted in part in Druery, 1910). Easy to grow and deserves to be more common.

'Cristatum' Several different crested cultivars are known. Each has a crest on the tip of the frond and on the pinnae. Only one named clone is believed to be in cultivation at present.

'Cristatum Mrs Thompson', syn. 'Thompsoniae' H38–60cm (15–24in). Found in north Devon in 1860 by Mrs Thompson. When young its fronds are ramose and crested; in middle age it produces many capitate fronds but once mature it reverts to a straight cristatum with pinnules the same shape as the species.

'Cruciato-pinnulum' H45–60cm (18–24in). Found in Dorset by James Moly in 1873. As the type plant except the tip of the frond is elongated with short cross-shaped pinnae. Not a beauty.

'Dahlem' H75cm (30in). Fronds narrowly triangular to lance-shaped, stiffish, held at around 30 degrees to the vertical, becoming tripinnate. Really a form of 'Divisilobum'. Plants in cultivation are usually sporelings and doubtfully resemble the original clone. This is a fairly new cultivar distributed from Dahlem in Germany. It may be completely new or it may be an old unidentified cultivar given a new name. It is certainly worth growing in its true form as the nearly erect evergreen foliage is a great asset in a fern bed.

'Divisilobum' (Plate XII) A number of cultivars of P. setiferum can be classed as 'Divisilobum'. This is a natural division, based on frond morphology, but over the years it rarely seems to have been understood and has often been confused with 'Multilobum', 'Plumoso-multilobum' and 'Plumoso-divisilobum'. I am indebted to the late Jimmy Dyce for his logical approach to this issue, which makes it possible to place any given cultivar into the correct category (see pp.42–43). However, it is still not easy to name all individual plants to a specific clone

PLATE XII
Polystichum setiferum I

'Broughton Mills'

'Grandidens'

'Multilobum'

'Acutilobum'

All fronds shown approximately half size

'Plumoso-
divisilobum'

'Plumoso-multilobum'

'Gracillimum
Cristulatum'

'Divisilobum'

'Divisilobum Laxum'

'Plumosum
Green'

within 'Divisilobum', hence it is convenient to refer to plants as 'Divisilobum' or Divisilobum Group. Named clones include:

'Divisilobum Allchin' H60cm (24in). Raised by Dr Allchin at Kew in the early 1850s. Fronds narrowly triangular to oblong-lanceolate, usually spreading, tripinnate. More leathery and darker green than the species. Pinnules and pinnulets narrow and acutely pointed. Certainly a cultivar of *P. setiferum* but having the appearance of cultivar of *P. aculeatum*. Over the years very many additional forms of 'Divisilobum' have been selected and named, in addition many plants originally named 'Proliferum' and 'Acutilobum' really belong here. Almost all forms have the ability to produce bulbils along the rachis. These will grow into new plants if laid down onto a suitable compost (see pp.176–177). Many plants can only be considered as Divisilobum Group but there are some distinct clones still in cultivation (see also 'Dahlem', 'Herrenhausen', 'Iveryanum' and 'Mrs Goffey'). Old forms can still be found in old gardens: I found a fine form in the garden at Langmoor Manor in Dorset, the old home of James Moly, possibly the most successful fern hunter in the Victorian period.

'Divisilobum Congestum' H30cm (12in). Raised by Philip Coke around 1975. Fronds short, broadly triangular, tripinnate, spreading. Pinnae crowded, triangular; pinnules long, giving congested form to frond, approaching 'Plumoso-divisilobum'. Copiously bulbiferous. A very neat cultivar.

'Divisilobum Crawfordianum' H38–60cm (15–24in). Found near Crawfordsburn, Northern Ireland in 1861 by a labourer. Fronds broad, ovate-lanceolate, bipinnate, not leathery. Pinnae also broad and overlapping. Proliferous. Plants in cultivation under this name occur from time to time but the original clone needs re-establishing. It was widely distributed and must surely be lurking in an old garden somewhere, but for the time being must be considered extinct: although Reginald Kaye in *Hardy Ferns* (1968) thought it was back in cultivation, I have never seen it.

'Divisilobum Laxum' *(Plate XII)* H60–90cm (24–36in). Frond triangular, tripinnate with pinnae, pinnules and pinnulets all well spaced from each other. The frond is very airy. Pinnules can be up to 3.5cm (1½in) long. A beautiful group of plants, unfortunately rarely bulbiferous. One clone raised by Vivien Green around 1980 is particularly good. It is virtually quadripinnate with the ultimate divisions slightly more leafy than usual.

Polystichum setiferum 'Divisilobum', found recently at Langmoor Manor, the former garden of James Moly.

I have named this 'Vivien Green'.

'Divisilobum Ramo-pinnatum' H60–90cm (24–36in). Pinnae branched, particularly in mid-part of frond.

'Divisilobum Ramosum' H60cm (24in). Tip of frond repeatedly branched. Quite distinct from 'Iveryanum' (see below).

'Divisilobum Trilobum', syn. 'Caput Trifidum', 'Ramulosum' *(Plate XIII)* H45–60cm (18–24in). Reintroduced from North America by Judith Jones in about 1990. Almost certainly an old British cultivar, perhaps taken to Canada by Joseph Wiper around 1900 (see *Polypodium australe* 'Grandiceps Parker'). Fronds triangular or oblong, bipinnate to tripinnate, branching near tip, often into three large heads. Pinnae bifid or flat crested. Abundantly bulbiferous.

'Divisilobum Wollaston' Found in a Devon hedgebank in 1852 by G. Wollaston. Fronds spreading, triangular, very neatly tripinnately divided. Usually sparingly proliferous. Plants under this name are common in cultivation but I am unsure how many are true: they are often sporelings which would probably be better named as Divisilobum Group.

'Nick Hards' (Divisilobum Group) H60–75cm (24–30in). Found by Nick Hards in Gloucestershire in 1978. Fronds lance-shaped, tripinnate, mid-green, fairly leathery. Pinnae, pinnules and pinnulets not overlapping. Pinnulets are particularly widely spaced along the pinnule. Probably the best recent wild find in Divisilobum Group.

'Eaves Wood' H15–25cm (6–10in). Found by Reginald Kaye pre-1985, this is a brachiatum-cristatum cultivar. Basal pair of pinnae greatly elongated, often equalling the length of the rest of the lamina. All other pinnae normal size. All tips crested. There were several nineteenth-century finds of this cultivar. I believe all are now extinct.

'Foliosum Walton' *(Plate XIII)* H38–60cm (15–24in). Raised by Walton about 1913. Fronds narrowly triangular, bipinnate, crispy, pale green. Pinnules have serrated margins, they are expanded, overlapping each other, and papery. Fertile. A fine foliose form.

Polystichum setiferum 'Grandiceps', sometimes thought to be a cultivar of P. aculeatum.

'Gracillimum' H45–60cm (18–24in). Raised from 'Plumosum Bevis' around 1905. Fronds lance-shaped, bipinnate, lax, spreading, darkish green. Pinnules slender and elongated, distant along the pinna midrib. Tips of pinnae and pinnules look a little cristulate but in reality there is usually only an uncrested tuft of foliage. Very rare, very beautiful. Sterile. Can be a bit delicate if not well cared for; however, I have seen this well established in a few gardens for 40 or 50 years. The stipe is often weak, allowing the fronds to rest on the soil; in a pot the fronds often hang down. Side crowns are very rarely produced. Propagated from spores of 'Plumosum Bevis' when available, or by tissue culture. See 'Green Lace'.

'Gracillimum Cristulatum' *(Plate XII)* H45cm (18in). Extremely rare form that has occurred with 'Gracillimum'. The tassels at the end of the pinnules are more pronounced and the whole frond is more feathery.

'Grandiceps' H38cm (15in). Fronds erect. First found as 'Grandiceps Talbot' in 1861 in Eire. Fronds narrow, oblong with a large terminal, polydactylous crest. Pinnae gently crested. Pinnules acutely angled at base, reminiscent of *P. aculeatum*.

'Grandidens' *(Plate XII)* H60cm (24in). Fronds nearly

Polystichum setiferum 'Mrs Goffey' – a distinct form approaching 'Plumoso-divisilobum'.

erect, lance-shaped, bipinnate, always depauperate lacking occasional pinnae and pinnules. Tip often truncate. Margins of pinnules deeply serrated. I include 'Truncatum' here. Despite its depauperations, this is a pretty fern. Rare in cultivation but deserves to be more widely grown. I found my plants wild in Devon in the 1970s.

'Green Lace' H60cm (24in). Raised from spores of 'Plumosum Bevis' in Holland by Cor van de Moesdijk around 1987. Very similar to 'Gracillimum' but more robust and with more finely cut pinnule sections. Cor raised quite a few plants of 'Gracillimum'. 'Green Lace' was selected for tissue culture on the basis that it was a much more robust form than all the others. Like 'Gracillimum', it is sterile.

'Herrenhausen' H60–75cm (24–30in). Fronds spreading, triangular to lance-shaped, tripinnate. More leathery and darker green than the species. Like 'Dahlem', a recent introduction from Germany that may actually be a long-lost older cultivar. It seems to come true from spores more commonly than many other cultivars of *P. setiferum* but, nevertheless, not all plants are correctly named.

'Hirondelle' H60cm (24in). Found by Moly in Dorset about 1870, although some sources attribute the find to Wills. Fronds lance-shaped, bipinnate, pinnules narrowed with a narrow lobe pointing down the pinna parallel to the pinna midrib. Pinnae viewed as pairs, either side of the midrib, can be likened to the silhouette of a swallow, hence 'Hirondelle', which is French for swallow. This cultivar is now extinct but I found a very similar form at Chardstock in Devon in 1980. I call this 'Chardstock'. The sori are usually visible from above the plant as they are wider than the pinnulet.

'Iveryanum', syn. 'Divisilobum Cristatum Ivery' *(Plate XIII)* H60–75cm (24–30in). Raised in 1870 by Messrs. Ivery. Fronds spreading, triangular to lance-shaped, more leathery and darker green than the species. Neatly tripinnate, crested at tip of frond and pinnae. Often proliferous. Comes more or less true from spores. Many crested forms of 'Divisilobum' are safely placed here.

'Leinthall Starkes' *(Plate XIII)* Raised by me about 1980 from a wild form found in Devon. Fronds lance-shaped, tripinnate, pale green, not leathery. Pinnae overlap but pinnules are spaced out. The frond has a feathery, airy appearance due to the lower-half frond pinnulets being leafy, pointed, and ending in a bristle, and the abundantly soriferous sporing pinnulets on the upper half of frond being noticeably narrowed. A beautiful fern, one of the best I have been lucky enough to raise. So far all spore-lings have been plants of comparable quality. Jimmy Dyce commented that the pinnules were sickle-shaped (falcate) curving towards the tip of the pinna, as in 'Pulcherrimum', but we agreed it would probably best be classified in the Plumosum Group.

'Lineare', syn. 'Confluens' H60cm (24in). Found several times in the wild in the 1870s. Fronds bipinnate, lance-shaped, pale green, slightly leathery. Pinnules linear, and widely spaced. Pinnules confluent at tip of pinnae. A pretty, airy little cultivar. 'Hirondelle' is similar.

'Manica-infantis' H45cm (18in). Found in Devon by Moly. Fronds lance-shaped, dark green. Pinnules reduced in size, said to resemble the outline of a child's mitten.

'Mrs Goffey' H45cm (18in). Introduced by Reginald Kaye, but I believe the plant was brought to him by a Mrs Goffey. Fronds triangular to ovate, tripinnate, spreading, pale to mid-green. Pinnule segments extremely narrow and delicate in appearance, narrower than in 'Divisilobum'. Here the frond is dense and approaches 'Plumoso-divisilobum'. In the 1960s this was changing hands for £50. It does produce occasional bulbils and, while still rare, is in quite a few collections and would be unlikely to reach £50 today.

'Multilobum' *(Plate XII)* H75–90cm (30–36in). Found in Devon by Robert Gray in 1865. Fronds nearly erect, tripinnate, narrowly triangular or lance-shaped, light green. Usually abundantly proliferous. Pinnulets resemble small versions of the pinnules of the species; in fact, apart from being once more divided, 'Multilobum' is much like the species, whereas in the Divisilobum Group pinnules and pinnulets are narrow and acutely pointed. Decompositum is another group of cultivars so similar to 'Multilobum' that I have included it here. There are many minor forms, one worthy of a name.

'Coke's Foliose' (Multilobum Group) H90cm (36in). Raised by Philip Coke in the 1970s. Fronds triangular, near erect, tripinnate, not leathery. Pinnae triangular; pinnules long with ultimate segments broad, giving foliose character. Very close to 'Plumoso-multilobum'.

'Percristatum' H60–90cm (24–36in). Frond tip, pinnae and pinnules crested.

'Perserratum' *(Plate XIII)* H60–90cm (24–36in). First found by Wollaston in South Devon in 1869. Thought to be extinct until re-found by N. Schroder in Sussex in 1972. Frond lance-shaped, bipinnate – or tripinnate at

The densely feathery fronds of *Polystichum setiferum* 'Plumoso-divisilobum Baldwinii' progeny have delicately cut pinnules.

base of pinnae – dark green, glossy, not leathery. Pinnules deeply serrated, with tips of serrations elongated into prominent bristles. A very pretty, somewhat feathery fern. Fertile, comes true from spores.

'Plumoso-divisilobum' *(Plate XII)* H50–75cm (20–30in). Fronds triangular, quadripinnate, not leathery, light green, very feathery. Divisions of pinnulets narrow, acutely angled at their point of attachment to the midrib, as in 'Divisilobum', hence 'Plumoso-divisilobum'. Fronds not usually as dense as 'Plumoso multilobum' (below). The ultimate divisions being narrower give the fern a more airy appearance. There are several selected clones; all are very rare, but all are occasionally proliferous, however, and it is not unknown for bulbils to sport and give new forms.

'Plumoso-divisilobum Baldwinii' Raised by Jones and Fox but given to Baldwin as a young plant in 1878. Frond triangular, quadripinnate, not leathery, foliage dense like 'Plumoso-multilobum' but more feathery. The original is extinct but there are plants in cultivation that appear to be this cultivar. This was considered the best of all the Plumoso-divisilobums.

'Plumoso-divisilobum Bland', syn. 'Divisilobum Bland' H60cm (24in). Found by Bland near Belfast in Northern Ireland around 1910. Fronds quadripinnate at base with pinnae overlapping strongly, tripinnate at top with pinnae not overlapping. This is considered the best wild find in the Divisilobum or Plumoso-divisilobum Groups.

'Plumoso-divisilobum Deltoideum' H60cm (24in). Fronds strongly triangular, the width across the basal pair of pinnae often greater than the length of the lamina. Raised by Dr Stansfield in the 1920s, still in cultivation but very rare. For those uncomfortable with Latin cultivar names this is as bad as it gets!

'Plumoso-divisilobum Esplan' H60cm (24in). Origin obscure, but possibly raised by Jones and Fox. Like 'Plumoso-multilobum' but ultimate divisions are acutely angled at point of attachment to the midrib. Characteristically all the fronds curve slightly in the same direction, reminiscent of a starfish, giving an illusion of movement.

'Plumoso-multilobum', syn. 'Plumoso-densum', 'Densum' *(Plate XII)* H35cm (14in). Raised by Jones and Fox in 1878. Fronds quadripinnate, triangular, not leathery, light green. Divisions of pinnulets are not acutely angled at their point of attachment to the midrib, and resemble very small versions of the pinnules of the species – as in 'Multilobum' – hence 'Plumoso-multi-

The densely feathery *Polystichum setiferum* 'Plumoso-multilobum' is almost like a small conifer.

lobum'. Bulbiferous when well grown. All parts are highly developed, pinnae overlap each other as do the pinnules, creating a dense, multi-tiered frond. A real beauty which virtually always comes true from spores. It is hard to believe that this fern is a cultivar of *P. setiferum*. The name 'Plumoso-multilobum' is possibly unacceptable as it may not have been coined until after 1959. However, it is a helpful name, advocated by Jimmy Dyce.

Plumosum Group A diverse group of cultivars united by their feathery form and the almost total lack of sporangia, although in exceptional circumstances at least one form ('Plumosum Bevis') can produce spores.

'Plumosum Bevis', syn. *P. aculeatum* 'Pulcherrimum Bevis', *P. setiferum* 'Pulcherrimum Bevis' H60–120cm (24–48in). Found in Devon by 'Jno.' Bevis in 1876. Fronds lance-shaped, bipinnate, darkish green, tapering to an almost plaited tip. Pinnules narrow, tapering to an acute angle at point of attachment to the midrib. Usually lacks spores. Bevis was employed to cut the hedgebanks. He noticed this plant was different and took it along to local fern man Dr Wills who immediately confirmed its importance and named it after its finder. This cultivar is now one of the most prized in collections. For many years the plant was thought to be a cultivar of *P. aculeatum*, but in the 1930s Stansfield started to doubt this, and subsequent chromosome counts have confirmed it to be a cultivar of *P. setiferum*. Soon after its discovery, Wollaston realised it was in fact a plumosum, not a pulcherrimum (see below). Despite its age, this plant is widely grown – the rootstock splits freely into separate crowns, allowing frequent division, but never freely enough for it to be mass-produced by nurserymen, so it remains a collector's fern. It is easy to grow in a well-drained situation.

'Plumosum Drueryi', syn. 'Pulcherrimum Drueryi' H60–110cm (24–42in). Raised by C.T. Druery around 1900. Sterile. The plant superficially resembles 'Plumosum Bevis' but the pinnules are themselves pinnatifidly divided making it more feathery and even more beautiful. It is very rare and in very few collections. Unlike 'Plumosum Bevis' side crowns are produced only slowly from the rootstock. This plant was raised from the first batch of spores discovered on the normally sterile 'Plumosum Bevis'.

'Plumosum Green' *(Plate XII)* H45–60cm (18–24in). Raised from 'Plumosum Bevis' by C.B. Green around 1900. Fronds spreading, lance-shaped to triangular, tri- or quadripinnate, pale green. Sterile. The pinnule sections are slender and acutely angled at their bases. I am not alone in thinking this is the most beautiful hardy

Polystichum setiferum 'Plumosum Bevis', the parent of several classic cultivars.

fern. The first spores discovered on 'Plumosum Bevis' were found on Green's plant. Druery sowed some and Green the rest. As mentioned above, Druery raised several 'Plumosum Drueryi' among his sporelings, while Green produced this cultivar as a single plant! I believe it is, in fact, a hybrid between a 'Divisilobum' plant and 'Plumosum Bevis' as it has never been re-raised since. Green's single plant is still in cultivation and has the unenviable distinction of being probably the rarest surviving fern cultivar. It has been multiplied over the years by splitting the crown, and very rarely from bulbils, but it is probably currently in fewer than a dozen collections. Not difficult to grow in a well-drained site.

Recently one or two plants reminiscent of 'Plumosum Green' turned up in a batch of 'Gracillimum' plants that had been tissue cultured. How this could happen is a mystery and does call into question my conjecture above that 'Plumosum Green' is a hybrid.

'Plumosum Kaye' *(Plate XIII)* H90cm (36in). Raised by Kaye at his nursery in Silverdale. Similar to 'Plumosum Moly' but less foliose; the pinnulets do not overlap. Fertile. A beauty that should be more widely grown.

'Plumosum Moly', syn. 'Plumosum Grande Moly' H1–1.2m (3–4ft). Found in Dorset by James Moly around 1870. Fronds lance-shaped, tripinnate, foliose, sterile. Pinnae overlapping, pinnules overlapping and greatly expanded and divided into broad, leafy, overlapping pinnulets. A large, dramatic fern. Slow to produce side crowns and, therefore, very rare in collections.

'Proliferum' A frequently used name which is now defunct as so many forms of *P. setiferum* are proliferous.

'Pulcherrimum' H45–60cm (18–24in). Found several times around 1870, but not since. Now extinct as a group apart from 'Moly's Green' (below) Typically the tips of the pinnules are greatly elongated. A very beautiful form, but difficult to grow and with a tendency to revert to normal. Sterile. Should be looked for wherever the species is common.

'Pulcherrimum Moly's Green' H60cm (24in). Found by James Moly along the Devon/Dorset borders around 1870. Fronds lance-shaped, bipinnate, dark green, pinnules sometimes producing an elongated sickle-shaped (falcate) tip; very often only one or two pinnae on a plant are in character, but occasionally a whole frond or whole plant may perform. When not in character, this cultivar is still easily recognized by its stumpy, sickle-shaped pinnules. A form of true pulcherrimum. Rare but in a few collections.

PLATE XIII
Polystichum setiferum 2

'Iveryanum'

'Smith's
Cruciate'

'Perserratum'

Cruciatum Group

'Foliosum Walton'

'Cristato-pinnulum'

'Divisilobum
Trilobum'

'Plumosum Kayc'

'Leinthall Starkes'

Congestum'

*All fronds shown
approximately half size*

Polystichum setiferum 'Rotundatum Phillips' is a beautiful form with rounded pinnules.

'Ramo-pinnatum' H45–60cm (18–30in). Pinnae branch near tip. Tip of frond usually uncrested. Not a great beauty.

Ramosum Group H30–45cm (12–18in). A group of cultivars whose fronds branch several times along their length but do not crest at tips. This sounds unexciting but, in practice, the best are first-class garden plants. The continuous branching of the fronds means they get broader with height, hence the plant is ball-shaped, rather than the usual open shuttlecock.

'Revolvens' H60cm (24in). First found by Dr Wills in Somerset in 1872. Pinnae rolled back forming a partial tube the length of the frond. Probably extinct. I found the same fern in the Wye Valley, Wales in about 1985, but unfortunately it died. A different form, where the pinnules are rolled back forming a partial tube along the length of the pinnae, was found in E.J. Lowe's garden. This form is in cultivation as 'Revolvens Lowe'.

'Rotundatum Phillips' H30–45cm (12–18in). Found by W.H. Phillips in Northern Ireland in 1877. Fronds lance-shaped, lamina tapering to tip and narrowed towards base, bipinnate. Pinnules round. A remarkable, graceful plant, sadly rare in cultivation. It comes true from spores. (Maintaining the family tradition, Phillips' great-grandson, Patrick, is planting a large fernery at Kentwell Hall near Long Milford, Suffolk.)

Rotundilobum Group H30–60cm (18–24in). A range of cultivars all with rounded pinnules but differing from 'Rotundatum Phillips' by always being slightly irregular with blunt pinnae tips and, usually, heavy cresting and normally bulbiferous. Pinnules serrate.

'Smith's Cruciate', syn. 'Ray Smith' *(Plate XIII)* H45–60cm (18–24in). Discovered in a garden by Ray Smith around 1986. Fronds tripinnate, cross-shaped (cruciate), narrow: a cruciate divisilobum. Fertile and bulbiferous. No reference to it has been found in the old literature: thus, it is named in honour of the finder here.

'Tripinnatum' H60–90cm (24–36in). Common in the wild – simply a tripinnate (pinnules cut into pinnulets) form of the normal species. Well-grown plants often develop the tripinnate character. Referred to as 'tripe' by some fern lovers!

'Wakeleyanum' H60cm (24in). Found by a navvy named Russell working on the railway near Axminster in 1860. He donated it to a Miss Wakeley. Fronds oblong lance-shaped, bipinnate, cross-shaped (cruciate), at least in mid-part of frond. The pinnae fork into two equal parts at the point of attachment to the rachis, giving the appearance of a series of crosses along the rachis (see also *Athyrium filix-femina* 'Cruciatum'). A rare form that is not usually in good character until a few years old. The original clone probably no longer exists but it comes fairly true from spores as Cruciatum Group *(Plate XIII)*.

P. setigerum, syn. *P. alaskense*
North-west America, H45–60cm (18–24in), E, Dry/Wet, Zone 6. Fronds lance-shaped, bipinnate, mid-green. Pinnules hairy, less prominently stalked than *P. braunii*. Basal acroscopic pinnule enlarged as a 'thumb' (not so in *P. braunii*). Differs from the also similar *P. andersonii* by lacking proliferous buds towards tip of rachis. Another useful garden plant if available.

P. silvaticum, syn. *P. sylvaticum*
New Zealand, H30–45cm (12–18in), E, Dry/Wet, Zone 9. Fronds lance-shaped, bipinnate-pinnatifid, blue-green. Pinnae narrowly triangular with a drawn-out tip. Pinnae and pinnules quite distant giving frond an airy, elegant appearance. Sori have no indusium. In nature a plant of dark forests, best cultivated in a shady, sheltered corner.

P. squarrosum
Himalaya, east Asia, H60–75cm (24–30in), E, Dry/Wet, Zone 7. Fronds lance-shaped, glossy dark green on upper surface, bipinnate to sometimes tripinnate. Pinnules conspicuously pointed at tip. Stipe is a quarter the length of frond. Stipe, rachis and pinnae midribs covered with dark

brown scales. Underside of lamina thinly covered with pale brown hairs. A beautiful fern all year round with the added bonus of bright red fronds in spring.

P. stenophyllum
Himalaya, China, H10–30 × 2.5cm (4–12 × 1in), E, Dry/Wet, Zone 6. Fronds very narrow, leathery, oblong, pinnate, with a proliferous bud near the tip on the rachis. Pinnae short rhomboid to ovate. Whole frond has a slightly pinkish hue. The very similar *P. craspedosorum*, from Japan and China, differs in not having a 'thumb' at the base of each pinnae on the acroscopic side.

P. thompsonii
Himalaya, China, Taiwan, H7–20 × 2.5–3.5cm (3–8 × 1–1½in), D, Dry/Wet, Zone 7. Fronds bipinnatifid, narrowly lance-shaped, mid-green. Pinnae bristly and serrate. An unusual deciduous polystichum (see also *P. prescottianum*, p.146).

P. transkeiense
South Africa, Zimbabwe, H60cm (24in), E, Dry/Wet, Zone 8. Fronds broad ovate, bipinnate, slightly glossy dark green. Pinnules ovate shallowly toothed. Stipe long. Rhizomes shortly creeping. My material originated from the Vumba Mountains in Zimbabwe and has thrived outdoors here for about 15 years.

P. tripteron
China, Japan, H30–60cm (18–24in), E, Dry/Wet, Zone 7. Fronds slightly glossy, pinnate, with basal pair of pinnae greatly elongated and pinnate, the whole frond shaped like a dagger (see also *P. hancockii*, which is smaller with shorter basal pinnae). Pinnules narrowly triangular with a sharp-pointed apex.

P. tsus-simense
Korea, China, Japan, Taiwan, H30cm (12in), E, Dry/Wet, Zone 7. Fronds bi- to tripinnate at base of larger pinnae, triangular to broadly lance-shaped, dark dull green, leathery. Pinnae narrow drawn out into a long acutely pointed tip. Pinnule and pinnae sharply pointed. Scales on rachis and stipe black. Forms a small clump. Very pretty and neat. Similar to *P. luctuosum* but the fronds are more finely divided and the pinnae are distant.

P. vestitum
New Zealand, H30–90cm (12–36in), E, Dry/Wet, Zone 8. Fronds lance-shaped, bipinnate, dark green and glossy on upper surface. Pinnae well spaced, not overlapping. Pinnules ovate, small, quite crowded on the pinna midrib. Rachis abundantly covered with brown scales. Stipe a quarter the length of frond. A beautiful fern that does well in central England. In the mild, wet climate of

north-west Scotland at Inverewe Gardens it flourishes, with fronds up to 90cm (36in) tall.

P. wilsonii
Himalaya, H30–40cm (12–15in), D, Dry/Wet, Zone 8. Fronds erect, oblong, bipinnate, pale green, rachis covered with pale scales. Croziers very scaly. Unusual and very attractive.

P. xiphophyllum
China, H30–45 × 7–10cm (12–18 × 3–4in), E, Dry/Wet, Zone 7. Fronds lance-shaped, mostly pinnate, dark glossy green. Pinnae slender, entire apart from detached 'thumb' on acroscopic side at base.

P. yunnanense
Himalaya, China, H60–90cm (24–36in), E, Dry/Wet, Zone 7. Fronds narrowly triangular, glossy dark green, bipinnate-pinnatifid. Pinnae quite widely spaced. Pinnules deeply serrated, almost pinnate. Stipe has two types of mid-brown scales and is a third the length of lamina. A very robust grower surviving neglect with style. Even in wet clay this has luxuriated.

PSEUDOPHEGOPTERIS

There are two or three rather similar species in this genus from the Himalayas, all probably hardy in zone 7.

P. levingei, syn. *Leptogramme levingei (Plate IX)*
Himalaya, H30–45cm (12–18in), D, Wet/Dry, Zone 8, possibly 7. Fronds lance-shaped, bipinnate, with pinnules roundly lobed. Pale green, copiously covered with hairs. Rhizomes creeping, potentially invasive but sufficiently attractive to be forgiven.

PTERIDIUM

Bracken (*Pteridium aquilinum*) can get very tall. It is a straggly plant and very invasive with only very limited use in large estates where landscaping is necessary.

P. aquilinum (bracken)
Northern hemisphere, including British Isles, H to 4m (12ft), D, Dry/Wet, Zone 4. Fronds broadly lance-shaped tripinnate. Stipe long. Rhizomes creeping several centimetres underground. Very invasive in acid or neutral soil, and known to be carcinogenic. Not a garden plant but sporelings of bracken often appear in spore sowings. The North American form, which also occurs in northern Europe, is slightly shorter and called var. *latiusculum*, syn. *P. latiusculum*. Purists may like to grow the cultivars.

'Cristatum' Really a percristatum as pinnules, pinnae and frond tip are crested. There is a garden in Kendal in the Lake District where this fern has taken over – it has to be mown to stop it invading the lawn.

'Grandiceps' A sporeling of 'Cristatum' with much heavier crests. Slightly depauperate and nowhere near as invasive as the type. Worth growing as a curiosity but rare.

PTERIS

A genus of mainly subtropical ferns with a few species hardy in zone 9 or 8.

P. cretica (ribbon fern)

Worldwide in tropical and warm temperate regions, including, rarely, on sheltered walls as an escapee from cultivation in British Isles, H15–60cm (6–24in), D in cold areas, Dry/Wet, Zone 9, possibly 8. Fronds usually pinnate with simple linear pinnae; in larger plants some pinnules are produced, particularly on the lower pinnae. A distinctive fern often offered as a houseplant. Many cultivars have been described. Collections from high altitudes, particularly in the Himalayan region have survived several winters outside in central England, but they are not reliable.

P. wallichiana

Himalaya to Taiwan, Samoa, H1–1.5m (3–5ft), D, Wet/Dry, Zone 8. Fronds erect with horizontal and fan-shaped (pedate) lamina. The fan area is usually split into 7 radiating pinnae: each pinna is pinnate-pinnatifid. Rhizomes thick, creeping. This is effectively the Himalayan bracken. It is a magnificent plant that luxuriates in the mild zone 9 climate of far south-west England. In central England it survives but rarely exceeds 60cm (24in) in height. The rhizome seems to be tasty to a boring mammal, causing death to some of my plants. Acid or neutral soil preferred.

PYRROSIA

A medium-sized genus, closely related to *Polypodium*. Fronds are normally strap-shaped and leathery. They are usually epiphytic with their creeping rhizomes growing over the surface of tree or tree fern trunks.

P. eleagnifolia, syn. *P. serpens*

New Zealand, Australia, H2.5–5cm (1–2in), E, Dry/Wet, Zone 9. Fronds simple, unbranched, round to ovate on a short stipe. Fertile fronds larger, up to 7cm (3in), narrower and more oblong. Sori arranged in two rows along the fertile pinnae. Dark fleshy green above but silvery below due to the abundance of hairs. A wonderful fern that does very well at Logan Botanic Gardens in southwest Scotland growing on the trunks of *Dicksonia antarc-*

Pyrrosia polydactylis (left) and *P. sheareri (right)* are two epiphytic ferns from Taiwan.

Plants of *Sadleria cyatheoides* can produce short trunks. This specimen is in the garden at Leinthall Starkes, Herefordshire.

tica. It survives in my unheated polytunnel on a dead tree fern trunk, but seems to prefer a warmer, moist climate.

P. lingua (tongue fern)

Eastern Asia, H7–15cm (3–6in), E, Dry/Wet, Zone 9. Fronds entire, lance-shaped with an acute tip, unbranched. Upper surface dark green, underside pale brown. I have never grown this fern but it is a good candidate for hanging baskets. It may be able to survive outdoors in central England (zone 8), but it would probably be safer to bring it inside over winter. There are several cultivars with forked or lacerated fronds.

P. polydactylis

Taiwan, H7–15cm (3–6in), E, Dry/Wet, Zone 9. Fronds palmately forked, with the lamina continuous between each section. Green above, silvery beneath due to the thick covering of hairs. Sori numerous and small, scattered over the undersurface. This has survived several years in my unheated polytunnel. Best grown as an epiphyte.

P. sheareri

Taiwan, China, H7–15cm (3–6in) but larger in wild, E, Dry/Wet, Zone 9. Fronds simple, unbranched. Under-sides covered with brown hairs. A most attractive species that has survived in my unheated polytunnel for many years now. Much admired for its colour at successive Chelsea Flower Shows.

RUMOHRA

A small genus of one or two species from the southern hemisphere.

R. adiantiformis (leather leaf)

South Africa, Australasia, H30–90cm (12–36in), E, Dry/Wet, Zone 9, possibly 8. Fronds triangular, bi-pinnate-pinnatifid, shiny dark green, very leathery. Rhizomes thick, creeping. Can grow on the ground or on rocks or trees. This is the fern widely sold by florists as long-lasting greenery – it is grown commercially in Florida. It has survived outdoors here for two winters on the trunk of *Dicksonia antarctica*, on which it was imported. Plants I have seen in Australia have always been smaller than South African material. It would be interesting to grow them both side by side.

SADLERIA

A small genus of ferns confined to Hawaii, closely related to the blechnums. Can form sizeable trunks; new foliage often reddish.

S. cyatheoides

Hawaii, H90cm (36in) or more, E, Wet/Dry, Zone 9, possibly 8. Fronds pinnate, glossy, often pinkish when young. Very handsome, forms a trunk with age. I over-wintered a specimen with a 15cm (6in) trunk for several years protected alongside some tree ferns – the red fronds in spring were spectacular. Younger plants seem much more difficult to overwinter as they do not like damp, stagnant air.

SELAGINELLA

A huge genus of very pretty fern allies. Very unfern-like, often mistaken for a moss. Small, entire leaves are arranged in rows along midrib. Two kinds of spores are produced. Many species would be worth growing but few hardy species seem to be in cultivation in Europe. Richard Rush (1984) gives quite a few additional species from Asia and North America that would probably be hardy in zone 8, but I have never grown them and they seem to be too rare in cultivation to describe here.

Selaginella kraussiana makes a useful mossy ground cover in sheltered sites.

S. apoda

North America, Berlin, H2.5cm (1in), Wet/Dry, Zone 6. Fully frost hardy. Plant mat-forming. Superficially rather similar to *S. kraussiana*, but leafy stems only 3–3.5mm (⅛in) wide.

S. denticulata

Europe, H less than 2.5cm (1in), Sporing spikes 2cm (¾in), Wet/Dry, Zone 8. Mat-forming with sterile leaves of two distinct types. Stems plus leaves about 5mm (¼in) wide, branching. Sporing spikes are stemless. Died out quickly with me, perhaps too dry, too cold or too neglected!

S. helvetica

Europe, H less than 2.5cm (1in), Sporing spikes 5cm (2in), E, Wet/Dry, Zone 7. Mat-forming with sterile leaves of two distinct types. Darkish green, stems plus leaves about 5mm (¼in) wide, branching. Sporing spikes on an erect stem. Native to damp, acid rocks. I have failed to keep this alive for long but it is reported hardy in Britain by S. Czeladzinski.

S. involvens (tree spike-moss)

East Asia, H15–25cm (6–10in), E, Wet/Dry, Zone 6. Stems erect, much branched into a ferny frond shape, all the branches covered with tiny leaves. Spreads by an underground rhizome. I grew a plant under this name for a few years, but I suspect it may have been *S. sinensis*. It died right back every year and was late reappearing in the summer, but was fully frost hardy. I eventually lost it through drought.

S. kraussiana

Africa, H2.5–5cm (1–2in), E, Wet/Dry, Zone 6. Ground cover. Pale green leafy stems about 5mm (¼in) wide, branch repeatedly to create an attractive carpet. Sterile leaves of two distinct types. There are many cultivars of *S. kraussiana*, some coloured, which are often available at garden centres. I have not grown them but I expect them to be as hardy as the type.

'Aurea' Leaves golden-yellow and more compact than the type. Fully frost hardy.

'Brownii' Leaves pale green, forming compact, dome-shaped clumps.

'Poulteri' Not remarkable, a rather more straggly form of *S. kraussiana* of garden origin.

'Variegata' Leaves variegated creamy-white. Fully frost hardy.

S. oregana (Oregon spike-moss)

North-west USA, H10cm (4in), E, Dry/Wet (high humidity), Zone 6. Fully frost hardy. Plants often form

Thelypteris japonica, doing well in the shade of a yew tree on clay at Kyre Park.

festoons rather like some of the bromeliad airplants. Can form a loose, creeping mat with the stem tips upturned.

S. peruviana (Peruvian spike-moss)
South-western USA to Peru, H2.5–5cm (1–2cm), E, Dry/Wet, Zone 6. Fully frost hardy. Mat-forming with sterile leaves all alike. Branch tips curl up when dry.

S. rupestris (rock spike-moss)
Eastern North America to Newfoundland, H2–4cm (¾–1½in), Dry/Wet, Zone 3. Forms grey-green flat mats of sterile leaves that are all alike. Rather compact, not easily fragmented. Very attractive on rocks in the wild; could be good in a rock garden.

S. sinensis
Manchuria, China, H10cm (4in), D, Wet/Dry, Zone 7. Fully frost hardy. Sometimes confused with *S. involvens*. A very attractive plant, one of few frondose selaginellas suitable for colder gardens.

S. tamariscina
Asia, H12cm (5in), E, Wet/Dry, Zone 7. Rosette-forming species. Fronds dark green. Stem short, upright; fronds crowded on stem, much branched, slightly curved upwards to collectively form a leafy cup-like shape. 'Probably hardy', Richard Rush, 1984.

SPHENOMERIS

A medium-sized genus mainly found in the tropics. At least one species is worth trying.

S. chinensis
East Asia, H30cm (12in), D, Dry/Wet, Zone 9. Delicately divided, tripinnatifid fronds, ultimate segments fan-shaped. Ideal for a cold greenhouse or warmer garden. 'Perhaps hardy', Richard Rush, 1984. Certainly undamaged in my unheated polytunnels for several winters.

STEGNOGRAMMA

For many years included in the genus *Thelypteris*.

S. pozoi
South-west Europe, Africa, H30–60cm (18–24in), E, Wet/Dry, Zone 8. Fronds ovate-lanceolate, pinnate or pinnate-pinnatifid with pinnae divided about halfway to the midrib, pale green on a moderately long stipe. Stipe, rachis and both sides of pinnae hairy. Fronds have been described as erect in some floras, but whenever I have seen them in the wild in France and Spain or in cultivation here for many years, they have been prostrate or even pendent. I grow this in a shady, very sheltered spot at the base of a rockery. Initially I protected it with straw over winter but eventually neglect demonstrated this was unnecessary.

STICHERUS

A genus of climbing ferns closely related to *Gleichenia* (see for general tips on cultivation), but not forming a thicket in the same way. A bank covered with a colony of any fern in the genus is extremely attractive with the palmate fronds hanging down like lop-sided umbrellas to form a discontinuous sheet. The related *S. cunninghamii* from New Zealand is called the umbrella fern.

S. urceolatus, syn. *S. tener* (silky fan fern)
Australia, H30–60cm (18–24in), W, Wet/Dry, Zone 8. Fronds palmate with the rachis forking 2 or 3 times to produce 4 or 8 pinnae. Each pinna is deeply pinnatifid. Rhizomes creeping. So far with me, this is proving tolerant of my unheated fern house. It should also succeed outdoors here given some overwinter protection.

THELYPTERIS

Until a few years ago this genus contained hundreds of species. Recent investigation has, however, removed most to several newly created genera.

T. confluens
Southern hemisphere, H60cm (24in), D, Wet/Dry,

Todea barbara showing typical spore production on the bottom section of each pinna.

Zone 8. Similar to *T. palustris* except that it has scales along the pinnae midribs.

T. japonica, syn. *Parathelypteris japonica*

Japan, H38–60cm (15–24in), D, Wet/Dry, Zone 7. Fronds triangular, pinnate-pinnatifid with a long scaly stipe. Lowest pair of pinnae point forward, rather as seen in *Phegopteris connectilis*. This has spread quite rapidly with me. A good garden species making a handsome clump.

T. noveboracensis (New York fern)

Eastern North America, H45–60cm (18–24in), Usually D, Wet/Dry, Zone 4. Fronds pinnate-pinnatifid, oblong, yellow-green, with quite a long stipe. Rhizomes creeping and very invasive, not common in European collections.

T. palustris (marsh fern)

Europe, including British Isles, H60–90cm (24–36in), D, Wet, Zone 4. Fronds pinnate-pinnatifid, bluish-green, lance-shaped, erect with a long stipe produced at 2–3cm (³⁄₄–1¹⁄₄in) intervals along the creeping rhizomes.

Sporing fronds are taller, with pinnae and pinnae segments appearing more slender because the margins are rolled under. The entire undersides of these fronds appear to be covered with the brown sporangia. Can be very invasive but if the space is available it makes excellent ground cover among reeds and suchlike. In drier sites it does quite well and is less invasive, but the fronds are shorter. Altogether not an unattractive garden plant.

var. pubescens from North America differs only by being slightly hairy. **'Pufferae'** A crested form.

T. simulata (Massachusetts fern)

North-eastern North America, D, Wet, Zone 4. Another species similar to *T. palustris*; differs in that the veins in the lamina are not branching. Likes wet, acid conditions.

TODEA

A small genus, related to *Osmunda*. Spores green.

T. barbara

Australia, South Africa, H1.2m (4ft), D, Wet, Zone 8. Very handsome upright, bipinnate fronds produced on a massive rhizome. Available in Britain for 2 or 3 years and surprisingly hardy so far.

TRICHOMANES (bristle ferns)

A genus of filmy ferns in the family Hymenophyllaceae (see *Hymenophyllum*). The common name refers to the bristle-like receptacle that projects from the centre of the sorus. Collectively the bristles, which may be over 6mm (¹⁄₄in) long, can be very conspicuous. Cultivate as *Hymenophyllum*.

T. caudatum, syn. *Macroglena caudata* (jungle bristle fern)

Australia, some Pacific Islands, H5–15cm (2–6in), E, High humidity with good drainage, Zone 9, possibly 8. Frond lance-shaped, tripinnate, pinnule segments narrow, translucent dark green. Rhizomes short creeping, near erect. *T. caudatum* is occasionally being imported on the trunks of *Dicksonia antarctica*. In the wild it is confined to dark forests.

T. speciosum (Killarney bristle fern)

Western fringes of Europe, including British Isles, H10–25cm (4–10in), E, High humidity with good drainage, Zone 8, possibly 7. Fronds triangular or broadly ovate, bipinnate-pinnatifid, translucent, dark green. Rhizomes far creeping, 1–2mm (¹⁄₁₆in) diameter. In the wild an extremely rare fern protected by law, but easy in cultivation when available preferring well-drained, acid soil. Good quantities are on show at several specialist public botanic gardens in the British Isles, including Kew in

London, Glasnevin in Dublin and Glasgow Botanic Garden. It is established outdoors in a few gardens in Cornwall and south-west Eire, but for most of us its cultivation will be limited to a terrarium or specially built filmy fern house as it needs close to 100 percent humidity. To establish, pin sections of rhizome down firmly and mist occasionally. Only when new fronds unfurl is success proven – old fronds have a tendency to look alive when they are, in fact, dead!

T. venosum, syn. *Polyphlebium venosum*

Australia, H2.5–5cm (1–2in), E, High humidity with good drainage, Zone 8. Fronds broadly lance-shaped, pinnatifid, translucent. Rhizomes creeping, slender. Quite frequently imported on trunks of *Dicksonia antarctica*. If kept on the trunk (roots not disturbed), it seems to be remarkably tolerant of less than high humidity. I exhibited a good clump at both the Chelsea and Hampton Court Flower Shows without any detrimental effect. I suspect it would do well outdoors on a tree fern in a very sheltered site, even in drier areas. It would be important to angle the trunk in such a way that the filmy fern was on the north side. Alternatively, it will grow in a terrarium. It has been established in an artificial grotto in a garden in Cornwall for very many years, possibly even more than a hundred.

WOODSIA

Small alpine ferns ideal in a rock garden or an alpine house. All like good drainage and plenty of light. Foliage flushes early in spring, maturing much earlier than most other ferns. Some species are wintergreen. All bulk up with age, forming an attractive tuft. Woodsias can be recognized when mature by their cup-shaped indusium.

W. alpina (alpine woodsia)

Northern Europe, including British Isles, Northern America, H2.5–12cm (1–5in), D, Dry/Wet, Zone 3. Fronds narrowly lance-shaped, pinnate-pinnatifid. Stipe black at base, darkish green above. Pinnae equilaterally triangular. Very rare in the wild and in cultivation, sometimes mistakenly confused with *Cystopteris dickieana*. Needs good drainage.

W. elongata

Himalaya, H12–25cm (5–10in), D, Dry/Wet, Zone 5. Fronds very narrowly lance-shaped, pinnate-pinnatifid. Hairiness of pinnae gives a silky appearance to the upper frond surface. A very pretty species, ideal in a situation where the fronds can hang over rockwork, unfortunately rare in cultivation.

W. fragilis (Plate IX)

Caucasus Mountains, Russia, H15–30cm (6–12in), D, Dry/Wet, Zone 5. Frond pinnate-pinnatifid, lance-shaped, pale green. Pinnae triangular, pinnae segments often pointed. Fronds arch gracefully.

W. glabella

North and central Europe, North America, Asia, H7–20cm (3–8in), D, Dry/Wet, Zone 4. Fronds lance-shaped, bipinnate, pale green. Stipe black at base but green above. Superficially like *Cystopteris fragilis* but mature specimens can be distinguished by their cup-shaped indusium (bladder-shaped in *Cystopteris*). Likes limy soil, usually in shade.

W. gracilis

Source unknown, H15–30cm (6–12in), D, Dry/Wet, Zone 7. Fronds bipinnate or pinnate-pinnatifid, lance-shaped, pale green. Pinnae triangular, tapering to a point. Pinnules oblong, very prominent at point of attachment to rachis. The plant in cultivation under this name is very attractive but the name may prove to be incorrect. *W. × gracilis* is a hybrid between *W. alpina* and *W. ilvensis* and is distinct from *W. gracilis* of gardens.

W. ilvensis (oblong woodsia)

Northern hemisphere, including British Isles, H2.5–15cm (1–6in), D, Dry/Wet, Zone 3. Fronds narrowly triangular, pinnate-pinnatifid, pale green. Pinnules oblong to narrowly triangular. Lower surface covered with scales and hairs. Apparently common in North America and

Woodsia alpina, here on Ben Lawers, Scotland, is one of the rarest British ferns.

The very pretty little fern *Woodsia polystichoides* growing in an alpine trough.

Scandinavia but extremely rare in the rest of Europe. Rarely in cultivation in Europe – the European plant seems difficult to establish. Plants under this name are common in collections but they are almost always *W. intermedia*. The North American form may be easier in cultivation. Likes a well-drained, neutral to acid soil with good light.

W. intermedia
Japan, east Asia, H7–15cm (3–6in), D, Dry/Wet, Zone 5. Fronds narrowly lance-shaped, pinnate with some lobing of the basal pinnae. Pinnae hairy. Similar to *W. ilvensis* but the upper surface of the frond is hairy – and it is easier to grow!

W. obtusa
Eastern North America, H15–30cm (6–12in), D, Dry/Wet, Zone 3. Fronds lance-shaped, bipinnate, light green with a few glands, none on the indusium. Pinnae triangular; pinnules with a rounded tip. A very easily grown species, the one most often seen in collections.

W. plummerae
Southern USA, Mexico, H15–30cm (6–12in), E, Dry/Wet, Zone 7. Fronds lance-shaped, bipinnate, light green copiously covered with stalked glands, also on the indusium. The abundant glands give the frond a slightly felty look. They are easily seen with a hand lens.

W. polystichoides
Japan, eastern Asia, H5–15cm (2–6in), Dry/Wet, Zone 5. Fronds narrowly oblong, pinnate. Each pinna has a small lobe on the acroscopic side at its base, resembling a polystichum, hence its specific name. A very pretty little fern especially in spring when the frond tip hangs down under the weight of the crozier as it unfurls. There is a form of this species in cultivation which is reported to have originated from Kamchatka in Russia. It is very similar but has a slightly shiny upper surface when the fronds are young.

W. scopulina (Rocky mountain woodsia)
North America, H10–20cm (4–8in), E in mild winters, Dry/Wet, Zone 3. Fronds lance-shaped, bipinnate, mid-green. Pinnae quite long, triangular with hairs and glands. Prefers acid to neutral, well-drained soil and good light.

WOODWARDIA (chain ferns)

Many of the woodwardias are excellent garden plants, often creating a dramatic effect. Chain fern refers to the sori which create a pattern reminiscent of a chain on the upper surface of the pinnule. Woodwardias are closely related to the blechnums and, like that group, prefer an acid or neutral soil, although I have grown *W. unigemmata* satisfactorily in a soil rich in Wenlock limestone. Two of the species listed here, *W. virginica* and *W. areolata*, differ so markedly from the others that they seem completely unrelated, but the key characters of the indusium and the venation show the connection.

W. areolata, syn. Lorinsora areolata
Eastern North America, H30–60cm (18–24in), Wet or Wet/Dry. D, Zone 4. Fronds pinnatifid, reddish when young, erect on a long stipe. Rhizomes creeping; can be invasive. Fertile fronds similar, except that the pinnae are much thinner, as often seen in species of blechnum. Native to acid bogs in America but it can do well in drier conditions. I try to give it lime-free soil. If supplied with adequate water, it can tolerate full sun.

W. fimbriata (giant chain fern)
Western North America, H0.6–2m (2–6ft), Wet/Dry, E, Zone 8. Fronds pinnate-pinnatifid, lance-shaped, green, even when young. Fronds more or less erect except when very large. They are not so elegantly elongated, nor do they normally arch over to touch the ground like

Woodwardia fimbriata is one of the tallest evergreen (or wintergreen) ferns that are hardy in zone 8.

W. unigemmata and *W. radicans*. No bulbils on fronds. A magnificent large, evergreen species, but unfortunately proving difficult to propagate. When more readily available, it should be more widely grown. I have grown it for around ten years outdoors in central England. Initially I was cautious and protected it with straw, but for many years now it has been left unguarded over winter and has thrived. It may prove hardy in zone 7.

W. martinezii

Central America H30–60cm (18–24in), Wet/Dry, E, Zone 8. Fronds pinnate-pinnatifid, arching, triangular and carried on a long stipe. I have never seen any buds on the fronds of this species, and it is distinguished from the arching frond species by the more broadly triangular laminae. *W. martinezii* seems to be hardy throughout central England.

W. orientalis

East Asia to Himalaya, H0.6–1.5m (2–5ft), Wet/Dry, E, Zone 9. Fronds pinnate-pinnatifid, ovate with a long stipe. Young fronds green. Upper surface of sporing sections of fronds abundantly covered with bulbils; there are none on the main rachis near the frond tip. Plants sold under this name may be *W. radicans*. I have never succeeded in overwintering this outdoors in central England.

W. radicans (European chain fern)

South-west Europe, including Atlantic Islands, H0.3–2.5m (1–8ft), Wet/Dry, E, Zone 9. Fronds pinnate-pinnatifid, ovate with a long stipe. Young fronds green. One or more vegetative buds are formed on the main rachis near the tip of the frond. The fronds are arching and tend to touch the ground at this point; the bud then roots and creates a new plant. In this way magnificent thickets of woodwardia can be formed, as at Glanleam in the south-west of Eire. Unfortunately not reliably hardy in central England.

W. spinulosa

Central America, H45–90cm (18–36in), Wet/Dry, D, Zone 8. Fronds pinnate-pinnatifid, ovate, elegantly elongated, arching, pale green. Pinnae well spaced; pinnule margins spiny. No buds near tip of frond. This is one of the high-altitude Mexican species that has proved reliably hardy for many winters in central England.

W. unigemmata

Himalaya, H0.3–2.2m (1–7ft), Wet/Dry, E, Zone 8. Like *W. radicans* except the new fronds are a beautiful deep red. The colour combined with greater hardiness makes this one of the most sought-after ferns, admired by Her Majesty the Queen at a recent Chelsea Flower Show. I grow it with the crown protected by a stone. I have seen this species produce a thicket from the buds near the frond tip in the glasshouses at Edinburgh Botanic Gardens, but I have not seen this happen outdoors as it is relatively new to cultivation. In defiance of the specific name, it does not always have only one bud. In fact there is a possibility that the plant in cultivation is not true *W. unigemmata*: it differs from material first collected in Taiwan in being larger and more deeply bipinnatifid, and in having more than one bulbil. Future research will tell but it is possible that the Himalayan plant should be included in the Philippine species *W. biserrata*.

W. virginica

Eastern North America, H30–60cm (18–24in), Wet/Dry, D, Zone 4. Fronds pinnate-pinnatifid, ovate on a long stipe. Young fronds reddish-brown. Rhizomes creeping; can be invasive. If supplied with adequate water it can withstand full sun. When well grown it is a pretty fern, somewhat reminiscent of *Osmunda cinnamomea*.

Woodwardia unigemmata has beautiful deep red new fronds. Here it grows in the garden of Veronica and Giles Cross in Stoke Lacy, Herefordshire.

5 Propagation

Most gardeners with a few ferns, and surprisingly quite a number of specialist fern growers, do not propagate ferns. True, a reasonable range of more generally available species and cultivars can be acquired from good garden centres, and additional species and cultivars can be bought from specialist nurseries or exchanged with other growers. However, special ferns can be quite difficult to find, and if you want to exchange, you need spare plants; if you want to grow something new and perhaps completely different it is best to grow it yourself. You, therefore, really need to do some propagation.

Growing ferns from spores is the best way of building up stocks. It can take rather a long time but the result should be lots of plants. Before explaining the technique involved in growing from spores, it is useful to understand the fern's lifecycle – it is not as simple as you might expect!

THE FERN LIFECYCLE

Ferns have what is termed alternation of generations: the plant we see is only part of the lifecycle; there is another stage, or generation, the prothallus. The mature fern is the sporophyte – the plant that produces spores. The prothallus is the gametophyte – the part that produces gametes. Until the middle of the nineteenth century, no-one associated the prothallus with fern plants. The lifecycle was, therefore, not understood and the gametes were unknown; ferns were classed as cryptogams or as having 'hidden gametes'.

The sporophyte, or mature fern, typically has two sets of chromosomes per cell. In the production of the spores, a reduction division takes place so the spores have only one set of chromosomes. The spore germinates into a prothallus, which in a short time develops male and female sex organs on its undersurface. The male organs are called antheridia and the female organs archegonia. The antheridia produce many antherozooids, the male gametes. The antherozooids are free-swimming; they move around in the film of moisture ever-present on the

underside of a healthy prothallus until they are attracted chemically by an archegonium. They then swim down the archegonium's neck and the first one in fertilizes the egg cell, the female gamete. The antherozooids and the egg cell have one set of chromosomes each; when they fuse, the complement returns to two sets. (It is clear that the reduction division that occurs when spores are produced is necessary: if there were no reduction division, the number of chromosomes would double in every cell with every additional generation, and the process would not be sustainable.)

Once fertilized, the egg cell grows rapidly by normal cell division into a young version of a fern plant. Depending on species, it may take anything from four months to several years before the first tiny true fern frond appears. It may then take a further year or two for the sporophyte to mature and produce spores of its own.

Reflection on this process always reminds me how humble we human beings should be – like the primitive fern, we reproduce via free-swimming male gametes!

Reproduction from spores is a sexual process and, therefore, there is an opportunity for the genetic material carried on the chromosomes to be mixed slightly in the process and not all offspring will be identical to the parent. This is particularly true if the spores are sown from a cultivar. This is the great advantage of building up a collection by sowing spores as the chances of growing something very special and perhaps new are good. Long-extinct cultivars may also be re-raised. Certainly, I have acquired some of my best plants in this way.

Ferns produce spores usually on the underside of mature fronds in globular structures called sporangia, each normally holding 64 spores. The sporangia are usually formed in groups of perhaps a hundred or more together, covered by a simple flap of tissue. The flap is the indusium; the whole structure is the sorus. A mature frond may carry several thousand sori. Charles Druery once calculated that a single fern could produce up to 1,120,000,000 spores, or one thousand one hundred and twenty million.

These spores are shed and carried on the wind. Perhaps fortunately, very very few land in a spot suitable for the spore to germinate. If they do germinate, they grow

Previous page: The somewhat evil-looking croziers of *Dryopteris neorosthornii* unfurling in spring.

LIFECYCLE OF A FERN

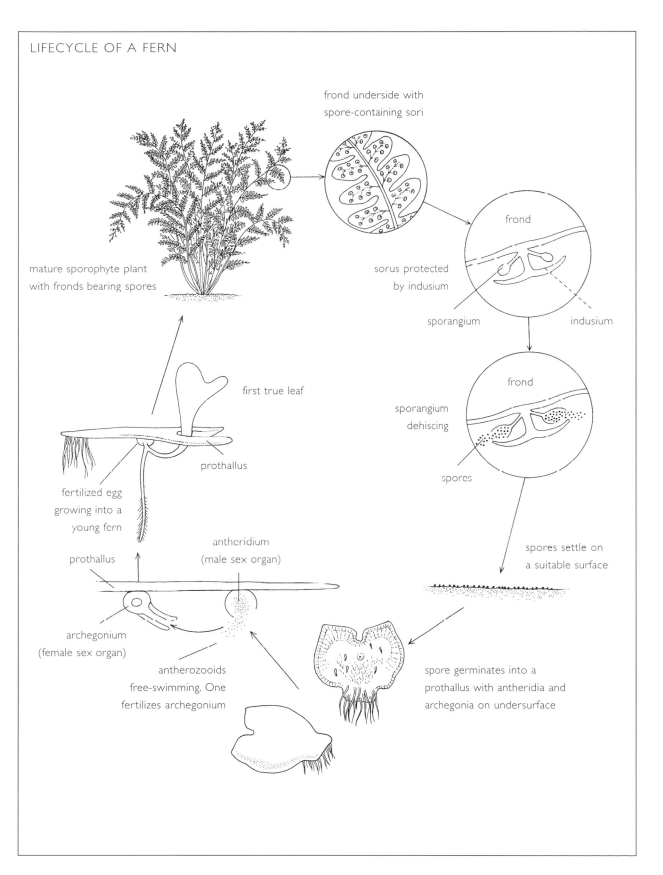

frond underside with
spore-containing sori

mature sporophyte plant
with fronds bearing spores

sorus protected
by indusium

frond

sporangium

indusium

frond

sporangium
dehiscing

spores

first true leaf

prothallus

fertilized egg
growing into a
young fern

spores settle on
a suitable surface

prothallus

antheridium
(male sex organ)

archegonium
(female sex organ)

antherozooids
free-swimming. One
fertilizes archegonium

spore germinates into a
prothallus with antheridia and
archegonia on undersurface

into a heart-shaped prothallus, a flap of tissue up to 5mm across. With luck, each prothallus will produce a new baby fern – Druery once succeeded in raising seven ferns from a single prothallus.

The whole process may sound quite complicated but, in fact, Mother Nature takes care of most of it; all the fern grower has to do is provide the right conditions for the spore to germinate and then nurse the young fern to maturity.

SPORES

The first step is to collect your spores. For most species, this is best done in midsummer (July in the northern hemisphere). To select ripe spores, examine the sori on the underside of the frond: if the sporangia are exposed, glossy, dark brown or black, they are probably ripe; if they look rough or shaggy, they have probably already shed their load and all you can see is the broken sporangia walls; if they are green or only pale brown, they are probably not ripe. Spores normally ripen in sequence from the base to the tip of the frond, therefore you can often find ripe and unripe spores on a single frond.

When you have selected a section of the frond with ripe spores, break off a small piece, perhaps a pinna, and put it in an envelope. Leave this in a dry place for 48 hours, then tap the envelope vigorously and, with a little luck, a very fine dust should be visible at the bottom of the envelope. Check whether you have spores or just rubbish by examining the dust with a good hand lens. If good spores have been harvested, the dust will contain thousands of specks mostly of identical size; if the dust is not spores, it will contain particles of many different sizes. Once the spores are safely gathered, they can be stored for several months but germination is much better if sown sooner rather than later.

Some growers like to clean their spores. This can be done by pouring the collected dust and spores onto a sheet of paper. Hold the paper at 45 degrees and tap it gently. The spores tend to stick while most of the debris will slide off. Once all the rubbish has been removed, hold the paper in a funnel and tap it more vigorously to collect spores back into a packet. It is important to use a room with still air for this process. I do not bother to clean my spores. All that is achieved is the removal of a normally harmless waste product. It is not possible to separate the spores from different species by this method – nor by any other that I know!

Next, prepare your compost. I prefer to use ericaceous compost with a low nutrient content but other growers use peat with equally good results. Fill the number of washed pots you need and prepare to surface-sterilize the compost. Sterilization is essential otherwise fungi, bacteria, mosses or liverworts may grow and swamp the the fern prothalli. I sterilize my compost by pouring boiling water over the compost until I am satisfied that all the surface has been scalded. Place the treated pot in a new (therefore clean) polythene bag, fold the top of the bag over so that no unwanted spores can intrude, then leave it to cool down. The next day sprinkle your spores onto the sterile surface, label the pot and return it to its polythene bag. Ensure you do the sowing in a still atmosphere. If several different lots of spores are being sown in one session, I like to move around so that each sowing is in a different room to minimize the risk of cross contamination. When finished, store the culture in good light but not direct sun; it will not need watering.

If the spores are sown in midsummer, a film of green should be seen over the surface of the compost within a month or two; the first true fronds may be produced before the onset of winter, but it is more likely they will appear in the following spring. Autumn sowings take much longer to develop. For the time being keep the culture in the polythene bag. This ensures high humidity, so the prothallus does not dry out and the antherozooids underneath can continue to be able to swim freely. Once sufficient true fronds have been produced, remove the culture from the polythene bag, place it in indirect light, and lightly lay the polythene bag over the top of the pot; water the surface very carefully as necessary. This is a way of hardening-off the young plants: immediate exposure to dry air can be fatal.

After a few days, gradually expose the culture to the open air and, when you are satisfied the young ferns are tough enough, prick the little plants out into seed trays. It is wise to surface-sterilize these trays 24 hours before use. Prick out in clumps so there is a good chance that at least some young plants' roots will survive the operation – do not try to transplant individual plants as they will be too small to stand individual disturbance. It is often a good idea to place a polythene sheet over the freshly pricked-out ferns for a few days to help prevent drying out until their root systems have recovered. Once they have been hardened-off, the plants should grow away strongly and can be potted-on into plugs or individual pots.

This technique holds true for most commonly grown

ferns, but, of course, there are exceptions! Some ferns have green spores when ripe, notably *Osmunda* and *Lygodium*. Their spores tend to be ripe in mid- to late summer. *Matteuccia struthiopteris* and *Onoclea sensibilis* also have green spores but they are shed in midwinter. It is an exciting experience to pick seemingly dead sporing fronds of either species in midwinter, bring them into the warm and see a thick green dust appear under a frond within half an hour. All green spores need to be sown as soon as possible after collection; they are only viable for about two weeks under normal conditions. Although not green, all tree-fern spores also tend to be shortlived and should ideally also be sown within a fortnight of collection. If immediate sowing is not possible, all spores can be stored for longer if kept cool: the top of a fridge is suitable.

Hybrids between two species do not normally produce viable spores, but all true species and most cultivars are best increased by propagation from spores. For the

Polypodium vulgare 'Jean Taylor' combining well with *Cyclamen hederifolium*.

more adventurous grower, mixed sowings can be tried – hybrids may be formed.

DIVISION

Ferns can be divided either when they have creeping rhizomes or when the main crown splits.

Creeping rhizomes

Once a fern with a creeping rhizome has divided and produced at least two growing tips, the parts can be separated with a sharp knife and planted out separately. In practice, creeping ferns are only split when a good colony has become established. This can then be cut into small parts without worrying about whether or not there is a growing point on each.

Ferns to propagate by this method are all species of *Gymnocarpium, Polypodium* and *Pyrrosia, Phegopteris connectilis, Phegopteris hexagonoptera, Onoclea sensibilis*, some creeping *Athyrium* and, of course, other rhizomatous ferns. *Matteuccia struthiopteris* is slightly different because it spreads by stolons but in effect each individual crown can be easily separated. With the polypodiums, cutting up

clumps into smaller units is by far the commonest way of propagating the best cultivars. Spore sowings from polypodiums are rare, so plants in cultivaton are very likely to be the original clone – a great advantage when trying to give names to cultivars. Unfortunately, as always, there are exceptions to the rule: *Polypodium australe* 'Wilharris' has been known to revert vegetatively to a form of 'Pulcherrimum', but this phenomenon is very exceptional and need not worry the general grower.

Splitting main crowns

Splitting a main crown is a simple but very slow way to build up stocks. It is the only way to reproduce some of the most choice sterile cultivars. Unfortunately, not all are generous with their production of side crowns: *Athyrium filix-femina* 'Clarissima' seems to take about ten years before developing a split crown, and this may take more years before it is ready for the chop. Other sterile cultivars are more generous with their side crowns: *Polystichum setiferum* 'Plumosum Bevis' splits rapidly, giving a head of many crowns. These can be separated with care but it will probably take some time before each of the offsets settles down. Because spore-produced progeny are not necessarily the same as their parent, dividing the main crown can also be a useful way of propagating fertile cultivars. The original clone of *Athyrium filix-femina* 'Victoriae' is always a better plant than its progeny, and it is always very rare! Although some straight species can be split, many stay as single crowns throughout their lives. Sometimes a bunch of crowns may seem to have been produced but this may be because the plant has been raised in a nursery and a pinch of young plants was pricked out in the first place – in other words the multiple crowns may each be a separate plant!

The actual splitting process can be carried out with a knife or, in the case of large clumps, with two forks. The two forks method gently teases the crowns apart and is my preferred technique. Select the line where the division is to be made, insert one fork vertically along this line, then insert the other fork in the same line but back to back with the first fork so that the two handles are leaning away from each other. Use pressure to bring the two handles together and gently separate the two sections of rhizome. If further splits are required repeat the process on the fragments.

Large splits can be planted straight into the garden but small pieces are probably best potted up and grown on before planting out.

BULBILS ON FRONDS

Quite a few ferns produce bulbils on their fronds. With care these can be grown on into new plants. Propagating by this means has the advantage that all offspring should be identical to the parent. There are, however, rare exceptions – bud sports have been reported on polystichums in the past – so it is worth keeping an eye open for breaks.

Bulbils are produced most commonly on cultivars of *Polystichum setiferum*, such as 'Divisilobum', 'Plumosodivisilobum', 'Cristato-pinnulum', 'Multilobum' and others. In each of these, the bulbils are formed along the top of the rachis at the point of attachment of each pinna. They are more frequent towards the base of the fronds. Other species of *Polystichum*, including *P. proliferum*, *P. andersonii*, *P. lentum* and *P. stenophyllum*, also produce bulbils, but usually only one or two near the tip of the frond. Other species with bulbils near the tip of the frond include *Woodwardia unigemmata*, *Asplenium flabellifolium* and *Camptosorus rhizophyllus*.

Bulbils may be produced all over the upper surface of the frond. Notable examples of this are *Woodwardia orientalis* and *Asplenium bulbiferum*, neither of which is really hardy under the terms of this book. Such bulbils also occur on the upper surface of fronds of *Polypodium vulgare* 'Elegantissimum'. These have been noticed many times over the past 100 years but so far no one has reported any success with their culture, including me! Even the great Charles Druery failed to keep them alive. If you grow this cultivar, please keep your eyes open for more bulbils. I will be interested to hear of any success with their cultivation.

In some related species of *Cystopteris*, such as *C. bulbifera* and *C. tennesseensis*, bulbils are produced along the underside of the rachis. Unlike all the bulbils reported above, these fall off and grow happily without any connection to the parent plant. In time quite a colony may build up and the species can even become a bit of a weed – not really possible with a fern!

Some cultivars of *Athyrium filix-femina*, for example 'Plumosum Superbum Dissectum Druery' and 'Clarissima', produce bulbils as replacements for sporangia in the indusia, or elsewhere on the frond. They are difficult to see even with a lens, but if a mature frond is laid down (see below) young plantlets can be raised quite easily. Curiously, ferns produced from bulbils on 'Clarissima' are likely to be inferior to the original. This form of reproduction is a type of apospory.

Growing frond bulbils

All the cases listed above, except the *Cystopteris*, which propagates itself, and the *Polypodium*, which seems unviable, can be induced to grow by following this procedure.

Fill a seed tray with peat. Scrape a shallow groove in the peat, then sterilize the surface with boiling water. Allow to cool. Select a frond with ripe bulbils (usually already with conspicuous small frondlets), lay it in the groove and anchor it firmly in position by either pegging it to the peat or sprinkling grit lightly over it. Water it and then lay a polythene sheet loosely over the tray. I do not normally put the tray into a polythene bag as it may get too damp; the polythene sheet just helps to control water loss and helps establishment. Keeping an eye on the watering, leave the frond undisturbed in a greenhouse or coldframe for a few months. Usually by the following spring there are obvious rows of little plantlets and these can be carefully teased out of the tray and potted up. Peat is the perfect substrate because it carries little nutrient, forcing the bulbils to produce roots. In a well-fertilized medium it is possible for the plantlets to produce a lot of top and few roots, making them difficult to establish.

The bulbils of the *Athyrium filix-femina* cultivars mentioned above can be treated in the same way but it is best to keep them frost free because the parent frond is deciduous.

LEAF BASE BULBILS

Ferns produce clumps of crowns in two ways: the crown can either split into two equal halves, as in *Athyrium filix-femina* 'Clarissima', or it can produce side crowns from little bulbils that are produced at the base of the frond at its point of attachment to the rhizome, most usually associated with *Asplenium scolopendrium* cultivars. Careful dissection of the plant enables the harvesting of these leaf bases without destroying the parent clump, although the process invariably sets it back a little. I normally confine my use of this technique to *Asplenium scolopendrium*, but I have successfully propagated *Dryopteris filix-mas* 'Bollandiae', which is sterile, by this means and in the past *Oreopteris limbosperma* was grown in this way.

Growing leaf base bulbils

Select the most mature parent plant possible. Dig it up and wash off all the soil. Low down in the clump there will be old sections of rhizome covered with short, dead-looking leaf bases. Peel these downwards, oldest first, so that they break off cleanly from the rhizome; you will notice they are green at the point of attachment, but no bulbil is normally visible. Working systematically over a mature plant of *Asplenium scolopendrium* you can often harvest over 100 leaf bases. Keep the detached leaf bases in a polythene bag until you are ready to continue. Do not take bases of existing green fronds: they are still doing a job for the plant and would probably not be ripe enough to produce bulbils anyway. When sufficient leaf bases have been collected, replant the parent, perhaps back in the garden, but usually in a pot. Give it some tender loving care until it has recovered from the operation. If only a few bulbils are required, the damage to the parent plant is far less and it will recover more quickly.

Wash the leaf bases, cleaning off remnants of old frond and removing any root material – many bases will have a single root attached. Prepare a pot or tray of sand or low-nutrient compost. Surface sterilize it with boiling water. Allow to cool. Plant the leaf bases upside down, with the cut end (the point of attachment to the parent) facing upwards. Space them about a centimetre apart. Place the pot or tray into a new or very clean polythene bag and place it on a windowsill in good indirect light. In one or two months examination of the tips of each base should reveal a green swelling; this is the bulbil. On some bases five or six bulbils may form. Do not do anything to the culture at this stage, except keep it in the polythene bag. After a few months, little fronds will appear and once little plantlets are formed and are about 1–2cm (½in) tall, the plastic bag can be removed. A day or two afterwards the plantlets can be pricked out. Harden them off just as with all small ferns.

This process is extremely useful for the sterile cultivars of *Asplenium scolopendrium*, such as 'Crispum', as these can only otherwise be propagated by division of the crown.

TISSUE CULTURE

This is a specialized technique that remains something of a mystery to me. For the time being it is not likely to be available to amateur gardeners. However, it is worth mentioning because certain cultivars are now being propagated commercially by tissue culture – to my knowledge *Polystichum setiferum* 'Gracillimum', *Polystichum setiferum* 'Plumosum Bevis' and *Cyathea cooperi* 'Cristatum' are becoming increasingly available.

6 Pests and Diseases

Fortunately ferns suffer from few pests and diseases. What diseases there are can often be eliminated or at least kept in check by following general and commonsense good husbandry rules.

Principally I like to cut off all old fronds. This job is best done before the new ones unfurl, when it is quick and easy to perform; if it is left until the new croziers have appeared, it can take hours to clean up just a few plants. This breaks any disease cycle from one year to the next, thus it has to build up from scratch annually so there is less chance of it doing lasting damage. Cutting off the old fronds has the added advantage of keeping the plants looking tidy.

It is also not a good idea to water fronds for the sake of it: water straight to the roots wherever possible, not to the crown, just in case there are any rots around. The two most serious rot problems are *Milesina scolopendri* on *Asplenium scolopendrium* and *Taphrina wettsteiniana* on *Polystichum setiferum* and related species of *Polystichum*. Both of these diseases and their control are covered under the host species in An A–Z of Ferns pp.42–169.

Polystichums, particularly the densely foliose forms, such as *Polystichum setiferum* 'Plumoso-multilobum', can be disfigured at the base of old fronds by a black rot, which is possibly a species of *Rhizoctonia* or *Botrytis*, if allowed to stay too wet. As with all ferns it is, therefore, a good idea to try to avoid wetting the crown during watering. If the rot develops in the garden, either spray with a systemic fungicide or clear all debris away from the crown to facilitate good air circulation. Tree ferns are cold hardy but not fully hardy: this means that they, too, can suffer from rots developing in the crown. Again, it is good practice to avoid watering the crown, especially during the cold, damp months of autumn, winter and early spring.

PESTS

Greenfly, Blackfly and Capsids

More common problems are greenfly and blackfly, although problems with either are rare on ferns grown in the garden – they are more likely to occur on house or greenhouse plants. I am reluctant to spray ferns with insecticides unless absolutely necessary. Instead, I prefer to use insecticides formulated to act as vapours. These are sold in blocks that are impregnated with the insecticide and enclosed in plastic containers. The containers can be open or closed as required. When I find a plant infested with aphids I simply open the pack, place it beside the fern over night and by morning all the aphids are dead. It is as well not to stay in the room where the product is being released as it may not be suitable for long-term exposure to humans.

If spraying is unavoidable, soapy water can be tried, but I have little confidence in its activity. I prefer to resort to a pyrethroid insecticide, used at half dose, when necessary. Some scorching is quite common with insecticides so I try to do any spraying in the evening when there is no risk of the sun burning the sprayed fronds. One pest that seems to be controlled only by spraying is capsid, which grazes the frond creating tiny white blotches at random. Capsids are not often a real worry unless the ferns are being prepared for show – then, of course, any insecticide scorch is doubly undesirable.

Slugs and Snails

One of the commonest of all garden pests are slugs and snails. Happily, they are very rarely attracted to ferns. The most notable exceptions are some of the thicker-textured fronds found among the spleenworts, such as *Asplenium fontanum* and *Camptosorus rhizophyllus*. Whenever they do become a nuisance try sharp grit around the plant or, failing that, resort to slug pellets. In my polytunnels I find frogs are quite an effective means of control!

Vine Weevil

Another common pest is the vine weevil whose grubs eat any part of the plant, usually starting with the roots and moving on to the leaf bases. Unfortunately, this damaging beast is a problem for a wide range of plants. It is common in gardens in much of the British Isles, but rarely causes any problems outdoors: it is with pot-grown plants that the real damage is done. With ferns, certain species are more susceptible than others. Of all those that I grow, *Asplenium scolopendrium* is the worst affected, but in bad years, following mild winters, many different species can be attacked.

Specimens of *Polystichum setiferum* Ramosum Group have fronds that branch several times.

The first visible symptoms of attack by vine weevil are plants wilting while their soil is moist so it is obvious that drought is not the problem. Gently pull the fronds: if they come away easily, vine weevil is almost certainly the cause. Tip the remains of the plant out of the pot and sift through the compost. Look for white banana-shaped grubs, anything up to 5mm (¼in) long. These may be anywhere in the pot but look particularly closely among the remains of the crown. If you have caught them early, the weevils may not have irretrievably damaged the crown. Remove it immediately and repot it. With care it might recover; however, recovery is usually a long process and, to be honest, I do not usually try to resuscitate weeviled plants unless the damaged fern is something rather special.

Unfortunately, weevil damage is not confined to grubs eating the parts under the soil; the adult weevils nibble at the margins of fronds, leaving otherwise straight margins irritatingly scalloped. Fortunately, this is not too serious to the health of the plant, unless they are being grown for showing. The adults are easily recognized. They are black crawling insects with a long pointed snout. They are more readily found at night and if seen should be crushed. A gentle squeeze will not do as they are tough little creatures: really crush them.

Control of weevils is not easy. Most of the various chemicals that have proved active over the years have been withdrawn from general use as potentially damaging to the environment, although one or two are still available to the horticultural trade. There is also a nematode that parasitizes weevils and can be added to the compost. I have never used it but I have heard mixed reports. I suggest regular inspection of the root ball – the grubs often rest against the side of the pot – together with night-time torchlight sessions in the greenhouse. Alternatively, try to avoid the problem by planting out *Asplenium scolopendrium* and other susceptible species.

Eelworm

I have never knowingly had an eelworm problem but I may have overlooked or misidentified it. Typically eelworm damage is seen as dead patches of frond confined by larger veins. Control is just about impossible. It is best to remove fronds suspected of being infected as soon as possible. The problem is most likely in damp, humid conditions.

Appendix I *Glossary of Terms*

Words printed in emboldened italic are defined elsewhere in the glossary.

Acroscopic Side of the *pinna* nearest the frond tip. See also *basiscopic*.

Annual Completes lifecycle in a single year.

Antheridia Male sex organ on the *prothallus*.

Antherozooid Male gamete.

Apical Towards tip of frond.

Aposporus Without *spores*.

Archegonia Female sex organs on the *prothallus*.

Basiscopic Side of the *pinna* nearest the frond base. See also *acroscopic*.

Bipinnate *Pinnae* divided into distinctly separate *pinnules*.

Bipinnate-pinnatifid *Pinnules* almost divided into *pinnulets*.

Chromosome Components of the cell nucleus carrying the inherited genetic material.

Crenate Margin roundly toothed.

Crested Forked tips.

Crozier Uncurling frond.

Depauperate Lacking parts of the frond.

Dimorphic Carrying fronds of two types.

Diploid Having two sets of *chromosomes*.

Distal Furthest point.

Epiphytic Growing on other plants, using them as a substrate (not parasitic).

Falcate Sickle-shaped, usually meaning that the *pinnae* are curved towards tip of the frond.

Genus (genera) Term for describing a closely related group of species.

Haploid Having one set of *chromosomes*.

Hybrid Result of a sexual cross between two different *taxa*.

Indusium Flap of tissue covering the *sorus*.

Lacerate Margin irregularly cut.

Lamina Leaf or frond blade.

Lanceolate Frond lance-shaped – frond broadest between the middle and the base.

Pedate Frond hand-shaped.

Pinna (pinnae) Primary divisions of frond.

Pinnate Frond divided into distinctly separate *pinnae*.

Pinnate-pinnatifid *Pinnae* almost divided into *pinnules*.

Pinnatifid Frond almost divided into *pinnae*.

Pinnules Divisions of *pinnae*.

Pinnulets Divisions of *pinnules*.

Polydactylus Many fingered.

Proliferous Bud bearing.

Prothallus Alternative generation (see lifecycle p.172).

Rachis Section of the frond midrib that bears the leafy part of the frond.

Rhizome The fern's stem. May be erect as in tree ferns, or creeping as in polypodiums.

Serrate Margin regularly cut into small points.

Sorus The spore-producing structure, includes *spores*, *sporangium* and *indusium*.

Sporangium (sporangia) Structures containing *spores*.

Spore Dust-like particles which germinate to produce a *prothallus*.

Sporocarps Spore-bearing structure.

Stipe Midrib of frond below the leafy part (see also rachis).

Stolon A relatively short-lived procumbent stem, usually not swollen and often rooting at the tip to form a new plant. May be above or below ground.

Taxon (taxa) A unit of classification.

Tetraploid Having four sets of *chromosomes*.

Tripinnate *Pinnules* divided into distinctly separate *pinnulets*.

Xerophyte Growing in dry habitats.

Appendix II *National Collections of Ferns*

Since the early 1980s the National Council for the Conservation of Plants and Gardens (NCCPG) has set up National Collections of almost all garden plants grown in British gardens. Similar schemes are run in France and Australia (where as yet no national collections of ferns are recognized) and are being set up in other countries.

Britain

General Ferns Savill and Valley Gardens, Windsor Great Park, Windsor, Berkshire SL4 2HT. Tel. 01753 860222.

British Ferns Alastair Wardlaw, 92 Drymen Road, Bearsden, Glasgow G61 2SY. Tel. 0141 942 2461.

Asplenium Sizergh Castle (National Trust), Kendal LA8 8AE. Tel. 015395 60496.

Asplenium Jack Bouckley, 209 Woodfield Road, Harrogate, Yorkshire HG1 4JE. Tel. 01423 566948.

Athyrium Nick Schroder, 2 The Dell, Haywards Heath, Sussex RH16 1JG. Tel. 01444 415271.

Cystopteris Sizergh Castle (National Trust), Kendal LA8 8AE. Tel. 015395 60496.

Cystopteris Martin Rickard, Rickard's Hardy Ferns, Kyre Park, Kyre, Tenbury Wells, Worcestershire WR15 8RP. Tel. 01885 410282.

Davallia Mr and Mrs Mick Craddock, 40 Russell Drive, Ampthill, Bedfordshire MK45 2TX. Tel. 01525 402378.

Dicksoniaceae Glasgow Botanic Garden, Glasgow G12 0UE. Tel. 0141 334 2422.

Dryopteris Harlow Carr Botanic Gardens, Crag Lane, Harrogate, Yorkshire HG3 1QB. Tel. 01423 565418.

Dryopteris Sizergh Castle (National Trust), Kendal LA8 8AE. Tel. 015395 60496.

Equisetum Anthony Pigott, Kersey's Farm, Mendlesham, Stowmarket, Suffolk IP14 5RD. Tel. 01449 766104.

Osmunda A.R. Busby, 16 Kirby Corner Road, Canley, Coventry, West Midlands CV4 8GD. Tel. 01203 715690.

Osmunda Sizergh Castle (National Trust), Kendal LA8 8AE. Tel. 0141 942 2461.

Polypodium Harlow Carr Botanic Gardens, Crag Lane, Harrogate, Yorkshire HG3 1QB. Tel. 01423 565418.

Polypodium Martin Rickard, Rickard's Hardy Ferns, Kyre Park, Kyre, Tenbury Wells, Worcestershire WR15 8RP. Tel. 01885 410282.

Polystichum Joan Loraine, Greencombe Gardens Trust, Greencombe, Porlock, Somerset TA24 8NU. Tel. 01643 862363.

Polystichum Lakeland Horticultural Society Garden, Holehird, Ullswater Road, Windermere, Cumbria LA23 1NP.

Selaginella Stephan Czeladzinski, Barbican Conservatory, Barbican Centre, Silk Street, London EC2Y 8DS. Tel. 020 7638 6114.

Thelypteridaceae Martin Rickard, Rickard's Hardy Ferns, Kyre Park, Kyre, Tenbury Wells, Worcestershire WR15 8RP. Tel. 01885 410282.

Woodwardia Diana Grenfell and Roger Grounds, Apple Court, Hordle Lane, Hordle, Lymington, Hampshire SO41 0HU. Tel. 01590 642130.

France

General ferns (epiphytic) Conservatoire et Jardins Botaniques de Nancy, 100 Rue du Jardin Botanique, 54600 Villers les Nancy.

General ferns Mairie de Paris, Direction des Parcs, Jardins et Espaces Verts, 1 Avenue Gordon Bennett, 75016 Paris.

United States of America

There are no national fern collections as yet but the Hardy Fern Foundation has set up a number of reference gardens across the United States where a wide range of species is grown and documented. The primary study garden is at the Rhododendron Species Botanical Garden in Federal Way, Washington, with satellite plantings at botanical gardens and arboreta throughout the country, from Florida to Alaska. See 'Where to See Hardy and Half Hardy Ferns' (p.183).

Appendix III *Fern Societies*

There are many small fern societies scattered around the world. These are best sought out locally, especially as some are short-lived. Larger well-established organizations include:

Australia

The Fern Society of Victoria

This thriving society is centred on Melbourne, where lecture meetings, plant shows and field visits are held. A journal is issued several times a year. Contact: The Fern Society of Victoria Inc., P.O. Box 45, Heildelberg, Victoria, 3081.

There are several other fern societies in Australia. They are probably best contacted through the Fern Society of Victoria.

Europe

British Pteridological Society

Celebrating its centenary in 1991, this is the oldest fern society in the world and has around 800 members living in about 50 countries and is run entirely by volunteers. Its three journals provide good cover of what is going on in the fern world: the *Fern Gazette*, usually published twice yearly, includes items mainly of specialist interest on international pteridology, the *Pteridologist*, published annually, includes topics of more general appeal, and the *Bulletin*, also published annually, has details of society business and reports. Back numbers of its journals are much sought-after for the valuable information they contain. The society also publishes occasional small books on specialist subjects. Meetings concentrate on lectures, garden visits and expeditions to the more ferny parts of the world. Services to members include a free spore exchange, a book sales scheme (where unusual and rare books are offered at very reasonable prices) and sales of fern merchandise.

In 1998 the Society was greatly honoured when His Royal Highness, The Prince of Wales agreed to be its Patron for a five-year period. The Prince is a great fern-lover with many parts of his garden in Gloucestershire given over to ferns. Contact: Mr M. Porter, 5 West Avenue, Wigton, Cumbria CA7 9LG.

Nederlandse Varenvereniging

This well-organized society holds very good symposia and publishes a journal. Contact: Mr J. Greep, Van Remagenlaan 17, 6824 LX Arnhem, Holland.

Schweizerische Verinigung der Farnfreunde

I have heard that this is a very friendly, well-run society. It publishes a journal, *Farnblatter*, in German.
Contact: Dr M. Zink, Institut fur Systematische Botanik der Universitat, Zollikerstrasse 107, CH-8008 Zurich, Switzerland.

New Zealand

Nelson Fern Society Inc. of New Zealand

This little society is run by enthusiasts in and around Nelson on South Island. They organize lectures, field meetings and special projects. Most notably they have planted a huge area down to ferns in one of the public parks of Nelson.
Contact: Mrs J. Bonnington, 9 Bay View Road, Atawhai, Nelson, New Zealand.

North America

American Fern Society

Although I have been a member of the American Fern Society for many years I cannot, unfortunately, report first-hand on any of their meetings. I do know, however, they have many field meetings throughout the USA. Their journals are excellent with the *American Fern Journal* covering topics of international Pteridology and the *Fiddlehead Forum* publishing items of more general interest. The American Fern Society was founded in 1893. Contact: Dr George Yatskievych, Membership Secretary, Missouri Botanical Garden, PO Box 299, St Louis, MO 63166-0299. Website: http://amerfernsoc.org/home.html

Hardy Fern Foundation

This organization takes over the horticultural side of fern interest in the USA. It sponsors fern collections throughout the States, evaluating hardiness in very wide-ranging conditions, and publishes an excellent quarterly journal. Contact: The Hardy Fern Foundation, P.O. Box 166, Medina, Washington 98039-0166.

There are many other regional fern societies in North America. Details can be obtained through the American Fern Society. Two are listed below.

Los Angeles International Fern Society

A large group with wide-ranging interests. Its journal, *Laifs Fern Journal*, is issued several times a year. Contact: P.O. Box 90943, Pasadena, CA 91109-0943.

San Diego Fern Society

Although effectively a sub-tropical fern society, its journal is of wide-ranging interest with good information on tree ferns and desert ferns. Contact: Robin Halley, 1418 Park Row, La Jolla, CA 92037.

Appendix IV *Where to See Hardy and Half Hardy Ferns*

Most, if not all, major cities in the world have a botanical garden where a good selection of ferns are likely to be grown. Those included in this list are known to have a good selection on display. See also 'National Collections of Ferns' (p.181).

Australia
Adelaide Botanic Gardens, North Terrace, Adelaide, South Australia 5000.
Australian National Botanic Gardens, G.P.O. Box 1777, Canberra A.C.T. 2601.
Rippon Lea, Elsternwick, Melbourne. Wonderful selection of mainly tree ferns in a Victorian fernery.
Royal Botanic Gardens, Melbourne. Tree ferns luxuriate in a woodland garden.
Sydney Royal Botanic Gardens, Mrs MacQuaries Road, Sydney, New South Wales 2000.

Europe
England
In addition to those listed below there are several gardens in Cornwall where tree ferns can be seen outdoors – Trebah, Glendurgan, Carwinion and Penjerrick (all near Mawnan Smith), Trengwainton (near Penzance), and Caerhays Castle and Heligan (on the Roseland Peninsula). In Devon they can be seen at Coleton Fishacre (near Brixham) and Hartland Abbey (near Clovelly).

At the time of writing there are several very good private fern collections. Many are open to visitors by appointment (again see National Collections of Ferns). However, it is the nature of such collections that they get broken up periodically. I have, therefore, not included many in the list.
Abbeydore Court, Abbeydore, Herefordshire HR2 0AD. Hardy ferns in garden.
Chelsea Physic Garden, 66 Royal Hospital Road, London SW3 4HS. Ferns in gardens and glasshouses, including research collections.
Greencombe, Porlock, Somerset TA24 8NU. National Collection of *Polystichum* set in one of the most beautiful gardens in England.
Harlow Carr Botanic Gardens (Northern Horticultural Society), Crag Lane, Harrogate, North Yorkshire HG3 1QB.
Knightshayes (National Trust), Knightshayes Court, Tiverton, Devon EX16 7RG. Hardy ferns in gardens.
Kyre Park, Kyre, Tenbury Wells, Worcestershire WR15 8RP. Large collection of hardy ferns in gardens.

Lakeland Horticultural Society Gardens, Holehird, Ullswater Road, Windermere, Cumbria LA23 1NP. National Collection of *Polystichum*.
Royal Botanic Gardens Kew, Richmond, Surrey TW9 3AB. Very large collection of ferns, mainly in glasshouses.
Royal Horticultural Society Garden Wisley, Wisley, Woking, Surrey GU23 6OB.
Savill Garden (part of Windsor Great Park), Wick Lane, Englefield Green, Egham, Surrey TW20 0UU. National Collection of hardy ferns in beautifully landscaped garden.
Sizergh Castle (National Trust), Kendal LA8 8AE. National Collections of *Dryopteris*, *Cystopteris*, *Osmunda* and *Asplenium*.
Tatton Park, Knutsford, Cheshire WA16 6QN. Magnificent Victorian tree fern house.
University Botanic Garden Oxford, Rose Lane, Oxford OX1 4AX. Ferns in borders and in glasshouses.
University of Cambridge Botanic Gardens, Bateman Street, Cambridge CB2 1JF. Ferns in garden, also glasshouses.

France
Conservatoire Botanique Nationale de Brest, 52 Allee du Bot. 29200, Brest.
Conservatoire et Jardins Botanique de Nancy, 100 rue du Jardin Botanique, 54600 Villers les Nancy.
Jardin Botanique Parc de la Tête d'Or, Ville de Lyon, Lyon Cedex 06, F-69459
Mairie de Paris, Direction des Parcs, Jardin et Espaces Verts, 1 Avenue Gordon Bennett, 75016 Paris.

Germany
Botanischer Garten und Museum, Königen-Luise-Strasse 6-8, 1 Berlin (Dahlem), D-14195. Originator of *Polystichum setiferum* 'Dahlem'.
Munich Botanical Garden, Munich.

Ireland
Many Irish gardens include good stands of *Dicksonia antarctica*, the soft tree fern from Australia. Good examples are Kells House, Kells, Kerry and Dereen Garden, Kenmare, Kerry.
Fota Estate, Cork Harbour, Cork. Good stand of tree ferns including *Dicksonia fibrosa*, and Victorian fernery outdoors.
Glanleam Gardens, Valencia Island, Kerry, Eire. Good range of tree ferns out of doors, also some ground ferns.
National Botanic Garden Dublin, Glasnevin, Dublin 9, Eire. Ferns in glasshouses, including filmy ferns.

Scotland

Glasgow Botanic Gardens, 730 Great Western Road, Glasgow G12 0UE. Ferns mainly in glasshouses, including the National Collection of tree ferns in the Kibble Palace.

Inverewe Garden, Poolewe, Ross-shire IV22 2LG. Mainly ferns in gardens, including tree ferns.

Logan Botanic Gardens, Near Stranraer. Tree ferns and other ferns in gardens.

Royal Botanic Gardens Edinburgh, Inverleith Row, Edinburgh EH3 5LR. Some ferns in garden but most, including a very good collection of tree ferns, in heated glasshouses.

Switzerland

Conservatoire et Jardins Botaniques de Genève, Chemin de l'Impératrice 1, Caisse Postale 60, Chambesy, Genève CH-1292.

Zurich Botanischer Garten, Zollikerstrasse 107, Zurich, CH-8008.

New Zealand

Pukekura Park, New Plymouth. Tree ferns and king ferns (*Marattia salicina*) abundant in gardens, with a wonderful range of fern houses including other species – mainly New Zealand natives.

North America

I am indebted to Sue Olsen of Seattle for the very helpful information on the best fern gardens in North America.

Hardy Fern Foundation (HFF)

P.O. Box 166, Medina, Washington 98039-0166, USA.

The Hardy Fern Foundation has sites scattered throughout North America to test the hardiness of different ferns in different areas. At the sites every attempt is made to display and label the plants, and keep public records on their performance in the garden. For more information contact the HFF.

The main fern garden is at **Rhododendron Species Botanical Garden**, 2525 S. 336th Street, Federal Way, WA 98003.

Bellevue Botanical Garden, 12001 Main Street, Bellevue, WA 98005.

Birmingham Botanical Gardens, 2612 Lane Park Road, ' Birmingham, AL 35223.

California State University Sacramento, 6000 J Street, Sacramento, CA 95819.

Coastal Maine Botanical Garden, Boothbay, ME.

Dallas Arboretum and Botanical Society,

8617 Garland Road, Dallas, TX 75218. Includes a mist garden.

Denver Botanic Garden, 1005 York Street, Denver, CO 80206.

Georgeson Botanical Garden, 309 O'Neill Building, University of Alaska, Fairbanks, AK 99775.

Harry Leu Botanical Garden, Orlando, FL.

Inniswood Metro Gardens, 940 South Hempstead Road, Westerville, OH 43081.

Lakewold Gardens, 12317 Gravelly Lake Drive, Tacoma, WA 98499.

Les Jardins de Metis, Case Postale 242, Mont Jolie, Quebec, Canada.

New York Botanical Garden, Bronx, NY 10458. Includes Foster Collection.

Stephen F. Austin State University Arboretum, P.O. Box 13000, Nacogdoches, TX 75962.

Strybing Arboretum, 9th Avenue at Lincoln Way, San Francisco, CA 94122.

University of Northern Colorado, Ross Hall Science Center, Greeley, CO 80639.

Whitefall Historic Home and Garden, Louisville, KY.

The following sites should also be of interest. They are selected from 'A Directory of Fern Gardens, Nurseries and Reserves in the United States, 1994' by Joan Gottlieb, *Hardy Fern Foundation Newsletter*, Vol.4, No.1, Winter 1994.

Atlanta Botanical Garden, 1345 Piedmont Ave. NE, Atlanta, GA 30309.

Bartholomew's Cobble, Weatogue Road, Ashley Falls, MA 01222.

Bloedel Reserve, 7571 N.E. Dolphin Drive, Bainbridge Island, WA 98110.

Brooklyn Botanic Garden, 1000 Washington Avenue, Brooklyn, NY 11225. A general fern collection and planned Japanese garden with fern glade.

Chicago Botanic Garden, 1000 Lake Cook Road, Glencoe, IL 60022.

Fairchild Tropical Garden, 10901 Old Cutler Road, Miami, FL 33156.

Fern Canyon, Prairie Creek Redwoods St.Pk., 15336 Highway 101, Trinidad, CA 95510.

Fernwood Botanical Garden, 13988 Range Line Road, Niles, MI 49120.

Garden in the Woods, 180 Hemenway Road, Framingham, MA 01701.

Institute of Ecosystem Studies, Millbrook, NY 12545.

Leach Botanical Garden, 6704 S.E. 122nd Avenue, Portland, OR 97236.

Leonard J. Buck Garden, 11 Layton Road, Far Hills, NJ 07931.
Longwood Gardens, Kennett Square, PA 19348.
Missouri Botanical Garden, 4344 Shaw Blvd, St Louis, MO 63110.
Mount Cuba Center, P.O. Box 3570, Greenville, DE 19807.
Norcross Wildlife Sanctuary, 30 Peck Road, Monson, MA 01057.
Planting Fields Arboretum, Planting Fields Road, Oyster Bay, NY 11771.
University of California Botanical Garden, 200 Centennial Drive, Berkeley, CA 94720. Includes an outstanding collection of desert ferns.

University of North Carolina, Charlotte, NC 28223. Specialist *Dryopteris* garden including duplicates from W.H. Wagner Jr. research collection.
Wild Gardens of Acadia, Sieur de Monts Spring, Bar Harbor, ME 04609.

South Africa
Lowveld National Botanic Garden, P.O. Box 1024, Nelspruit 1200.
National Botanic Gardens, Kirstenbosch, near Cape Town. Ferns, including *Cyathea dregei*, flourish in the garden. Above, in Skeleton Gorge, a very good selection of native South African species can be seen in the wild.

Appendix V *Where to Buy Ferns*

Over the last few years ferns have become more popular with gardeners and, as a consequence, many garden centres and general nurseries offer a reasonable selection. In addition, there are a few specialist retail nurseries. The following are the current principal suppliers.

Australia
I was fortunate enough to visit Victoria in Australia recently. My impression is that there are few specialist retail nurseries but several trade suppliers to garden centres. Hence, a good collection of ferns is offered at many places. The one specialist I came across was Fernworld in Melbourne, which has a wide range of Australian native species, especially tree ferns.

Britain
The Fern Nursery, R.N. Timm, Grimsby Road, Binbrook, Lincolnshire LN3 6DH. I have never visited this nursery but the proprietor is a committee member of the British Pteridological Society. Send SAE for list.
Fibrex Nurseries, Honeybourne Road, Pebworth, Stratford-on-Avon, Warwickshire CV37 8XT. Hardy and tender ferns. Also begonias, gloxinias, hederas, hydrangeas, primroses, arum lilies and plants for the cool greenhouse.
Mrs Marston, Culag, Green Lane, Nafferton, Driffield, East Yorkshire YO25 0LF. Hardy and greenhouse ferns especially *Adiantum*. Also garden leadwork. Send £1 for catalogue.
Reginald Kaye Ltd., Silverdale, Lancashire LA5 0TY. British ferns and their varieties. The nursery is now run by Reginald Kaye's daughter-in-law and his grandson, Linda and Dominic Kaye. It also grows alpines and hardy perennials.
Rickard's Hardy Ferns Ltd., Kyre Park, Kyre, Tenbury Wells, Worcestershire WR15 8RP. My nursery is devoted solely to ferns. Most main groups are covered with a special emphasis on tree ferns. We hold the National Collection of *Polypodium*. Send 5 first-class stamps for a catalogue.

North America
There are many nurseries scattered across North America that sell ferns. The first two given below are the only true specialists, but the others are also excellent sources of ferns.
Fancy Fronds, Post Office Box 1090, Gold Bar, WA 98251. North American and British hardy ferns. Proprietor Judith Jones. Send $2 for a catalogue.
Foliage Gardens, 2003 128th Avenue SE, Bellevue, WA 98005, USA. Wide range of ferns from around the world. Also sells acers. Proprietors Sue and Harry Olsen. Send $2 for a catalogue.
Humber Nurseries Limited, RR No.8, Brampton, Ontario L6T 3Y7, Canada. $2 (Canadian) for a catalogue.
Plant Delights Nursery, 9241 Sauls Road, Raleigh, NC 27603, USA, Send 10 first-class stamps or a box of chocolates for a catalogue.
Rainforest Gardens, 13139 224th Street, Maple Ridge, BC V2X 7E7, Canada.
Russell Graham Purveyor of Plants, 4030 Eagle Crest Road Northwest, Salem, OR 97304, USA. Send $2 for a catalogue.
Siskiyou Rare Plant Nursery, 2825 Cummings Road, Medford, OR 97501, USA. Send $3 for a catalogue.

Appendix VI *Further Reading*

Beddome, Col. R.H., *The Ferns of British India*, Madras, 1865-70.

Beddome, Col. R.H., *Handbook to the Ferns of British India*, Thacker, Spink and Co., Calcutta, 1883.

Bolton, James, *Filices Britannicae*, Leeds, 1785.

Boyd, Peter D.A., 'Pteridomania: the Victorian Passion for Ferns', *Antique Collecting*, November 1993, pp.9-12.

Brown, Donald, F., *A Monographic Study of the Fern Genus Woodsia*, Weinheim, 1964.

Brownsey, Patrick J. and Smith-Dodsworth, John C., *New Zealand Ferns and Allied Plants*, David Bateman, 1989.

Burrows, John E., *South African Ferns and Fern Allies*, Frandsen, 1990.

Ching, Ren-chang, *Icones Filicum Sinicarum*, Vols. 3, 4, 5, Peiping, 1935, 1937, 1958.

Cody, William J. and Britton, Donald M., *Ferns and Fern Allies of Canada*, Ottawa, 1989.

de Vol, Charles E., et al, *Flora of Taiwan*, Vol. 1, 2nd ed, Epoch, 1980.

Dhir, K.K., *Ferns of North-Western Himalayas*, Cramer, 1980.

Dhir, K.K. and Sood, A., *Fern-flora of Mussoorie Hills*, Cramer, 1981.

Druery, Charles T., *The Book of British Ferns*, Country Life, London (1903).

Druery, Charles T., *British Ferns and their Varieties*, Routledge (1910).

Duncan, Betty D. and Isaac, Golda, *Ferns and Allied Plants of Victoria, Tasmania and South Australia*, Melbourne, 1986.

Dyce, James W., 'Classification of Fern Variations in Britain', *Pteridologist*, 1, 4, pp.154-155, 1987.

Dyce, James W., *The Cultivation and Propagation of British Ferns*, British Pteridological Society, 1993.

Dyce, James W., *Fern Names and their Meanings*, British Pteridological Society, 1988.

Fisher, Muriel E., *Gardening with New Zealand Ferns*, Coolins, Auckland, 1984.

Foster, F. Gordon, *Ferns to Know and Grow* (third revised and enlarged edition of *The Gardener's Fern Book*), Timber Press, Portland, Oregon, 1984.

Francis, George W., *An Analysis of the British Ferns and their Allies*, London, 1837.

Franco, Joao D.A. and Afonso, E. Maria, *Distribuicao de Pteridofitos e Gimnospermicas em Portugal*, Lisboa, 1982.

Fraser-Jenkins, Christopher R., *A Monograph of Dryopteris in the Indian Subcontinent*, British Museum, London, 1989.

Fraser-Jenkins, Christopher R., *New Species Syndrome in Indian Pteridology and the Ferns of Nepal*, International Book Distributors, Dehra Dun, 1997.

Goudey, Christopher J., *Maidenhair Ferns in Cultivation*, Lothian, Melbourne, 1985.

Goudey, Christopher J., *A Handbook of Ferns for Australia and New Zealand*, Lothian, Melbourne, 1988.

Goulding, Jeanne H., 'Early publications and Exhibits of New Zealand Ferns and the Work of Eric Craig', *Rec. Auckland Inst. Mus.* 14: 63-79, 1977.

Gunckel, L. Hugo, *Helechos de Chile*, Santiago, 1984.

Gurung, Vidja L., *Ferns – the Beauty of the Nepalese Flora*, Sayayogi Press, Kathmandu, 1991.

Hall, Nigel and Rickard, Martin H., *A Bibliography of Books and Related Items exclusively about Ferns and Fern Allies appearing before 1900 and written in English*, in press.

Hooker, William J., *Species Filicum*, Pamplin, 1845-1864.

Hope, C.W., *The Ferns of North Western India*, 1899, republished by International Book Distributors, Dehra Dun, c.1973.

Hoshizaki, Barbara Joe and Wilson, K.A., 'The Cultivated Species of the Fern Genus Dryopteris in the United States', *American Fern Journal*, 1999, 1, pp.1-100.

Hutchinson, George and Thomas, Barry A.T., *Welsh Ferns*, Cardiff, 1996.

Jacobsen, W.B.G., *The Ferns and Fern Allies of Southern Africa*, Butterworths, Durban, 1983.

Jermy, A. Clive and Camus, Josephine, *The Illustrated Field Guide to Ferns and Allied Plants of the British Isles*, Natural History Museum, London, 1991.

Jones, David L., *Encyclopaedia of Ferns*, Lothian, Melbourne, and Timber Press, Portland, Oregon, 1987.

Judd, Warren, 'Seuffert & Son', *New Zealand Geographic*, pp.39-53, 1990.

Kaye, Reginald, *Hardy Ferns*, Faber and Faber, 1968.

Khullar, S.P., *An Illustrated Fern Flora of West Himalaya*, International Book Distributors, Dehra Dun, 1994.

Lellinger, David B., *A Field Manual of the Ferns and Fern Allies of the United States and Canada*, Smithsonian Institution Press, 1985.

Lloyd, Robert M., *Systematics of the Onocleoid Ferns*, California Press, 1971.

Lowe, Edward J., *Our Native Ferns*, Groombridge, London, 1862-1867.

Lowe, Edward J., *British Ferns and Where Found*, Swan Sonnenschein, London, 1890.

Lowe, Edward J., *Fern Growing*, Nimmo, London, 1895.

Mickel, John T., *How to Know the Ferns and Fern Allies*, The Pictured Key Nature Series, Iowa, 1979.

Mickel, John T., *Ferns for American Gardens*, Macmillan, 1994.

Mickel, John T., and Beitel, Joseph M., *Pteridophyte Flora of Oaxaca, Mexico*, New York Botanic Garden, 1988.

Moore, Thomas, *The Ferns of Great Britain and Ireland*, London 1855.

Moore, Thomas E., *The Octavo Nature Printed British Ferns*, Bradbury and Evans, London, 1859-60.

Newey, Vic, 'Bulbil Production in Lady Ferns', *Pteridologist*, 1, p.115, 1986.

Newman, Edward, *A History of British Ferns*, London, 1840.

Newman, Edward, *A History of British Ferns*, London, 1844.

Newman, Edward, *A History of British Ferns*, J. Van Voorst, London, 1854.

Page, Christopher N., *The Ferns of Britain and Ireland*, Cambridge University Press, 1982.

Prelli, Remy and Boudrie, Michel, *Atlas Ecologique des Fougères et Plantes Alliées*, Lechavalier, 1992.

Rasbach, Kurt, Rasbach, Helga and Wilmanns, Ottilie, *Die Farpflanzen Zentraleuropas*, Heidelberg, 1968.

Rush, Richard, *A Guide to Hardy Ferns*, British Pteridological Society, 1984.

Schneider, George, *A Book of Choice Ferns*, Upcott Gill, London, 1890-1894.

Scully, Reginald W., *Flora of County Kerry*, Hodges, Fidges and Co., 1916.

Small, John K., *Ferns of the Vicinity of New York*, Dover, New York, 1975.

Smith, Alan R., *Flora of Chiapas, Part 2, Pteridophytes*, California Academy of Sciences, 1981.

Tagawa, Motozi, *Coloured Illustrations of Japanese Pteridophyta*, Hoikusha, Osaka, 1959.

Tutin, T.G. et al, *Flora Europaea*, Vol. 1, 2nd ed, Cambridge, 1993.

Ward, N.B., *On the growth of plants in closely glazed cases.* Second edition, London, 1852.

Wu, Cheng-yih, *Flora Xizangica*, Vol. 1, 1983.

Wu, Y.C., Wong, K.K., and Pong, S.M., *Polypodiaceae Yaoshanensis, Kwangsi*, Canton, 1932.

Index Page numbers in *italic* refer to illustrations